SHELTER WHAT YOU MAKE
MINIMIZE THE TAKE

Beverly Tanner
Marvin Pheffer
Alex Laurins

Published in San Francisco by
HARBOR PUBLISHING

Distributed by G.P. Putnam's Sons

For information, write Harbor Publishing,
1668 Lombard Street, San Francisco, CA 94123.

Printed in the United States of America.

Composition and design: WB Associates
Copyeditor: Sara Boyd
Cover design: Hal Lockwood, Bookman Productions
Printer and binder: Fairfield Graphics

ISBN 0-936602-45-7 Casebound

CONTENTS

A PERSONAL NOTE

As a client and friend of the author, I have been asked to write a brief introduction to this book.

How does one explain, disclose or reveal a Beverly Tanner? Say that she is a licensed, experienced investment counselor and a certified financial planner? The woods are full of such properly qualified (if frequently dull) people. Say that she is thorough, does careful research, and rigorously cross-checks investment opportunities — via a small but hardworking, dedicated, loyal staff — before making recommendations to clients? So does any good planner. Rated against a checklist of the standard requirements/expectations one seeks in an investment counselor, Beverly would probably score as well as, but not necessarily better than, most of her peers. But she is much more than they are; I must find a way to communicate the reasons why this is so.

Beverly Tanner is that rare combination in the financial community — a tough, calculating, ruthlessly goal-oriented money operator who also is simultaneously a person of great charm, gentleness, patience and persuasive ability. When I balk, for instance, at an investment suggestion she may make, her quizzical, amused look and her subsequent reaction is always directed simply at my inability to understand investment principles, and never at my general intelligence level or courage quotient. Beverly will patiently explain what I must do, why her recommendation will prove sound and profitable, and why delay in a decision may be expensive. I am *always* eventually convinced.

The result has been a steadily expanding portfolio of investment commitments, each more interesting than the last, all exiciting to contemplate as they grow in value, and every one of them a financial opportunity I would never have chosen (or even been aware of) by myself.

Beverly Tanner has earned my loyalty and trust, as she has patiently shown me that there are always new, better, and more profitable ways to manage money. She has taken away my imagined terrors, given me financial self-confidence and enthusiasm, and taught me to truly enjoy money and how to use it. For this I shall always be grateful.

Mason Ingram

FOREWORD

Three primary obstacles today prevent individuals from achieving financial independence: inflation, taxes, and interest rates. While you can do little personnally to curb inflation and interest rates, you can reduce the taxes you pay.

"Shelter What You Make, Minimize the Take" discusses how lowering your taxes is the key to economic survival. If you can reduce your taxes, you can increase your current cash flow and build your assets. Through prudent tax planning, this can be accomplished.

The new tax bill has changed the attractiveness of various tax shelters. The following chapters contain the most up-to-date information reflecting these changes. Some writers have indicated that tax shelters are not as important now as in the past since the maximum tax bracket is now 50%. This change actually makes little difference in the investor's desire for the tax relief, but it makes the investor more selective in choosing tax shelters, which is a healthy trend.

It is important to save taxes but this should be balanced by seeking economic merit. Initially, people may be anxious to reduce their tax bills, that as the years go by they begin to be more interested in the residual value — what is their investment worth in dollars and cents?

For this reason it is wise to diversify your tax shelter investments. This book discusses the various types of shelters ranging from the most basic — your retirement plan — to the more exotic investments, such as movies and art. Seeking investments suited to your particular circumstances is also important. This is where your choice of a good advisor becomes critical. This book guides the investor to select a compitent advisor as well as suggesting intelligent questions to ask the advisor.

While you may be aware of how much you owe in taxes, you may need guidance as to which investment to use to reduce your bill. This varies with the individual. What other assets do you have? How are they invested? How secure is your current income? What is your risk tollerance? All these factors and many more should be considered by your advisor before selecting the right tax shelter for you.

This is why this book is particularly useful to the individual investor. Different types of shelters are described with particular emphasis on economic merit as well as tax advantages. A tax shelter can be an excellent investment. After reading "Shelter What You Make" you should be well prepared to work with an advisor effectively to reduce your taxes and build your assets.

— Alexandra Armstong, CFP

WHAT IS FINANCIAL PLANNING?

Financial planning is a concept that is relatively new to a lot of people. Stated simply, financial planning is to your finances what physical training is to your body or family planning is to your household.

Family planning permits a couple to determine the size of their family. According to current statistics, more than 75 percent of American couples exercise some sort of family planning. Physical training is also a kind of planning. If you want to develop your arteriovascular system to minimize the chance of a heart attack, you may take up jogging.

But whether it is family planning or physical training or financial planning, the common element is preparation. Being prepared means setting a goal and then taking the necessary steps to achieve it. Runners, for example, follow regimented training programs because they have specific fitness goals.

The same holds true for financial planning. First we must identify our financial goals and, once they are identified, devise a plan to achieve them.

Financial planning is not a difficult task; yet many people fail to plan their financial future. Why? Procrastination is probably the single biggest reason.

Consider yourself. If you're like most people, 99 percent of your time is spent coping with the concerns of the moment. You may have a family that you need to provide with such necessities as food, clothing, shelter, transportation, education, and emotional support. To handle these immediate needs, you probably have a salaried job or work for yourself as an entrepreneur or professional. You use your immediate income to pay for your immediate needs. Again, if you're like most of us, any disposable income, or money left over after needs are paid for, usually gets spent on small luxuries such as better furniture or a new television set.

But, although we live for the moment, we also need to plan for the future. Somewhere down the road, your children may want to go to college. There may be weddings to pay for or a long trip you want to take. And then there's retirement. It's now obvious that Social Security alone will not take care of our retirement needs.

At this point, it's important to mention something which may or may not be obvious: the financial objectives you set for yourself can only be met if they reflect a realistic picture of your present financial condition. The word to be emphasized here is *realistic*. That is why, when people seek financial advice, one of the first things they are asked to do is fill out a simple data sheet like the one shown here. The data sheet helps identify financial objectives, helps determine where you are right now, and indicates your financial goals.

Let's begin this process by looking at some common financial objectives. On the front of this particular form in big, bold letters is the heading *Financial Objectives*.

Common goals include:

Income Now
Income at Retirement
Maximum Tax Advantage
Children's Education
Travel
Build Estate
Other (explain)

Many of you will have several or all of them as your personal goals. But, if you carefully list yours *in order of importance*, your primary goal becomes clear.

Depending on what your primary goal is, your plan of action will vary. For instance, if your goal is "income now," you would aim toward putting your money in short-term high-yield investments. On the other hand, if your primary goal is "income at retirement," your investments would be concentrated in areas of long-range growth and capital appreciation. Remember, what you do financially is determined first by your goals.

WHAT ARE YOUR GOALS?

To determine your personal financial goals, review your list of objectives. If you are married, be sure that you and your partner discuss this matter to make sure you have common goals. It is not unusual for couples to have different ideals and goals. Now is the time to determine that, not ten years from now.

Now that you've established what your goals are, or at least what you would like them to be, you must find out if these goals are realistic. To do so, fill out the following data sheet, listing all assets and liabilities as well as income.

Planned Investments, Inc.

CONFIDENTIAL
PERSONAL FINANCIAL PLANNING QUESTIONNAIRE

Family Information   Date _____

Name _____ Occupation_____ Date of Birth _____

Spouse's Name _____ Occupation_____ Date of Birth _____

Address _____

Phone Number (Home)_____ Phone Number (Business) _____

Employer's Name _____ Employer's Address _____

Social Security No. (Husband) _____ (Wife) _____

Children	Age	Dependent	Self-Supporting
_____	_____	| |	| |
_____	_____	| |	| |
_____	_____	| |	| |
_____	_____	| |	| |

Other Dependents — Explain

_____

_____

_____

Annual Income

	Husband	Wife
Salary (including bonus)	$_____	$_____
Fees and Commissions	$_____	$_____
Limited Partnerships	$_____	$_____
Real Estate	$_____	$_____
Dividends	$_____	$_____
Interest	$_____	$_____
Trust Income	$_____	$_____
Other: _____	$_____	$_____
_____	$_____	$_____
Total Income	$_____	$_____

Annual Expenses

	Husband	
Family Living Expenses	$_____	
Taxes	$_____	
Debt Amortization and Interest	$_____	
Insurance	$_____	
Total Expenses		$_____

700 Larkspur Landing Circle, Suite 109, Larkspur, California 94939, 415/461-4800

3

ASSETS

Fixed Dollars

Checking Accounts . . . . $_____

Savings Accounts (describe) . . . . Interest _____% $_____

Money Market Account . . . . $_____

Credit Union . . . . Interest _____% $_____

Time Certificates . . . . _____ Years, matures ___/___/___ $_____

_____ Years, matures ___/___/___ $_____

Bonds (describe) . . . . $_____

Cash Value — Life Insurance . . . . _____ Net $_____

Notes, Loans, and Mortgages Receivable . . . . $_____

Pension Plan(s) . . . . $_____

Individual Retirement Account(s) . . . . $_____

Other Fixed Assets . . . . $_____

Total Fixed Dollars . . . . $_____

Variable Investments

Common Stocks* . . . . $_____

Mutual Fund Shares* . . . . $_____

Real Estate* (other than home) . . . . _____ Equity $_____

Business or Professional Practice — Net Worth . . . . $_____

Limited Partnerships _____ $_____

_____ $_____

_____ $_____

Gold, coins, art objects, etc. . . . . $_____

Other Variable Investments _____ $_____

Total Variable Investments . . . . $_____

Non-Income Producing Property

Home (estimated market value) . . . . $_____

(less outstanding mortgage) . . . . $_____ $_____

Personal Property . . . . $_____

Total Non-Income Producing Property . . . . $_____

TOTAL ASSETS . . . . $_____

LIABILITIES

Bank loans . . . . $_____

Accounts Payable . . . . $_____

Other Debts . . . . $_____

Total Liabilities . . . . $_____

NET WORTH . . . . $_____

*See details next page.

Planned Investments, Inc.

ASSET DETAILS

Insurance

Company	Face Amount	Cash Value	Annual Premium	Beneficiary
_____	$_____	$_____	$_____	_____
_____	$_____	$_____	$_____	_____
_____	$_____	$_____	$_____	_____
Total	$_____	$_____	$_____	

Variable Dollars (Mutual Funds and Stocks)

No. of Shares	Company	Cost	Date Purchased	Market Value
_____	_____	$_____	_____	$_____
_____	_____	$_____	_____	$_____
_____	_____	$_____	_____	$_____
_____	_____	$_____	_____	$_____
_____	_____	$_____	_____	$_____
_____	_____	$_____	_____	$_____
_____	_____	$_____	_____	$_____
	Total Value of Mutual Funds and Stocks	$_____		$_____

Real Estate

Description	Mortgage	Market Value	Equity
_____	$_____	$_____	$_____
_____	$_____	$_____	$_____
_____	$_____	$_____	$_____
_____	$_____	$_____	$_____
_____	$_____	$_____	$_____
Total	$_____	$_____	$_____

Any additional information or clarification on assets _____
_____

(Attach additional sheets as necessary)

Planned Investments, Inc.

PERSONAL FINANCIAL OBJECTIVES

Financial Independence

How many years before retirement? _____

Desired monthly income at retirement $_____

Expected Sources of Monthly Retirement Income:

Social Security . . . . $_____

Company Pension or Profit Sharing Plan . . . . $_____

Other (Keogh, Annuities, etc.) . . . . $_____

Childrens' Education

Name	Years to be Funded	Annual Cost
_____	_____	$_____
_____	_____	$_____
_____	_____	$_____
_____	_____	$_____

Disability

Disability Income Needed $_____ per month   Company provided benefits $_____ per month

Premature Death

Do you and spouse have wills now? _____   When Drafted? _____

Trusts? _____   When Drafted? _____

Estimated required monthly income for surviving Spouse and Dependent Children in case of death:

Capital Needs:

Emergency Fund. . . . . $_____

Mortgage Cancellation Fund (if surviving spouse will continue to live in family house) . . . . . . $_____

Notes and Loans Payable . . . . $_____

Total Education Expenses . . . . $_____

Income Needs:

What is your estimate of the monthly income which will be needed during the following periods:

Until your youngest child is self-supporting . . . . $_____

To provide life income for surviving spouse after your youngest child is self-supporting . . . . . $_____

Do you plan on retaining assets for your children or depleting assets over the life expectancy of your spouse?

Planned Investments, Inc.

An area that should receive special attention is the Unusual Financial Demands category. For example, the ages and dependency status of any children listed on the data sheet are important factors to consider in formulating a financial plan.

Perhaps you have a child who is 21 years old. In your mind you may be saying, "Oh, she's already grown up, I don't have to worry about her." But that child may want to go to graduate school or may remain in some other way financially dependent on you for years. Or you may have an older parent who will not need support if things go well, but what if they don't?

Your ability to commit your present income and assets to long-term or short-term investments is in some part related to your responsibilities to your dependents. The sooner you realize this, the sooner you can formulate a realistic financial plan.

After completing the financial portion of the data sheet, listing your income, liabilities, assets, and those special obligations that you may have, you arrive at the bottom-line figure: disposable income.

WHAT IS DISPOSABLE INCOME?

Disposable income is the money that is left over after all immediate and necessary financial obligations are met. It is the money you can put to work to achieve your financial objectives. In many cases, disposable income can be increased substantially through tax-advantaged investments, that is, by investments that are essentially subsidized by the government because they reduce your taxes. We'll go into that in detail in the next chapter. But for now, let's simply say that the amount of disposable income available determines what financial objectives are realistic. It may turn out that after determining your disposable income, you will need to reevaluate your objectives. If you don't want to change objectives, you may have to change jobs, or even careers, to keep your objectives realistic.

To illustrate how your financial objectives and your current financial position work together in financial planning, let's look at a typical case history.

THE HERBERTS

Joe and Marian Herbert are a working couple, both aged 40. They have three children aged 12, 11, and 8. When they filled out their data sheet, they listed their primary financial objective as their children's education. When asked about retirement, the Herberts commented that retirement was more than 20 years away, and while that might be a goal sometime in the future, their children's education was far more important to them at the present time.

Once their primary financial objective was defined, their current financial position could be analyzed:

Joe Herbert, engineer, annual salary	$35,000
Marian Herbert, teacher, annual salary	22,000
Total annual income	$57,000

In addition to their salaries, they had some income from investments:

Certificate of deposit — annual interest	$ 1,700
Stocks — annual dividends	500
Investment property — annual cash flow	1,000
Total investment income	$ 3,200
Total annual gross income	$60,200

The Herberts have a little more than $60,000 in income. Assuming average deductions, they will be in the top, or 50 percent, marginal tax bracket, when both federal and state taxes are combined.

Before we continue our discussion, let's take a moment to discuss tax brackets. When someone is in the 50 percent bracket, it does not mean that every dollar earned is taxed at 50 percent. Rather, income is taxed on a sliding scale of 12 to 50 percent. As the tax tables show, a married couple's income over the $3400 base figure is taxed incrementally at 12 percent, 14 percent, and so on.

Tax Rate Schedules for Single Individuals

Taxable Income	1981* Pay	1981* % on Excess	1982 Pay	1982 % on Excess	1983 Pay	1983 % on Excess	1984 Pay	1984 % on Excess
0 — $2,300	—0—	—0—	—0—	—0—	—0—	—0—	—0—	—0—
$2,300 — 3,400	—0—	14	—0—	12	—0—	11	—0—	11
3,400 — 4,400	$154	16	$132	14	$121	13	$121	12
4,400 — 6,500	314	18	272	16	251	15	241	14
6,500 — 8,500	692	19	608	17	566	15	535	15
8,500 — 10,800	1,072	21	948	19	866	17	835	16
10,800 — 12,900	1,555	24	1,385	22	1,257	19	1,203	18
12,900 — 15,000	2,059	26	1,847	23	1,656	21	1,581	20
15,000 — 18,200	2,605	30	2,330	27	2,097	24	2,001	23
18,200 — 23,500	3,565	34	3,194	31	2,865	28	2,737	26
23,500 — 28,800	5,367	39	4,837	35	4,349	32	4,115	30
28,800 — 34,100	7,434	44	6,692	40	6,045	36	5,705	34
34,100 — 41,500	9,766	49	8,812	44	7,953	40	7,507	38
41,500 — 55,300	13,392	55	12,068	50	10,913	45	10,319	42
55,300 — 81,800	20,982	63	18,968	50	17,123	50	16,115	48
81,800 — 108,300	37,677	68	32,218	50	30,373	50	28,835	50
108,300 —	55,697	70	45,468	50	43,623	50	42,085	50

The preceding table shows federal tax rates only; state tax rates must be added. For example, a couple filing in California in 1982 must have more than $45,800 in taxable income to be taxed at 50 percent. (Federal taxes account for 39% and state taxes for 11%.)

The Herberts' income has to cover the family's personal expenses — food, clothing, medical bills, insurance, car maintenance, mortgage payments, educational fees, and taxes. Very little is left to be invested. The Herberts, like so many families, are caught in the middle. They don't make enough money to have a substantial portion left after taxes; yet they make enough to be in the top tax bracket.

At first, the Herberts were a bit dismayed by what they learned. It appeared that they simply did not have enough disposable income to achieve their goal of sending their children to college.

At that point, it became necessary to modify their financial objectives. Instead of their children's education being the primary goal, it changed to "growth." What the Herberts needed was to place whatever disposable income they had in an investment where it would grow. With the Growth game plan, at some later date, perhaps six or eight years down the road, the money they save in the meantime can be reinvested to produce income. Their financial objective became more specifically defined as *growth now* and *income later*.

But, no matter what investment they choose, the Herbers are going to run into one big problem. They are going to end up paying taxes on their investment income at the 50 percent rate — their current tax bracket. If, for example, they invest $5000 and it shows a return after one year of 25 percent, or $1250, the Herberts would only be able to keep about $625, since the other half would be paid to the government in taxes. Therefore, before making any kind of investment, the Herberts should find a way to protect their investment income from taxes.

One way to do this is to take whatever disposable income is available and either lend or give it to (or put it in trust for) the children. Under the 1981 Economic Recovery Tax Act, gifts of up to $10,000 a year can be given to each child. Once the money is in the children's names, with the parents as guardians, any income it earns is taxable to the children.

Since most children have little or no income, they pay little or no tax. The entire $1250 earned by the Herberts' investment could be retained and added to the original investment. This money, compounding without taxation, provides for optimum growth.

After giving money to their children, the Herberts wanted to invest it for growth. There are a variety of areas in which they can invest to achieve growth potential, including, but not limited to, real estate, stocks, and energy. Money can be constantly added to these investments just by making additional loans or gifts. To ensure the tax-favored status of loans or gifts to children, we recommend that you consult a financial advisor to be certain that the note is drawn properly. Trust documents should be written by an attorney.

With all these options, the Herberts became a little concerned. Joe and Marian both worked hard at their jobs. When they were at home, they liked to relax with the children. They did not want to have to spend their free time making investment decisions. What the Herberts wanted was someone to manage their investments so they could free themselves from that worry. They wanted to be *passive investors*.

PASSIVE INVESTING

There are many vehicles for passive investing. We'll briefly cover three. Each offers the investor the opportunity to invest money, obtain tax shelter, and profit — essentially without lifting a finger.

Real Estate Investment Trusts (REITs)

One kind of professionally managed investment is a REIT (Real Estate Investment Trust). Money is invested by many individuals to form a larger pool that is managed by real estate investment specialists. This pool of money may be invested in equity such as apartments, office buildings, and shopping centers, or in mortgages. Once a REIT is fully subscribed it is traded on the over the counter market and is, therefore, quite liquid.

In 1974, many of the REIT's invested in mortgages fell into serious financial trouble and declared bankruptcy. However, the equity REIT's survived and became financially strong and profitable. Today there are some excellent real estate investment trusts on the market that can be quite safe and profitable.

Limited Partnership

Other professionally managed investments are limited partnerships, sometimes referred to as *syndications*. These will be discussed in detail in a separate chapter. Essentially, in a limited partnership, there are two types of partners — the general partners, who manage the entire deal together, and the limited partners, who pool their money to be managed by the general partners, the experts in the field. With this type of relationship, the investor has certain tax benefits, will receive distributions from cash flow, and will participate in the profits once the properties are sold.

Any REIT, limited partnership, or other managed investment must be analyzed thoroughly. You want to know who the general partners are, their experience in the particular field, past performance records, financial statements, and what the sharing arrangements are up front, during operations and upon sale.

Stock Fund

Another investment area is stocks. One of the advantages stocks have over real estate is liquidity. While you can pull your money out of stocks overnight, investments in real estate often take months to retrieve. Depending on your personal situation, liquidity could be an important factor. For example, if the Herberts want the money they invest to act as an emergency fund as well, they would want to be able to get at it on a moment's notice.

Funds have many advantages. They are professionally managed, shares are easily sold, dividends can be automatically reinvested, and the investment risk is reduced because a fund owns a part of many companies. You can receive a monthly distribution check if you are in need of the income. There are two funds which have particularly good track records: the Oppenheimer family of funds and the American General funds. An advantage of a family of funds is that you can transfer from one fund to another within the group for a nominal fee, usually only $5. Today, there are several rating bureaus that track the performance of funds. (One of these is the Wiesenberger reports, another is Fundscope.) These reports let the investor know how well the fund is doing. Of course, for far less money, the investor can chart his own record from the market quotations listed in most daily newspapers.

For the Herberts to achieve their financial goals, they need to give or lend their disposable income to their children (so that the income generated would not be taxed at the 50 percent rate) and then select and invest that money in growth areas.

So far, we've looked at the Herberts' financial position, identified and clarified their financial objectives, and then involved them in a program of investments aimed at achieving their goals.

Even with as little as $3000 a year in disposable income, it is possible to invest in real estate, stocks, or energy. After six years of compounding at 15 percent, the $3000 a year without taxation (remember, it's in their children's names) will grow to around $50,000, depending, of course, on how much they make on their investments. That $50,000 could then be used by the Herberts to reinvest in a program that would produce a steady flow of income to finance their children's college education.

The plans the Herberts made are basically what financial planning is all about. It means ignoring, for a few hours, the financial concerns of the moment to establish a plan for the future. With a goal or destination point in mind, it is then possible to use the tools or money you have to reach your objectives.

Financial planning can really mean the difference between having what you want later on, or being stuck in the same place ten years from now. Financial planning is, of course, more complicated than it appears in the case of the Herberts. With the Herberts, we saw how one family took steps to achieve a single, relatively short-term goal.

A broader view of financial planning would have to include tax planning, estate planning, trusts and wills, all types of investments, insurance, and retirement planning. Financial planners, working with attorneys, accountants, insurance brokers, and realtors, will help you develop an appropriate line of action.

In the case of higher income taxpayers, financial planning emphasizes tax planning, as we will see in the next chapter.

CHAPTER TWO

WHAT IS A TAX SHELTER?

A lot of different things are called tax shelters. To generalize, we must say that a tax shelter is a kind of umbrella that shelters income from current taxation.

Some shelters are truly tax free. For instance, dividends received from municipal bonds are not taxed by the federal government; other investments have interest and dividend exclusions with certain limitations. Unfortunately, many investments that are truly tax free are often not very good investments.

TAX DEFERRAL SHELTERS: RETIREMENT PLANS

The vast majority of shelters are not tax free. They are actually tax deferrals. That is, taxes on current income are deferred, or transferred, to some future time. Perhaps the simplest forms of such tax deferrals are retirement plans such as IRA and Keogh accounts. The current maximum annual contributions are $2000 to an IRA account and $15,000 to a Keogh account. The amount invested in such an account is deducted from current income (that is, it is not taxed now). In addition, there are no taxes on the income this investment accumulates.

Therefore, if a person invests $10,000 in a retirement plan, he will pay no taxes on the original investment or the income it earns until some future date. On the other hand, if this same person makes a $10,000 investment without any tax advantages, he must first pay taxes on the $10,000. In the 50 percent bracket, this leaves only $5000 for investment purposes. The earnings on the $5000 investment are also fully taxable (for example, earnings will be cut in half for our investor in the 50 percent tax bracket). The table below shows what happens to $10,000 invested, first, in a Keogh account and, second, in a taxable account.

	Keogh	Taxable
Investment	$10,000	$10,000
Tax — 50% bracket	—	5,000
Amount at work	$10,000	$ 5,000
Interest at 15%	15%	7½%
Value after 10 years	$40,455	$10,305

As you can see, after only 10 years, the Keogh account is worth almost four times as much as the taxable acount. Should the taxpayer, at retirement, still be in the 50 percent tax bracket, he would have to pay taxes on the full $40,455. This would leave him with $20,227, or just about twice the amount in the taxable account. (In reality, however, most taxpayers will be in a lower tax bracket at retirement, thus profiting even more from their tax-deferred investments.) Let's say that our taxpayer, at retirement, is in the 30 percent bracket. The Keogh savings would be taxable at 30½, leaving him $28,318.

If this same person is able to invest $10,000 at the beginning of each year for ten years, and if the interest is compounded annually, his Keogh account will grow to $233,492, whereas his taxable account will grow to only $76,040. Assuming again a 50 percent tax bracket at retirement, the Keogh account would net, after taxes, $116,746, or $40,706 more than the taxable account.

I purposely chose a retirement plan for the first example of a tax shelter because it is the easiest to understand. A bit more complicated is depreciation, which is found mostly in real estate, and depletion, which occurs mostly in energy-related investments. Depreciation and depletion are also tax-deferral shelters. To see how these shelters work, let's take an example from real estate.

TAX-DEFERRAL SHELTERS: REAL ESTATE INVESTMENTS

In real estate, the owner of investment property is allowed to depreciate that property at various rates over various periods of time, depending on the type of property.

All buildings deteriorate. Most become obsolete in time and ultimately useless as income-producing investments. In a sense, an investor could buy a building, hold on to it for 50 years or so, and get rental income from it during that entire itme. Then, when it finally becomes obsolete, the investor could write it off as a loss. The government, however, allows investors to write off the eventual loss of their investment during the years of ownership; they need not wait until the building falls down to declare a tax loss. Today, real property is generally recovered over a 15-year period.

Let's assume you own an apartment building and are going to depreciate it over 15 years using the straight-line depreciation method. Straight-line simply means that you write off an equal amount each year. (Accelerated depreciation methods will be discussed in later chapters.) The building, exclusive of the land, is worth $500,000. Now you divide this amount by 15 years and arrive at the figure that can be written off each year, $33,333. If you write off this amount each year, at the end of 15 years there is nothing left.

Now, let's make an assumption that may not necessarily be true in the real world. Let's assume that the income from your apartment building exactly equals all expenses. (From your rental income you deduct various expenses, such as mortgage payments, real estate taxes, insurance, repairs, and maintenance. What is left is zero.) The building is a wash — no profit, no loss. On top of this you have depreciation. This is also considered an expense item. The $33,333 annual depreciation figure added to a profit/loss statement that otherwise balances out produces a $33,333 loss for the current year. What that means is that you now have $33,333 to deduct from your other income.

Think what this really means. If your other income happens to be $70,000 a year, this write-off drops it down to $36,667. You have now decreased your taxable income by a substantial amount. Assuming again a 50 percent tax bracket, this would give you an immediate saving of one-half of $33,333, or $16,666. That means that because of depreciation you are paying $16,666 less in taxes.

Owning — and depreciating — an apartment building is, therefore, a tax shelter.

At this point, you might think that the $33,333 is tax free. Unfortunately, this is not so. It is only tax deferred. It is money that you do not have to pay taxes on in the current year. But, at some time in the future it will become taxable. To see how and why, let's take a look at the accounting system that is used for your apartment building. The value of the building was determined on the basis of its cost (forgetting about the land for the moment). The cost of the building was $500,000, and this is your starting point, or basis.

When property is depreciated, the basis, or original value, of the property must also be lowered by that same amount. (This only makes sense. Depreciation is an accountant's way to handle a loss of value in real property brought about by age, physical deterioration, or obsolescence. Broadly, it is a loss in value from any source.) Note how the process works:

Basis at time of purchase	$500,000
Depreciation first year	33,333
Adjusted basis second year	466,667
Depreciation second year	33,333
Adjusted basis third year	433,334
Depreciation third year	33,333
Adjusted basis fourth year	400,001

•

•

•

•

It should be clear that if you continue this process for 15 years your final basis will be zero. You will have fully depreciated the property. Of course, during that time you were also taking $33,333 each year off your ordinary income as a tax write-off (assuming that income and expenses from your investment property continue to remain in balance).

Now, let's say that after 15 years you decide to sell your apartment building. It is still a relatively new building, in good condition and definitely not falling apart. (Depreciation is a paper loss and has very little to do with reality.) Let's assume further that you are selling the building for $500,000 — exactly what you paid for it. After 15 years you haven't made a dime in profit. Except, the building has not cost you anything, and it has given you $33,333 in write-offs each year.

The problem you have now is that as soon as you sell the building, you have to pay taxes on 15 years' worth of write-offs. If you add up all those $33,333 figures for 15 years, you will find that they equal exactly $500,000 — which becomes, in this case, your taxable income in the year of sale. It is calculated this way:

Sale price	$500,000
Less adjusted basis	000
Taxable gain	$500,000

What have you done here? What you've done is take $33,333 off your current income each year for 15 years, deferring taxes on it until some future date. In this case, the future happened to be 15 years down the road. You have not avoided paying taxes on the $33,333 a year. The money really was not tax free — it was only tax deferred.

What's the advantage? Perhaps the most important advantage is that by holding the building for more than one year the gain realized upon sale is treated as a long-term capital gain. The maximum federal tax rate on ordinary income is 50%, whereas the tax rate on capital gains is 20%. By deferring the sale of the property to the future, you have transferred current income out of a 50 percent tax bracket into a 20 percent bracket.

In the preceding example, you showed a taxable capital gain of $500,000. If this amount were taxed at the ordinary 50% rate, the tax would be $250,000, which is the same as paying 50% in taxes on $33,333 (the depreciation deduction) over 15 years. On the other hand, if our $500,000 long term capital gain is taxed at the maximum rate of 20%, your tax is only $100,000. Therefore, by deferring the sale into the future you have saved $150,000 in taxes.

For purposes of our example, we have assumed that the building was fully depreciated before it was sold. We also assumed that the building produced no income. (Remember, income and expenses were a wash.) The basic reason for becoming involved in the building, therefore, was a long-term shelter — a shelter that provided a yearly write-off, year after year. When the write-off is thus structured for ten or more years, it is commonly called a *deep shelter*.

DEEP SHELTERS

A deep shelter is normally bought by taxpayers who have a high (50 percent bracket) income and anticipate maintaining that income for ten or fifteen years. A deep shelter provides neither capital appreciation nor income. It provides only continuing write-offs. A HUD subsidized housing program is typical of this kind of investment, as we'll see later in the chapter.

EQUITY BUILDERS

If you had anticipated selling your apartment building sooner (say, in five or ten years) and for a profit, then you would have a different kind of shelter.

Let's say that there was appreciation and you were able to sell your building for $750,000 at the end of five years. (Remember, you bought it for $500,000.) Over the five years, you reduced your basis at the rate of $33,333 a year, or $166,665. Your gain is figured in this manner:

$33,333		Annual depreciation
×5		Years
166,665		Total depreciation taken
	500,000	Original basis
	−166,665	Less depreciation taken
	333,335	Adjusted basis
$750,000		Selling price (building only)
− 333,335		Less adjusted basis
416,665		Gain on sale

You must now pay taxes on this gain of $416,665. However, because the property was held for over one year, you can take a capital gains rate. You end up paying only 20 percent in taxes. The point to be understood here is that both the income you have written off for five years (166,665) and the profit you made on the sale ($250,000) are taxed at capital gains rates.

In the equity-builder shelters, therefore, the lower capital gains rate applies both to the ordinary income sheltered and to the equity it builds.

INCOME SHELTERS

The final kind of shelter we will consider is the income shelter. Here the property produces income that, for a while at least, appears to be tax free. Let's assume that your apartment building is not heavily financed. Annual income exceeds expenses by $25,000. You'll recall, however, that there is $33,333 of depreciation annually. That depreciation is an expense item that overtakes the positive cash flow.

$33,333	Depreciation
25,000	Positive cash flow
8,333	Taxable loss

Because your building continues to show a loss (due to depreciation), your cash flow is not ordinary income to you. It is income on which you do not have to pay taxes immediately. Rather, the tax on it is deferred to the future. That means that you get your $25,000 and can do anything you like with it. It is sheltered income. (In addition, you also have $8333 as a write-off against your ordinary income.)

MULTIPLE WRITE-OFF SHELTERS

Although multiple write-off shelters are available throughout the year, they become especially desirable toward the end of the year. probably because they are designed for people who need large write-offs, but do not have sufficient cash or foresight to achieve their objectives with ordinary shelters.

The way multiple write-off shelters work is fairly simple. The investor comes up with part cash and part letters of credit issued and guaranteed by a bank and due at some later date. These letters of credit are then used by the general partner as collateral to raise money from some bank or other lending institution.

Let's assume that an investor puts up $10,000 cash today and gets one or more letters of credit totaling $20,000. He has, in effect, guaranteed a total payment of $30,000. He is "at risk" for $30,000. His write-off is limited to the amount that he is at risk, in this case $30,000. Should this investment offer a 100 percent write-off the first year, he would have a 3 to 1 write-off. His cash outlay is only $10,000, but he can write off $30,000 from his income and save $15,000 in taxes if he is in the top bracket.

In one or more years, the letter of credit will come due, and the investor will have to come up with the balance of $20,000, for which there is no additional tax write-off. What happened in this case is that the investor needed a large write-off the first year. He accomplished this with his 3 to 1 write-off. Ultimately, of course, he has to make good the letters of credit.

Some multiple write-off shelters that require only promissory notes and not letters of credit are quite often inflated. A combination of these notes, overvaluation, depreciation, and the like, can result in a very large write-off.

The IRS, however, is trying to crack down on overvaluations. The 1981 Economic Recovery Tax Act contains penalties for overvaluating assets. These penalties, ranging from 10% to 30% of the tax underpayment, are nondeductible. Should the IRS find such an overvaluation, the write-off would be disallowed. In the above case, the $15,000 would have to be paid back. If the investor cannot pay it back immediately, he must pay interest (at prime rate) on the sum from the time he took the write-off until he pays it back. In addition, he must pay a penalty of 50% of the interest and an overvaluation penalty of 10% to 30% of the tax due. If you add all the penalties and interest, it becomes quite obvious that you would have been better off without this particular investment.

Multiple write-off shelters must be carefully analyzed. Only a few of these investments make good sense.

It is generally better to plan ahead so that your income can be sheltered through sound and proven investments. Sometimes, under certain circumstances, a high write-off shelter is needed anyhow. There are some that make good economic sense, but you must be very careful in choosing the right ones.

LIMITED PARTNERSHIPS

Limited partnerships will be discussed in detail in a separate chapter. At this point our only interest is the tax advantages that certain limited partnerships can offer. A properly structured limited partnership passes special tax benefits on to the investors, or the limited partners. If a partnership were taxed as a corporation, all the tax benefits to the investors would be lost. Before investing, therefore, it is important to have some kind of assurance that a limited partnership is truly a limited partnership and will not be taxed as a corporation.

The tax benefits of a limited partnership can be structured in a variety of ways. In one case, for instance, all the limited partners share equally in the tax benefits; in another case, the limited partners get cash flow only and receive no tax benefits until the property is sold. There are many variations on these two themes.

Not all investors have the same goals. A retired person with a small income needs cash flow or an income shelter. A younger investor at the peak of his earning years needs an equity-builder shelter. In order to accommodate both types of investors, a partnership can be structured to give all or most of the excess write-off to one person and all or most of the sheltered income to another person. In such a case, a person who needs write-offs may give up some income in favor of more shelter, and the other person may give up write-offs in favor of more income. A partnership can be structured to benefit both.

Investing in limited partnerships frequently results in substantial tax savings for the investor. Of course, the investment must be in an area that offers tax advantages such as depreciation or depletion.

Having thus gone through the main features of a tax shelter it is important to see how tax shelters and tax planning fit into the overall picture of financial planning. To do this let's look at the case history of Dr. Moore.

DOCTOR MOORE

Dr. Moore's situation is far different from the Herberts'. Dr. Moore is a medical doctor with an annual income of $150,000. He is married and his wife does not work. He has two children but is not worried about the cost of sending them to college. The approximate $10,000 that it will cost annually to send each child to school can easily be taken out of current income.

When I asked Dr. Moore what his biggest concern was, he confided that it was taxes. "Taxes are eating me alive — I need a tax shelter." Dr. Moore's initial financial objective was "maximum tax advantage."

Now let's analyze his financial picture a bit more thoroughly by looking at the information on his financial data sheet. For this purpose, we consider only his income and investment assets. His home, jewelry, furnishings, and art objects are not considered at this time.

	Income	Assets
Salary	$150,000	
Cash in bank & C.D.s	4,000	$ 25,000
Stocks	2,000	15,000
Real estate partnerships	2,000	50,000
Life insurance	_____	250,000
Total income	$158,000	

It is fairly obvious that Dr. Moore has a substantial income. It is just as obvious that he is not getting a good return on his investments. Dr. Moore has a definite problem. He is taxed at the 50% rate. Unlike the Herberts, who have only the last few dollars of their income taxed at the 50% rate, the majority of Dr. Moore's income is taxed at 50%. (In 1982, all income over $85,600 is taxed at 50% by the federal government. In California, income over $35,200 is taxed at 50% if you include both federal and state taxes.)

Over the years, Dr. Moore has bought into an assortment of real estate limited partnerships, some good and some bad, in an attempt to find tax relief. Dr. Moore's haphazard investment behavior is largely the result of his heavy workload. He is too busy with his practice to devote much time to investments.

Typically he waits until almost the end of the year to get some figures together and take a look at his tax situation. Then he realizes that he is going to have an enormous problem and generally buys the first shelter available. He looks only for a shelter, not for an investment that makes good economic sense in itself and offers some tax advantages in addition.

An investment should never be bought primarily for its tax advantages. It should be bought because it makes good economic sense. It should be bought because it will make a profit.

Dr. Moore's helter-skelter search for a tax shelter each December indicated to me that he was placing too much emphasis on his primary financial objective — maximum tax advantage. Upon further talking, I learned that Dr. Moore really had another objective that was quite important to him. His second objective, it turned out, was retirement. People like Dr. Moore think a lot about retirement. This is because they lead very hectic lives and think about slowing down sometime in the near future. But they seldom do anything about it. Dr. Moore's second most important objective has now been changed to retirement.

Now Dr. Moore suddenly has two major objectives. First, his taxes must be reduced. Second, an estate must be built to give him adequate cash flow at retirement. Dr. Moore does not, at this point, have to worry about the liquidity of his investments. He intends to work for at least another 10 years or so.

The tax shelters for Dr. Moore must have at least two major criteria. First, they must offer a large write-off in future years. and maybe some additional write-off in future years. Second, they must offer the possibility of excellent growth and capital appreciation.

Let's start with Dr. Moore's first investment criterion, write-off. Some of the following investments might be considered:

Oil and Gas. As we'll see in later chapters, certain forms of energy investments can result in a multiple tax write-off. A multiple write-off simply means that an investor gets over a 100 percent write-off in the first year. If he invests $10,000, he can deduct $10,000 from his taxable income. Since he is in the 50 percent tax bracket he would reduce his taxes by one-half or $5000. Should this same $10,000 investment have a first-year tax write-off of 200 percent, his taxable income would be reduced by two times his investment, or by $20,000. In the 50 percent bracket, this means a tax savings of $10,000. In other words, the entire investment is free, the government actually paid for all of it. Down the road, substantial profits of 3 to 1 or more are possible.

Research and Development is another area that Dr. Moore might want to pursue. This involves the financing of new products, primarily in high technology areas. Such investments can be handled directly or through a limited partnership. The write-offs are generally 100 percent of the investment the first year. Return can be as high as 10 to 1 on successful ventures.

HUD (Housing and Urban Development) Rehabilitation. This involves investing in the rehabilitation of moderate- to low-income housing. The government helps by subsidizing either a substantial portion of the mortgage payment or the rent. HUD programs offer a huge write-off since these buildings can be depreciated in only five years. Most of these programs are available through a limited partnership. Large write-offs, but little to no equity growth are possible in HUD investments.

Investments in limited partnerships such as the ones just mentioned can give Dr. Moore a write-off of up to 350%. As mentioned previously, a 200 percent write-off means that the investment is essentially free. If Dr. Moore is able to write off 200 percent, or two dollars for each dollar invested, he can reduce his taxable income by double the amount invested. Thus the government is paying the entire cost of his investment.

This type of investment would help to satisfy Dr. Moore's immediate financial objective. It would help to reduce the amount of taxes he has to pay. (The money thus saved could then be used for additional investments.) But Dr. Moore has a secondary objective, namely, retirement income in later years.

Planning for retirement involves taking current disposable income and investing it for growth and capital appreciation. (The shelters we've just considered, at least oil and gas and research and development, are also equity-builders. But they often involve higher risk than other equity-builders.)

Dr. Moore is planning for the future and is not concerned with getting income from his investments now. He wants his capital to grow as much as possible so that he can maintain his present lifestyle when he retires. To help him accomplish his secondary goal, I must first determine how much capital Dr. Moore needs at retirement and how much disposable income he really has. This process is somewhat different for a self-employed professional than it is for a salaried employee. After I determined how much income Dr. Moore earned from his practice, I deducted his expenses and arrived at a disposable income figure. Naturally, since he is self-employed and his income fluctuates monthly, a fairly large amount of reserve must be stored in a highly liquid form. He would want to have this money handy in case of an emergency, such as not being able to work because of illness.

A very liquid yet high yielding place to store money is a money market mutual fund. Dr. Moore would be wise to store his reserve in a money market account and use the rest of his disposable income for investing.

Now I need to examine the hodge-podge of investments that Dr. Moore has made over the past years in an attempt to shelter his income. Some may have done well and have a promising future. These he would keep. But other investments did not fare so well. Those are the ones that he undoubtedly bought simply because of their tax advantages and without consideration for their economic soundness. These nonprofitable investments should be liquidated if possible. The ones that are not liquid must be held. The proceeds from those investments he is able to sell should be added to the disposable income he will invest for the future.

Dr. Moore's disposable income will be invested in different areas — all in equity-builders. For many reasons, he needs diversification. To start out with, Dr. Moore might have his investments in such areas as:

Oil and gas
Real estate
Leasing
Mutual funds

Some will give him shelter, others growth. He needs them both. It is of utmost importance that these investments be reviewed at least annually. Should his objectives change, Dr. Moore might have to make an adjustment to the investments.

I believe that Dr. Moore's story illustrates how tax sheltering works together with financial planning. One cannot usually be done without the other. Depending on your particular financial situation, you may need more income and less tax shelters, but a consideration of tax consequences is always essential.

C H A P T E R   T H R E E

BENEFITS OF
PLANNING AND SHELTERS

In the first chapter, you learned that financial planning will help you identify your financial goals and give you a plan for achieving them. The last chapter showed you how to reach those goals by using tax shelters to reduce taxes and increase investment income.

There is still another important benefit to be derived from proper planning. We touched upon it briefly in the first chapter. Sometimes after analyzing their data sheets, people are forced to reconsider their financial goals. When they cannot meet their objectives with their current income, they are faced with two alternatives — to lower their objectives or to increase their income. Increasing income can be achieved by taking on a part-time job, or by having both spouses work, or by making a career change.

Then there are the self-employed who can make a fortune one year and be in the poorhouse the next. These people need proper financial planning in order to survive the lean years. This will be somewhat cleaner by taking a look at the case history of a woman named Helen.

HELEN

Helen is an entrepreneur, the owner and manager of a cosmetic sales distributorship. She is divorced, has two children to support, and has no source of income other than her business.

When Helen filled in her financial objectives on the data sheet, she listed as her primary goal "build estate." But after studying the data carefully, Helen began to realize that her true primary financial objective should be something else altogether. Her income over the past three years, according to her tax returns, was as follows:

First year	$35,000
Second year	$120,000
Third year	$43,000

Helen was already three months into the new year and still had no idea how much money she could expect to make that year. She felt it was crazy to be wealthy one year, skimping and saving the next. It was this state of uncertainty, Helen now believed, that was responsible for the frequent bouts of moodiness that were interfering with her relationships with her children, her friends, and her clients.

For Helen, then, building an estate really meant having enough money to live comfortably during the lean years of her business. When Helen realized that her true goal was "peace of mind," she set that as a primary financial objective. A college education for her two daughters was her second goal, and financial independence was her third. To achieve these objectives, Helen first had to determine exactly how much money she needed to support herself and family. Once this was done, Helen put away that amount in a reserve fund to pay for living expenses for up to six months. Helen invested her emergency dollars in a money market account where they would earn substantial interest but still be available at a moment's notice. Having a "peace of mind" fund made Helen a much happier person. She no longer had to worry about a regular paycheck from her business. As a result, she was able to devote much more energy to her business, and from that moment on, it really started to grow.

Later on, we reviewed Helen's situation to update her financial plan. She still had the six months of living expenses set aside. In addition, she had opened another money market account in which she deposited her savings from earnings each month. The second account had already accumulated a considerable amount of interest.

It's important to note at this point just what financial planning did for Helen. To begin with, it gave her peace of mind. Second, that peace of mind allowed her to improve her busines and therefore her income. And finally, with peace of mind, a good business, and money saved, Helen was well on her way to achieving her secondary goal, paying for her children's education. With continued financial planning and annual financial reviews. Helen should be able to achieve all her objectives.

It was pointed out earlier that putting money in a money market fund is a good idea when you are looking for a highly liquid form of storage rather than an investment. Money market funds simply allow you to keep up with inflation; they are not for long-term capital growth. Money market accounts should be used primarily for the following purposes:

1. to establish an emergency fund.
2. to accumulate savings which, once they reach a certain amount, will be invested elsewhere in accordance with your finance plan.
3. to accumulate earnings from investments. These earnings will be reinvested at a later time.

Helen had two money market accounts for entirely different purposes: the first was her emergency fund, to be used only if absolutely necessary; the second was her savings-from-earnings fund, to be used to finance the investments that will help her achieve her second and third goals — education for her children and financial independence for herself.

Now let's look at the investments Helen made. They are not like Dr. Moore's or the Herberts'. Because she is an entrepreneur, Helen is by nature a risk-taker. Therefore, she wanted to invest some of her money in ventures that might help her attain her goals more quickly. Naturally her investments needed to be sufficiently diversified to ensure that they would at least meet her minimum requirement — financing her children's education.

Since Helen is in a high tax bracket, she needs some type of tax shelter every year. These shelters could be in the form of a retirement plan, limited partnerships in oil and gas, leasing, cattle breeding, and others. Helen chose a properly drawn investment and diversification program that limited each investment to a certain percentage of her total assets. Such a program maximizes growth potential, yet minimizes risk.

Helen's story illustrates how financial planning can play a part in building a successful career. Not only does it help people achieve specific financial goals, as it did with the Herberts, or maximize tax savings, as it did with Dr. Moore, but it can also, by reducing financial uncertainty, free people to concentrate on the business at hand — their careers.

HOW YOU CAN DO IT YOURSELF

The data sheet is the starting point for your financial planning. You did some preliminary work on it in chapter 1, but now that you have had a chance to see how it actually worked in three case studies, you might want to go back and take a closer look at the sheet to make sure you filled in every detail. All the information you need for the form is on your income tax returns for the last three years. All sources of income, as well as all expenses, are listed on every return you file.

Once you have completely filled out your data sheet, put it away for a day or two, then reexamine it. Look carefully at your goals in terms of your income, trying to be as realistic as possible.

In light of your disposable income, are your financial objectives achievable? Perhaps you need to change your objectives somewhat or to restate them so that they more realistically meet your needs. Perhaps you need to consider changing or adding to your source of income.

Once you have defined your financial objectives, you will need help in achieving them. You are going to need to know what investments offer tax shelter — and how much, at what risk, and at what economic reward. You are going to need to know what investments offer growth, income, or a combination of the two.

The remainder of this book contains information that will help you determine the right investment for you. Through careful research and advice of specialists in all the investment areas, I have devised sound, clear guide to financial planning, growth, income, and tax-favored investments. Somewhere in this book, you will undoubtedly find ideas and investments that will help you achieve your financial goals.

CHAPTER FOUR

INVESTING THROUGH LIMITED PARTNERSHIPS

At some point in your investing careers, you will undoubtedly feel frustrated because you are not — and do not have time to become — experts at everything. Yet, you would certainly like to benefit from both the profits and the tax shelters offered by a wide variety of investment opportunities. What do you do, then, when you have money to invest and little or no knowledge of the world of investment opportunities?

For some people, the answer is that they limit their investments only to those areas which they do know something about. For example, some people invest only in real estate. Perhaps they began by buying their own home, then a rental house, then an apartment building. They feel they know real estate and they stick with it. Other investors feel equally comfortable investing in stocks or agriculture or oil and gas — areas they know something about.

Such investing requires active participation. The investment must be found, and the money raised to finance it. And once purchased, the investment must be expertly managed to make it profitable. Wouldn't it be simpler if there were a way for the investor to invest passively? To simply put up some capital and then pay someone else a nominal fee to handle the property search, the financing, the headaches of management?

The limited partnership is the solution for many passive investors. They can invest their capital and receive one or more of the following benefits:

Limited liability
Capital appreciation
Tax-shelter benefits
Immediate write-offs
Income

ADVANTAGES OF A LIMITED PARTNERSHIP

The major advantage of the limited partnership is that it gives the investor the benefits that would normally come to an individual investing alone. At the same time, it eliminates the problems of lack of expertise, liability, and active participation. Of course, limited partnerships are not foolproof. Later, we'll discuss what to watch out for when investing. But for now, let's explore how limited partnerships are put together and what they have to offer the passive investor.

If you were going to invest in, say, a research and development program, you would choose a particular product and company to go with. A partnership does the same thing. The partnership, however, has some distinct advantages over an individual investor when it comes to selecting an investment.

1. Because it can attract more investors and, therefore, more capital, a partnership can diversify. For example, you as an individual investor might only be able to invest in a single research and development product, whereas a partnership might be able to invest in ten. By diversifying, the partnership increases the chance of one of its investments paying off so well that it will cover the few that do not. If the product that you, the single investor, invests in fails, you lose everything.

2. A partnership, because it has more capital, is often in a better position to take advantage of opportunities, particularly in times of tight money, high interest rates, or depressed prices. A partnership with the capital of ten investors may be in a position to invest directly on a low leveraged basis while you as a single investor might only be able to invest through high leveraging. The difference in finance costs could mean the difference between a successful and unsuccessful investment.

3. A partnership, because some of its members are experts in the field, might be able to find investment opportunities that you as an individual might not be aware of.

A limited partnership does not protect against a bad investment. A partnership is not different from an individual when it comes to success or failure. In both cases, it's the success of the investment that counts. If, for example, it is cattle feeding, the cattle must eventually be sold for a profit. The limited partnership is only the investment vehicle. By itself, it won't protect the investor against a bad investment.

HOW A LIMITED PARTNERSHIP DIFFERS FROM A STANDARD PARTNERSHIP

Jane and Alice decide to open a boutique. They form a partnership, with each putting up half the investment and each agreeing to share equally in the management of their store. If their store's a hit, they'll share in the profits. If it's a loss, they'll share it equally. They are partners.

A limited partnership is different. In a limited partnership there are two categories of partners. The first category is the general partner or GP. The general partner has the same status as Jane or Alice. He or she usually finds the investment, raises the capital, puts in the time and effort to make it succeed, and bears full liability for loss (sometimes including personal liability).

The limited partner, however, is quite different. The limited partner contributes only capital, and often there is a ceiling on the amount one limited partner can invest. The limited partner does not, in fact cannot, take an active role in the business. In addition, the limited partner's liability is limited. *He or she cannot lose more than the amount of the original investment.* Hence the name "limited partner." This protection against loss extends to personal liability. In essence, the limited partner has a liability protection similar to that granted a stockholder who buys a share of stock in a corporation. He or she can participate in the profit, but can lose no more than the amount actually invested.

HOW LIMITED PARTNERSHIPS ARE FORMED

Typically, a limited partnership is formed when an individual, group, or even corporation finds an investment opportunity, but lacks the money to finance it. To raise capital, the individual or group offers limited partnership interests to those who are willing to contribute capital. The founding partner (or partners) becomes the general partner, and the investors the limited partners.

The general partner actively runs the partnership. The limited partners passively invest their money. Both hope to reap the profits.

HOW SIZE AFFECTS THE STATUS OF A LIMITED PARTNERSHIP

The size of the limited partnership is of major concern: it affects, of course, the amount of capital that can be raised, but more importantly, it determines whether or not it must conform to certain government regulations.

SEC Offerings

Large partnerships (generally those involving 35 or more people) or partnerships that cross state lines must be registered with the Security and Exchange Commission. These are referred to as *registered* or *SEC partnerships.* Partnerships purchased through stockbrokers and financial planners are in most cases SEC partnerships. Generally speaking, such investments involve millions of dollars because the investment pool must be large enough to warrant the expense and time of SEC registration.

Exempt Partnerships: 146 Partnerships and Private Offerings

The other form of syndication is the *exempt partnership,* a partnership that for one reason or another does not have to register with the SEC. Normally these partnerships are made up of just a few partners, all of whom reside within a single state. There are typically two types of exempt partnerships. One is the *146 partnership.* (The "146" refers to the IRS exclusion.) Its most obvious characteristic is that it cannot have more than 35 partners.

The second form of exempt syndication is the private or *friendly partnership.* Nearly every state allows for this type of syndication. There are usually limits on how many people may participate (in California, for example, the maximum number is 10), how potential investors may be contacted, what their relation to the general partner may be, and how much investment expertise the limited partners must have.

The private offering is generally for a small group of investors who join together for a particular investment. Both the private and the 146 exempts are often recommended by attorneys, accountants, and investment advisers.

RISK VS. GAIN IN TYPES OF PARTNERSHIP

Although success or failure of any partnership depends on a whole host of considerations (which we'll go into shortly), the risk of loss tends to decrease as the size of the partnership increases. The large SEC offerings usually have enough capital and expertise to succeed. Conversely, profits usually increase as the size of the partnership decreases. The greatest profit potential is found in small private offerings because far less capital is usually consumed in fees, commision, registration costs, and so forth, allowing for more capital to be channeled into the investment itself. If we were to chart risk potential with profit potential, our chart might look something like this:

> *Lowest risk*
> SEC offerings
> 146 offerings
> Private offerings
>
> *Highest profit*

TAX BENEFITS OF A LIMITED PARTNERSHIP

A limited partnership has been compared to a corporation several times in this chapter already. For example, limited partners, like stock owners, have limited liability. In addition, they participate only passively, not actively, and they get a share of the profits. But there are significant, even critical differences between a limited partnership and a corporation that give limited partnerships special advantages. These are in the areas of taxation.

A corporation is considered, for tax purposes, to be an entity. It is taxed as an entity. That means that the stock owner's potential earnings are taxed twice. They are taxed once when the corporation pays taxes on its earnings. Then they are taxed again when the stock owner pays his own personal income taxes on the dividends received from the corporation. This does not happen in a limited partnership. A partnership is not considered an entity for tax purposes; therefore, it is not taxed directly. Rather, any gain the partnership makes on an investment (including capital gains) is passed directly on to the individual partners. The partners, therefore, pay taxes only once — when they receive their profit.

There is another important difference. If a corporation has a tax loss or creates a tax shelter, the tax benefits go only to the corporation. The individual stock investors do not benefit (except, ultimately in higher dividends). In a limited partnership, however, tax benefits (including write-offs and shelters), like gains, are passed on directly to the investor.

The above tax advantages make a limited partnership a highly desirable investment vehicle. Limited partnerships offer the benefits of limited liability and passive investing that we normally associate with corporate stock investments. Yet, at the same time, they offer the benefits of direct pass-through of profits, shelters, and write-offs normally associated with individual investments. This is why so many investors today choose limited partnerships over other investment vehicles.

THE STRUCTURE OF THE LIMITED PARTNERSHIP

The benefits of the limited partnership that we have just discussed can be gained only if the structure of the partnership can withstand the scrutiny of the IRS. In the past the IRS challenged some syndications, refusing to allow them the tax status of partnerships. Write-offs and shelters were disallowed, causing severe tax problems for investors.

Today, the IRS seems less likely to challenge a properly structured partnership. The vehicle is becoming more and more accepted. Although a complete discussion of how a partnership must be structured to meet IRS requirements is beyond the scope of this book, there are a few conditions that all potential investors should be aware of. Generally speaking, to avoid being classified as an entity such as an association or a corporation, a limited partnership must not have more than two of the following characteristics:

Continuity of life
Free transferability of investment interest
Centralized management
Limited liability

Obviously every syndication has centralized management and limited liability. The question, then, is how to eliminate the other two. To avoid continuity of life, all partnerships should be set up to dissolve at a certain point in time. Upon sale of an investment, therefore, the hoped-for profit is split up and the partnership dissolved.

To avoid free transferability, often partnerships specify that limited partners may not freely sell their interests. Only the general partner at his or her discretion may allow the sale of a limited partner's interests. To be sure of a partnership's tax status, limited partners must be confident in the attorneys who structure it.

We've looked at the general picture of a limited partnership. Before investing in one, however, it might be worthwhile to spend a bit of time examining potential concerns more closely. Here are some questions that you might want to consider before investing as a limited partner:

1. *How strong is the general partner?*

The general partner is critical to the success of the limited partnership. It is his expertise that the limited partners are counting on. Remember, only the GP takes an active role in the partnership. The most important thing to look for in a general partner is his track record. How many successful (and unsuccessful) partnerships has he been involved in? The more experience he has had in the field of the current investment, the better protected you are.

The next most important requirement for a general partner is financial stability and strength. If the general partner is financially strong, he can weather the storm in case something goes wrong. Often the general partner has to come up with a substantial amount of money to cover unexpected expenses. A well-heeled general partner will be able to do it with no problem.

2. *How much does the general partner invest?*

An important consideration because the amount of the general partner's investment will probably have a direct bearing on his degree of involvement in the success of the partnership. If the general partner has invested at least as much as each of the limited partners, then it's a good sign that he has his eyes on the investment and not on your pocketbook.

3. *Is the partnership a specified partnership or a blindpool?*

Specified partnerships have the investment property already lined up before the money is gathered from potential limited partners. For example, the general partner may have an option to buy an apartment building and may now be raising money to make the down payment.

A note of caution. Potential investors must be sure that the property, whatever it is, is in fact in the general partner's name. If not, it could be a scam.

In a *blindpool*, individual investors combine their capital and then go out looking for property to buy or lease. Here, the property is found and acquired after the partnership is formed. If you are ever involved in a blindpool partnership, you yourself must know a great deal about the kind of investment you are planning to make, or you must have confidence in the general partner who will manage it for you. In this kind of offering, the goals of the group must be spelled out.

4. *Do the economics of the investment make sense?*

As you'll see, many investments offer enormous initial write-offs plus long term shelter. But, this may not be enough. Some exploratory wells offer a 100 percent or higher write-off. But, if no oil is found, the investors may suffer a big loss. The paper write-off, which is highly desirable, could become a real cash write-off, which is not desirable. Many investors who carefully examine the economic risks when they are investing individually can be swayed by the promises of large write-offs and tax shelters offered through syndication. The point is that both kinds of investments — individual and group — should make economic sense.

5. *What are the tax risks?*

You know the tax benefits of a limited partnership — passed-through gain, perhaps capital gain, and passed-through write-offs and shelter. Now it's time to look at the possible tax risks.

If the IRS disallows the partnership. As you have learned, the IRS may challenge the tax status of a limited partnership on the basis of structure. It may also disallow a partnership because it is "abusive." An abusive partnership is one that is created not to invest in property for economic gain, but to produce tax write-offs for its "investors." For example, there have been partnerships that offered an incredible 6 to 1 write-off. You invest $5000 and you can write off $30,000!

These offerings often involve a mine of some sort. Your large write-off is possible because a third party (someone not involved in the partnership) takes out options for the other $25,000, making it appear that you are at risk for the entire $30,000. If you become involved in such a partnership, you may be successful in claiming a significant write-off — initially. But, the IRS has been spending a great deal of its time investigating tax-shelter schemes, and you could fail an audit. The IRS might conclude that the limited partnership was abusive and that its real intent was to defraud the government of taxes. If that's the case, it could spell big trouble.

It is possible for the government to disallow any write-off taken in an abusive tax shelter. In addition, the government could charge interest on the taxes you deferred through the partnership. And it could even go so far as to demand penalties, perhaps as high as 40 percent of the money involved.

Abusive shelters should be avoided like the plague.

Generally speaking, abusive shelters tend to pop up at the end of the year when taxpayers are desperate for some sort of tax relief. Desperate taxpayers tend to be blinded by the possibility of huge write-offs promised and blind to the true value of the shelter as an economic and legal entity.

Beware of exotic limited partnerships offering huge write-offs at year's end.

If the investment fails. You'll recall that we spoke of a tax shelter as an instrument to defer taxable income from the present to the future. In addition, shelter may transfer money out of the ordinary income bracket rate into the more favorable capital gains rate. That may indeed be your investment goal. But, if you have not carefully examined the economic realities before investing (or if something should go wrong unexpectedly), you might end up

losing the investment. For example, in real estate, if the partnership over-leverages, and either the rental income cannot be collected or the resale market collapses, the property could go into
foreclosure. It — and all the capital invested in it — could be lost.

At first this may not seem so bad because you know that the
limited partner's liability is limited to the amount actually invested. But, let's see what else can happen.

Let's say that the property purchased was a building that had
been depreciated through an accelerated method. The building
was held for a number of years. Then, when rental income was no
longer sufficient to meet expenses, the building was lost through
foreclosure. How does that leave the limited partners? Assume
that each limited partner invested $10,000. During the course of
several years he or she was able to write off $30,000. This write-off
goes into the investor's "capital account." It includes the amount
of write-off minus the amount invested. In this case, the capital
account would show a deficit of $20,000.

$10,000	Investment
−30,000	Write off
−20,000	Deficit

When the property was lost, the partnership ended. The investor
obviously lost the original capital invested, or $10,000. In addition,
the investor must now bring his or her capital account back to zero
for tax purposes. That means showing a gain of $20,000.

Capital account deficit	−$20,000
Ordinary income	+20,000
	0

To bring the capital account back to zero, the investor now has
to show $20,000 of income on his or her income tax return. In other
words, the write-off taken has to be recaptured as ordinary income
even though the investment was lost through foreclosure.

We hope that our cautionary words will encourage investors to
seek out limited partnerships that make sound economic sense.

6. *How are the partners to share the gain?*

The profit-sharing arrangement is of critical importance to
limited partners. They determine how much — and how soon —
profit will be made. Three types of fees have a direct bearing on
the limited partner's profit: front-end fees, ongoing fees, and
back-end fees.

Front-End Fees. These are the fees that the partnership must
pay at the beginning of the investment. They cover the cost of
acquiring the property, legal and accounting fees, costs for setting

up the partnership, promotional fees for finding limited partners and commissions to sales people soliciting limited partners.

Front-end fees are usually paid out of the capital raised. What this means, of course, is that the more the partnership pays in front-end fees, the less it has for the actual investment. This situation accounts for the question so often asked in oil and gas partnerships: "How much of the investment is actually going into the ground?" Front-end fees in oil and gas, for example, should never be more than 20 percent of the capital raised. Fifteen percent would be an even better figure.

There is a huge variation in the amount of front-end fees limited partnerships pay. Small unregistered partnerships often have small fees because they don't need to advertise and promote (indeed are prohibited from it). Beware of small private offerings with large promotional fees going to the general partner.

Ongoing Fees. The general partner often charges a management fee. Additionally, there may be other fees like maintenance and insurance. The amount of these fees should be spelled out in advance so that the investor can take a close look at them to see if they seem reasonable. Beware of partnerships with high ongoing fees.

Back-End Fees. It's at the back end of the partnership that the profit is split up. As noted earlier, the split can be anything the partners agree upon. A 50-50 split between the general partner and the limited partners is not unusual. But, then again, neither is an 80-20 split, with 80 percent going to the limited partners.

What you as an investor should be wary of is a partnership where the general partner's interest is *nonsubordinated*. In a *subordinated partnership*, the limited partners get back all their original investment capital plus a modest return on it (usually in the range of 6 to 10%) before any of the remaining profits are shared.

In a *nonsubordinated partnership*, however, the sharing is done right away — before the limited partners get their capital back. Let's look at a case in which the partners initially put up $100,000. When the investment was sold, there was $200,000 to split up. Assuming a 50-50 split, here's how the money would be distributed in both a subordinated and a nonsubordinated partnership:

Subordinated split

$200,000	Proceeds of sale
−106,000	Limited partner's investment (plus 6%)
94,000	Profit
47,000	To general partner (50%)
47,000	To limited partners (50%)

Nonsubordinated split

$200,000	Proceeds of sale
100,000	To general partner (50%)
100,000	To limited partners (50%)

A close examination of these figures will reveal that the limited partners in the subordinated split made a profit of $53,000 ($6,000 in interest plus $47,000 in capital gains). In the nonsubordinated split, the limited partners only got back their original $100,000 investment. They made no profit at all.

Be wary of nonsubordinated sharing arrangements at the back end. It could take far longer for you as a limited partner either to get back your capital or to make a profit. The general partner could be making money at your expense.

Remember, *sharing arrangements have tax consequences.* Often the sharing arrangement will also determine how much write-off you may be allowed on an investment. Although at first glance this may seem so obvious that it is hardly worth talking about, there can be problems. One problem occurred in an oil partnership in which the promoter promised large year-end write-offs to potential investors. He put up one percent of the capital; the investors put up 99 percent. They were to share in the gain on a 50-50 basis.

The advantage to the oil promoter was obvious. To the limited partners, the advantage was the big write-off. Since they put up 99 percent of the capital, they felt they were entitled to 99 percent of the deductions. Unfortunately, that did not prove to be the case. The IRS felt that since the sharing arrangement was 50-50, the write-offs should also be 50-50. The promoter who put up one percent, got 50 percent of the write-off. And the investors who put up 99 percent had to be content with their 50 percent.

7. *Is the parternship assessable or nonassessable?*

If the partnership is nonassessable, the general partner cannot ask the limited partners for additional funds in the event something unforeseen happens. If the partnership is *assessable*, he can. Should you, then, avoid assessable partnerships at all costs? Not necessarily, as you shall see.

A limited partnership is an investment vehicle that must travel over bumpy roads as well as smooth ones. Unforeseen things do happen. If a partnership is locked into a nonassessable arrangement, it could mean that the entire investment could fail if something unexpected comes up. On the other hand, an assessable partnership has the means to raise the money to handle the unexpected. Sometimes it is better to be in an assessable partnership.

It is not uncommon in oil and gas, for example, for the general partner to assess the limited partners an additional 10, 20 or even 30 percent of capital to protect the investment. (Quite often an assessment has been required to complete a well or to drill an offset well. Such assessments are generally to the advantage of the limited partners.) The limited partners must now come up with this money. If they can't, the general partner can sell their share of the assessment. Or, if the general partner is strong, he might put up the money directly, thus reducing the limited partner's percentage of ownership.

8. *Are the suitability standards being observed?*

Federal and state laws specify that only "suitable" investors may enter into a limited partnership. These laws are designed to protect naive persons from promoters who might urge them to invest money they can ill afford to lose in risky ventures.

The offering circular must state the risks involved in the investment. In addition, the general partner must be sure that limited partners meet suitability tests. Generally these tests include such items as minimum annual income and minimum numbers of assets. Additionally, the general partner must be sure that the potential investors are sufficiently sophisticated to understand the risks involved. The GP must use *due diligence* in determining each partner's suitability.

All partners, limited and general, should make sure that suitability standards are met. If they are not, and if only one limited partner can show that the general partner did not use due diligence in determining his or her suitability, the appropriate government body could order recission.

Recission essentially dissolves the partnership, returning it to the way it was before the investment. If recission occurs several years after all the partners have taken big write-offs, it could mean horrendous tax bills for all concerned. Therefore, the limited partners should satisfy themselves that the general partner has screened all investors for suitability. Often a glance at the

Partnership Application forms will provide a clue. Typically, these forms include statements that reveal the limited partner's assets, income, and degree of financial sophistication.

Is a limited partnership for you?

Literally hundreds of thousands, perhaps millions, of investors participate successfully in limited partnerships in all sorts of fields. It is essential to get your financial planner's or your investment counselor's advice before investing in limited partnerships. But, ultimately, *you* must make the decision whether or not to invest.

IRA AND KEOGH PLANS: SOMETHING FOR EVERYONE

Keogh and Individual Retirement Account (IRA) plans should be considered by almost everyone who meets the requirements. These plans permit investors to accumulate money for retirement and to benefit from a strong tax shelter while doing so. They are also relatively simple to understand and safe to use.

In chapter 2, you saw how these plans save you money by deferring taxes on both the amount you invest and the income it earns until you are in a lower tax bracket. Now, we will look at the benefits and risks of retirement plans in greater detail.

BENEFITS

1. *Growth*. The most obvious benefit is growth. As you've learned, money that is not taxed grows at a much faster rate than money that is. The following chart shows the growth of two tax-deferred investments: a one-time $10,000 investment and a $2000-a-year annual investment, at various interest rates.

	Investment					
	$10,000 (one-time)			$2000 (per year)		
Interest rate	10 yrs.	20 yrs.	30 yrs.	10 yrs.	20 yrs.	30 yrs.
10%	27,070	73,280	198,373	36,015	133,500	397,362
15%	44,402	197,154	875,410	49,694	270,434	1,250,949

Note: Interest is compounded monthly.

2. *Retirement Capital*. The Keogh and IRA plans are designed to provide retirement capital for their investors. It is easy to figure out how much you should invest to achieve your retirement goals because taxation does not enter the picture until after you begin to withdraw the money. The following chart shows you how much money you should set aside each month to reach your goals.

Keogh and IRA Retirement Cost Timer

Age	Years to retirement	Monthly contribution necessary to accumulate $100,000	$250,000	$500,000	$1,000,000
25	40	16	39	78	157
35	30	44	110	219	439
45	20	130	325	653	1,306
55	10	484	1,210	2,421	4,841

Note: Figures are based on a 10 percent interest rate compounded monthly.

If the money in an IRA or Keogh account is withdrawn before age 59½, you may have to pay ordinary income taxes on the amount withdrawn plus a penalty of 10%, depending on the circumstances (as you will see later)

3. *Tax Deferral*. IRA and Keogh provide an immediate tax shelter. This shelter is perhaps better than any offered anywhere. Think of it this way. If you happen to be in the 50 percent tax bracket, the government is giving you an automatic 100 percent write-off. It's as if you went into a bank and deposited $1000, and the bank credited your account with $2000. You instantly pick up an extra thousand.

4. *Risk Factors*. Because an IRA or Keogh account gives you both immediate tax shelter and future security, you can invest your retirement money in low-risk ventures. Rather than looking for an immediate profit or a big write-off, you can concentrate on investments that pay good dividends now and will continue to grow over a long period of time. (Note: it is not necessary to keep your IRA or Keogh plan at a bank or at a stockbroker's office. It's possible to set it up so that you can invest it yourself in many other areas.)

IS AN IRA OR KEOGH PLAN FOR THE YOUNG INVESTOR?

A question that frequently comes up is whether people in their twenties should think about one of these pension plans. After all, they have many, many years before they will retire. Why worry now? This is a difficult question to answer. Generally, I tell young couples who are doing well (that is, both are working and are in a relatively high tax bracket) that a Keogh or IRA makes good sense for them.

On the other hand, if the couple is in a very low tax bracket and needs liquidity, then perhaps they should wait one or more years before participating. (Remember, you can't get the money out of

Keogh or IRA without a penalty except in special circumstances.) The tax bracket and the degree of liquidity needed are the real criteria on which the decision to invest in a retirement plan should be based.

CONTRIBUTIONS

We'll cover both the Keogh and IRA in detail in just a moment, but, first, let's consider one important point. In order to put money into one of these pension plans, you must first earn it. This is an important point. The government specifically requires that contributions to these plans come from earned income.

Earned income is basically income from salary or self-employment. It does not include income from dividends, rents, interest, and so on. Further, the amount of the contribution you can make in any one year is determined by the income you earned that year. The higher the earned income (up to the maximum limits), the more you may contribute.

THE 1981 ECONOMIC RECOVERY TAX ACT

The major change affecting retirement plans in the 1981 Economic Recovery Tax Act was to increase the maximum allowable contributions. Keogh's annual allowable contribution was increased from $7500 to $15,000 or 15 percent of earned income, whichever is less. This increased the desirability for a Keogh as a retirement plan, particularly for those in a high tax bracket.

IRA's annual contribution was increased from $1500 to $2000 or 100 percent of earned income, whichever is less. Everyone under the age of 70½ who is a wage earner can now have an IRA. (Even if you already have a pension plan through your work, you can open your own IRA account.)

THE KEOGH PLAN

The Keogh plan was created by the Self-Employed Individual Retirement Acts of 1962 (HR-10) and amended by the Economic Recovery Tax Act of 1981 (ERTA). It enables self-employed individuals (either full or part-time) to set up a personal retirement account on a tax-deferred basis. If you pay self-employed Social Security tax for yourself, you can qualify for a Keogh plan.

The maximum annual contribution to a Keogh plan is $15,000 or 15 percent of your earnings from self-employment, whichever is less. These payments are deductible from current income. Therefore, the true cost of a Keogh plan is considerably reduced.

Net taxable income	15 percent Keogh contribution	1982 federal tax bracket married-joint	Tax savings	Actual cost
$100,000	$15,000	50%	$7,500	$7,500
50,000	7,500	44	3,300	4,200
30,000	4,500	33	1,485	3,015
20,000	3,000	22	660	2,340

It is obvious that a person in a higher tax bracket benefits more from a Keogh plan. However, a $660 savings in taxes on a $3000 investment (for someone earning $20,000 in a 22 percent bracket) is not too bad either.

The Keogh plan is summarized in the following paragraphs.

1. Income and capital gains accumulate tax deferred in a Keogh account.

2. Should your earned income be less than $15,000, you can invest up to $750 a year in a so-called "Mini-Keogh."

3. Retirement withdrawals can start as early as age 59½ and must begin not later than the end of the year in which you reach age 70½. Premature withdrawals, before age 59½, are subject to a penalty of 10% on the amount withdrawn and are taxed at your regular income tax rate. Furthermore, you will be disqualified from participating in another Keogh plan for five years unless plan is terminated.

4. There are only two exceptions to the early withdrawal rules: disability and death. Your beneficiary may withdraw your investment in a lump sum or over a period of time. Beneficiary withdrawals are taxed as regular income.

5. At retirement, withdrawals may be made in installments or a lump sum. A lump sum withdrawal may be taxed favorably if you participated in the Keogh plan for at least 10 years. Under a special 10-year averaging method, the lump sum is divided by 10 and the quotient (one-tenth of the lump sum) is taxed using the tax tables applicable to single persons. That figure is then multiplied by 10 to arrive at the tax due. The benefit here is that the lump sum, because it is distributed before taxes are computed, is taxed at a much lower rate.

6. In case of death, your assets in a Keogh plan are not included in your estate, provided they are paid to a named beneficiary over

a period of at least two different taxable years. If paid out in a lump sum, the entire amount will be included in your estate.

7. Keogh plans do not affect Social Security benefits. The two are entirely separate plans.

OPENING A KEOGH

There are a number of ways to invest in a Keogh plan:

1. Banks and savings and loan associations offer Keogh plans, but your money must be invested in their accounts. The advantage here is that your money is insured to certain limits. The disadvantage is that the performance record of these accounts is very poor.

2. Mutual funds have prototype plans that offer investments in a variety of funds such as money market accounts, stock growth funds, bonds, and options. You may choose the funds in which you are interested, and for a nominal fee (about $5), you may switch to different funds within the same group.

3. Trust companies offer accounts where you may invest in an even broader group of vehicles. You may choose limited partnerships in real estate, oil and gas income, stocks, bonds, and the like. Fees to establish and maintain such trusts are higher than those charged by banks and mutual funds, but the advantages of diversification and the potential for greater capital growth might make a trust fund desirable.

Tax-Deferred Growth

Before leaving the Keogh plan, it is worth taking a few moments to compare the kind of growth possible in a Keogh with the kind available in a similar, non-tax-deferred investment. We'll assume a $15,000 annual contribution at 15% interest.

| | **Accumulations** | |
	With Keogh	**50% tax bracket Without Keogh**
10 years	372,707	115,754
15 years	905,450	215,387
20 years	2,028,254	360,161
25 years	4,394,671	570,528

The advantage of a tax-deferred investment is obvious. But, you must remember that money in a retirement plan is not liquid.

INDIVIDUAL RETIREMENT ACCOUNT (IRA)

Beginning January 1, 1982, anyone under the age of 70½ who earns income can establish an IRA. There are no exceptions. All earners covered by a company plan, a Keogh, or a government retirement system can have an IRA.

As in a Keogh, every dollar that you contribute is tax deductible. And all earnings in an IRA are tax deferred. This means you will not pay any federal taxes either on your contributions or your earnings until you begin to withdraw money at retirement. The maximum investment in an IRA account is $2000 per year or 100 percent of your earnings, whichever is less. If you are married, with a spouse that does not work, the law gives you an even bigger break. You may set aside up to $2250 and divide it in equal or unequal shares between two accounts — one for each spouse. You cannot put the entire $2250 in one account. The maximum is $2000 per account per year. If you are married and both of you work, each of you may contribute up to $2000 in two separate accounts, an annual total of $4000.

Investments

The investment opportunities for IRA are similar to those for the Keogh plan. In fact, to encourage the participation of IRA investors, most limited partnerships have lowered their minimum investment requirements from $5000 to $2000 (for IRA accounts only). Through custodial trust accounts, you may now invest your IRA money in various real estate, oil and gas income and leasing programs. This is an excellent way to share in high appreciation with a relatively low capital outlay.

Withdrawals

Retirement withdrawals can start as early as age 59½ and must begin not later than age 70½. Earlier withdrawals, unless due to disability or death, are penalized at 10 percent. You or your beneficiaries will have to use the five-year averaging method to compute taxes if they choose to withdraw the money in a lump sum. In case of death, the value of your IRA will not be included in your estate if your named beneficiary takes distribution over at least 36 months. If a lump sum distribution is taken (see above), it is included in your estate.

Rollovers

The rollover allows a taxpayer to transfer one retirement account to another account under certain circumstances. This generally happens when an individual receives a lump sum payment from a company pension or profit-sharing plan upon retirement or change of employment. Another often-used type of rollover is from a Keogh or IRA account to another IRA account. This is generally done when the investor is not pleased with the performance of his present retirement plan or when the investor has accumulated a great deal of money in a fixed account and would like to diversify for the possibility of greater growth.

The rollover can be made regardless of whether the account is in cash or in some other form. The critical thing here is that the transfer must be made within 60 days of the date the lump sum distribution was made. Such a distribution must go in its original form to the new trustee. The owners of a retirement plan cannot have constructive receipt of funds. If he or she does, the plan immediately becomes taxable!

IRA AND KEOGH TRUST ACCOUNTS

One final and important matter should be discussed with regard to pension plans. We see and hear a lot of advertising having to do with pension plans. Everyone wants our money. Banks suggest, naturally enough, that you put it in banks; stockbrokers suggest that it go to their companies, and so forth. The truth of the matter is that you can have fully administered pension plans or you can have self-administered plans.

In a fully administered plan, the trustee directs the investment. A bank requires the money to be placed in its accounts. A stock brokerage firm may frequently require that you keep it either in a mutual fund or in stocks and bonds. But, in a self-administered plan you can put the money where you wish, within certain rather broad legal constraints. (You can't, for example, invest it in highly speculative areas.)

You can establish as many Keogh and IRA plans as you wish, although the total contributions per year must remain the same regardless of how many plans you may have. Additionally, if you are dissatisfied with the trustee who now has your money, you can transfer at your option.

Some institutions acting as trustees may have your money invested in low interest accounts. When you walk into, say, a bank and demand to have your IRA plan transferred, the manager will offer to put your money in a higher paying account. (The response to this is, "If you have a higher paying account, why didn't you put my money into it before I asked to take it out?")

IRA and Keogh plans will probably be the major source of tomorrow's retirement incomes. In fact, they may be the only source. The baby boom generation will reach old age in just a few decades. There will be more older people entitled to collect Social Security than there are young people to pay into it. There may be no money to fund Social Security or government pension plans. They are going to be the bread and butter of older America. What this means is that the Keogh and IRA plans are going to become more and more important each year.

CHAPTER SIX

INVESTING IN OIL AND GAS

Almost all the investors I meet wish they had bought more real estate during the seventies — the great Real Estate Decade. The eighties will probably not be as kind to real estate investors, although selected investments should continue to increase in value. I believe the momentum has shifted to another area of tax-shelter investing.

Oil and gas will be the real estate of the eighties. It seems almost certain that fossil-based fuels will continue to rise in price as proven reserves dwindle.

If the current trend continues, in the year 2000 Americans will consume double the amount of oil and gas they do today. Even at today's rate of consumption, our current reserves (recoverable with current technology) of oil and natural gas will last only 40-60 years, according to the United States Geological Survey.

Oil, which, at the time of this writing, sells on the world spot market at $34 a barrel, could reach $100 a barrel by the end of the decade. Gasoline at $2.50 a gallon seems inevitable. In the colder parts of the United States, it could soon cost considerably more to heat a home than it does to rent one.

In the eighties, smart investors will finance their gasoline and home-heating bills by selling a barrel of "investment oil" every now and then. Don't laugh. For the past ten years or so, investors lucky enough to know a good financial planner or a very progressive stockbroker have been participating in a tax shelter known as an oil income program. In addition to a handsome income (oil prices have appreciated more than 1000 percent), this shelter has provided modest tax benefits because part of the income derived from selling the oil is tax free.

Oil and gas tax shelters, like real estate shelters, went through some growing pains in the seventies. Few reputable financial planners felt comfortable enough with gas and oil to recommend it to their clients. Now, most companies have had enough experience to recommend at least one program of each major type: (1) oil income programs for investors seeking income without great risk; (2) drilling programs for investors who want big tax write-offs and big gain potential; and (3) balanced programs that combine some features of both income and drilling programs.

I personally feel that oil and gas partnerships belong in almost any investment portfolio. Many of the problems of the past have disappeared simply because oil and gas have become part of the investment mainstream. For example, one problem in the past was a lack of liquidity. Recently, a major brokerage firm, Bache, Halsey, Stuart, Shields, formed a new corporation that will exchange its listed, liquid stock for your partnership interests in oil and gas.

The complete deregulation of natural gas prices, which now is inevitable, can only add to the value of partnership units, and in an energy-short world there is a psychological advantage to owning a little bit of the commodity that is on everyone's mind. As I tell my clients, even though owning oil and gas doesn't lower your monthly utility bill, it sure makes paying it less painful. To put it another way, rising fuel prices are not like the weather. Everybody complains about it, but something can be done about it. But what?

This chapter and the two immediately following tell you what you can do. This chapter relates the history of oil and gas shelters. Chapter 8 discusses the special risks of oil and gas, and chapter 9 surveys the rewards of programs on the market today.

MR. LEWIS'S PETRODOLLAR BANK

In 1970, long before news commentators had coined the word *petrodollar*, a man named Jerome Lewis founded a little company in Denver to engage in petrodollar banking. As you might have guessed, the bank's assets were calculated not in dollars but in barrels of oil and gas. Its vault was the earth itself, miles underground.

The minimum deposit in Mr. Lewis' bank was $2500, and for that a depositor received one unit in the Petro-Lewis Oil Income Fund. Mr. Lewis, who is a conservative man, invested his depositors' money only in producing oil wells or in new wells in proven areas. Before he put his investors' money in the ground, he had a very good idea how much oil it was buying. Then, just to be safe, he spread the investment among many wells, so that if one failed, others could make up for it.

People who put money in banks want interest on their deposits. Although Mr. Lewis could not guarantee his depositors quarterly or even annual interest, he did the next best thing. As soon as the oil started pumping, he sent them a quarterly income check which represented their share of the oil sold by the petrodollar bank.

Despite this planning, the idea of a petrodollar bank was not greeted with wild enthusiasm in 1970. Only 42 people invested in the first Petro-Lewis Oil Income Fund. They were entrepreneurs and college teachers, corporate vice-presidents and civil servants, doctors and lawyers, merchants and police chiefs. (Then, as now, the suitability standards for oil income programs were not restrictive: $25,000 in net worth, exclusive of personal belongings, and $25,000 in annual household income.)

I find that most investors, regardless of their assets or tax bracket, can't bear the idea that their money may be spent drilling a dry hole. Now that the cost of buying producing wells is very high, we have another conservative alternative for these people — the shallow well. In parts of Ohio and Pennsylvania, oil oozes relatively close to the surface of the earth, and 80 to 90 percent of the time these deposits can be tapped successfully. The oil never gushes forth in great quantity. It only trickles, but that trickle of oil can add up to a steady income, one that over time should hold up well against inflation.

Shallow well investments are the safest of the oil and gas partnerships, and when we leave them we move from petrodollar banking to petro speculation.

At first (in the earlier seventies), these investors received an annual income of only 6 to 8 percent of their investment — not bad in those days but not spectacular. Then, as oil climbed in price, from $3 to more than $30 per barrel, the value of their investment units increased in proportion. An investor who puts $10,000 in the 1970 program received four quarterly checks in 1980 totaling $8104, a return of more than 80 percent on the original investment in one year. The total return on this investment through 1980 was $42,287, more than four times the original investment. And the petrodollar pumps are still producing income.

About 100,000 individual investments have now been made in 81 subsequent Petro-Lewis partnerships, and even taking into account the company's strong investor loyalty (some people have invested in a dozen or more partnerships), perhaps 50,000 people have enjoyed petrodollar income, Petro-Lewis style. Now, another large oil program sponsor, Damson Oil of New York City, and several smaller producers have joined the oil income business, opening it up to even more investors.

The story of Mr. Lewis's petrodollar bank has undoubtedly raised a few questions in your mind. Do all people who invest in oil do that well? Are there other kinds of oil investments that make that kind of money? What are the risks? Perhaps the following tale will answer many of your questions.

LIFE ON THE PRAIRIE

Perhaps we can best understand how the different types of oil and gas programs work by looking at the life cycle of an imaginary oil field, Panhandle Prairie. The field will go through six phases before it is phased out. They are (1) information gathering, (2) leasing, (3) exploration, (4) completion, (5) primary production, and (6) secondary production.

Information Gathering. When we first look at Panhandle Prairie, we see nothing but gophers and sagebrush. However, if we look more closely, we will spot two sets of information gatherers at work. One is a team of seismic geologists, busy bouncing sound waves off subterranean rocks. The other is Wildcat Pete, the best divining-rod handler in the territory. At about the same time, the geologists complete their testing, and Pete's divining rod dips conclusively toward the ground.

Leasing. Now, with information in hand, the two sets of entrepreneurs go to work leasing mineral rights to Panhandle Prairie. (Very rarely do oil and gas explorers buy land outright.) The geologists work for an "independent oil man," who puts together financing and purchases his lease outright. Pete, on the other hand, borrows money from Aunt Bertha and Cousin Ned and, because he still doesn't have enough, cuts in the landowner.

Exploration. The exploration phase requires real risk money. The independent oil man sells his lease to a public oil and gas exploration company in exchange for cash and the promise of royalties on any oil produced. Pete raises his risk money in typical patch style. He finds three wealthy investors who finance the entire exploratory drilling operation in exchange for 75% of the action. Pete, the promoter, gets the other 25% in this kind of "third for a quarter" deal.

Pete, true to his nickname, drills the first well on the Prairie. Only about 75% of the wildcat wells drilled are successful, according to the American Association of Petroleum Geologists. The public exploration program drills the follow-up hole (this type of drilling is successful about 27% of the time).

Completion and Primary Production. Lo and behold, both exploratory ventures strike oil. Now comes the need for big medium-risk money to complete the drilling and bring the wells into production. The public program spends $50,000 to complete the initial well and get it pumping. It then uses the revenue from this first well, plus additional assessments from its limited partners if necessary, to finance six "developmental" wells in the same area, at a cost of $600,000. Pete has no such access to capital, and so he takes a different route. When he completes the drilling on his first well, he sells it to an oil income program to raise additional capital for developmental drilling. Aunt Bertha, Uncle Ned, the landowner, and the three "third for a quarter" investors continue to share the risk of developmental drilling with Pete. (Developmental wells have a success rate of about twice that of follow-up exploratory drilling.) On the other hand, the developmental risk-bearers have greater potential reward than the oil income program investors, who invest only in proven wells.

Secondary Production. Finally, the Prairie begins to play out as an active production site. All the investors are receiving regular cash, with the original risk-bearers getting the most, the developmental risk-bearers a little less, and the income program participants less yet. Pete, the original promoter, has joined the country club set. Uncle Ned has a new mobile home. The oil drillers, in an effort to extend the life of the wells, try secondary and tertiary recovery methods, which involve pumping water or pressurized gas underground to drive the oil upward.

The moral of Panhandle Prairie should be clear: The earlier an investor becomes a part of the oil field's history, the greater his risk and potential rewards. However, there is also a risk of getting involved too late — about the time a productive well starts to play out. The one drawback to oil income programs is that the investment value declines as the well plays out. (In one sense, an oil income program is like an annuity on the life of the well.)

A WORD OF CAUTION

What can we learn from the tale of Panhandle Prairie? I think it is obvious now that the risk of exploration should be borne only by sophisticated investors with deep pockets and a crying need for tax shelter. (The more risk you take, the more shelter you are likely to get.) Although most investors are initially excited by the prospect of striking a gusher, their fear of sinking their money into a dry hole is usually greater.

If an investor is almost, but not quite, a candidate for exploration or developmental drilling, I recommend a program like the Damson Development Drilling Program, where 20 percent of the money goes into exploration and the other 80 percent into proven income properties.

New ideas emerge each year in oil and gas, and I always urge caution in pursuing them. The latest new idea, called an *oil completion program*, buys the equipment necessary to pump oil out of the ground and then leases it to the well operator in return for a percentage of the production. The rules on depreciation have been liberalized, and the investors in these programs will benefit from higher tax write-offs for oil-producing equipment. But I remind all would-be investors in completion programs of a cardinal rule of tax-shelter investing: Look at the track record before you bet on the horse. Let somebody else's money finance the growing pains of oil completion programs and similar innovations.

How long does it take to earn a track record in oil and gas? My offhand answer is five years at least. Even Petro-Lewis with its conservatively structured programs did not earn the confidence of reputable financial planners until after its fifth or sixth year in business. It may take longer to test oil exploration and development sponsors. Oil exploration programs are only 30 years old, and their track record is not outstanding.

The first publicly registered program was offered in 1950 by two firms — Blackwood & Nichols and Davidson, Hartz, Hyde & Dewey. Only three companies were active in public programs during the fifties; two of them (Apache and McCulloch) have survived to the present. However, during the late sixties, Wall Street had a brief romance with oil tax shelters, thanks mainly to a master promoter named John M. King. In the late sixties, King's oil partnerships became intertwined with, and ultimately went down with, the Fund of Funds. The Fund of Funds empire was built by another master promoter, Bernard Cornfeld. About the same time, one of the great swindles in financial history, Homestake Oil, was being exposed. Because dozens of prominent Americans lost money in this sham deal, oil and gas partnerships received a great deal of unfavorable publicity.

Reeling from the exposure, the oil and gas syndication industry shrunk in the early seventies and did not regain momentum until about 1976. In a sense, then, investors in oil and gas partnerships are participating in a ground-floor industry.

I have a story, which most of my clients can identify with, that underscores just how new the "new world" of oil and gas is.

Anyone who has lived in Marin County (just north of San Francisco) for more than a few years remembers the brilliant false sunsets that once lit our night skies. These sunsets were in fact produced by the huge Standard Oil refinery in nearby Richmond. The refinery used to burn off millions of cubic feet of "excess" natural gas simply because the market price did not warrant harvesting and selling it.

The false sunsets of Marin burn no longer. Neither Standard Oil nor an energy-hungry world can afford them.

OIL AND GAS: THE RISKS

In real estate, the biggest risk lies in being in the wrong market at the wrong place at the wrong time. In oil and gas, the biggest risk is in the wrong relationship. Let me use an example to explain.

You are asked to participate in two business ventures. The first of these is a new apartment house. The promoter shows you the location, the blueprints, and an architectural rendering. He then produces a file bulging with all kinds of impressive statistical data: occupancy rates, projected construction costs and rent rates, mortgage amortization tables, and the like. Finally the promoter gives you a tour of the apartment houses he has previously developed and says with a confident gleam in his eye, "My track record is the best in town."

The second venture is in the fossil excavation field. The promoter leads you to a remote swamp and says earnestly, "Our reports indicate this is a fossil-intensive area."

"I see," you say politely. "What makes you think so?"

"Well, you see this rock formation here?" replies the promoter as he drops to his knees and scrapes back an inch of mud. "Our geologists believe it is evidence of a carbonate sedimentary substrata formation, and we have seismometric verification of a fault trend."

After some study of the rock, you think of another question: "Assuming fossils are buried here, how much will it cost to dig them up?"

"Oh, that depends on how deep they are and how much rock we have to dig through," says the promoter. "The cost of digging fossils is going up almost every day."

Rising from the mud, you ask a question which almost seems impertinent under the circumstances: "Well, tell me, Mr. Promoter, what experience have you had in fossil digging? Can you show me some fossils you've actually found?"

"Of course not," he says cheerfully. "You don't actually see or handle fossils. They would turn to dust in your hand. But they're quite valuable, and you can trust me. My track record is the best in the business."

Two different promoters, two different track records. In one case, virtually every piece of relevant data is available for inspection. Every variable has been tested in previous projects, and you can actually see (on paper at least) the finished product.

In the other case, you can see nothing. The evidence is buried both figuratively, within the argot of scientists and geologists, and literally, in the ground. As far as many investors are concerned, track record means blind trust.

Modern geology and drilling techniques have made oil and gas a more predictable proposition than fossil digging, but the analogy is not as farfetched as it might seem. For most investors in oil and gas (even those who have made small fortunes in it), the field remains a complete mystery. The remnants of vegetation that flourished during the dinosaur age are located by the divinations of geologists, pumped to the earth's surface, distilled through modern alchemy, and transported via pipelines longer and darker than the Amazon River. But, as long as the tax write-offs are permitted and the income keeps flowing, investors assume that all is well in the oil world.

"Not me," says the confident, expert oil investor. "The oil world is no mystery to me. I've actually seen the well where my money is invested. I've seen my oil flowing out of the ground." But has he?

While Homestake Oil was in the process of defrauding hundreds of people, it frequently led tours to deserted sites where the investors' money was "at work." With much drama, a Homestake employee would turn on a large spigot attached to a maze of pipes and out would gush gallons of crude black gold. In fact, Homestake had put part of the investors' money to work building a mock oil site, complete with an underground storage tank for shipped-in oil.

The oil and gas industry is much cleaner and more professional than it was at the time of the Homestake swindle, but there are still great disparities in expertise — and ethics — in the industry. Even if you are an excellent judge of business character, you will have a hard time telling the difference between the winners and the also-rans in oil and gas, a business with rules of conduct and measures of success that are all its own.

Even if you think you can size up real estate deals on your own, your investment in oil and gas begins with a financial planner you can trust. Most financial planners now have enough clients interested in oil and gas to justify spending many "due diligence" hours in this area. They have obtained a feel not only for the past records of companies but also for the strength of current management and the risk level of a given investment. Above all, the financial planner is trained to analyze whether the partnership deal is structured to give the investor a fair shake.

In real estate, you build your trust relationship on a series of precise assumptions. The syndicator will build x units, at a cost of y and rent them for z. And even if the variables change, you won't be hurt. If, for example, inflation makes the building cost more than projected, you can raise rents to compensate. You can appreciate the real estate syndicator's project without approving of his values or understanding how he thinks.

Not so with oil and gas. Before you sink money in an oil and gas partnership, you must have a rapport with the general partner regarding the sharing of risk and reward — come what may. You might compare this trust relationship to the buddy system scuba divers use for safety.

Whenever divers go to great depths, they take along another diver they trust, a buddy, and they have this understanding: Neither buddy will expose the other to greater risk than they have previously agreed to. If the unexpected happens, neither buddy will leave the other in the lurch. If one buddy runs out of air, the technique known as buddy breathing allows both divers to share one air tank. This type of sharing has a parallel in oil and gas investing.

If the syndicator (general partner) runs out of money before a project is completed, he may require an additional assessment from the limited partner investor, which usually is not more than 10 to 15 percent of the original investment. On the other hand, if the investor needs to withdraw some of the money invested in the partnership, he may take advantage of his *rights of presentment*, which allow him to sell units back to the partnership.

In both cases, the investor must understand the risk ahead of time: If he can't meet an assessment, his interests in the partnership may be diluted. If he exercises his rights of presentment and withdraws money, the true market value of his unit will usually be discounted, perhaps as high as 50 percent.

The risk that an oil and gas drilling partnership will run out of money is not as terrible as it sounds. Only partnerships that have discovered oil or gas in the first place will need more money to complete wells. Often, this risk is interchangeable with another:

61

The risk that you will not get a timely return on your money. Oil income programs usually begin paying cash distributions a year after the investor sinks his money in the ground, but drilling programs may take three or four years. Here's why. If the program is short on cash and does not raise it through additional assessment, it may instead use income from the first completed wells to drill or complete additional wells for the partnership. Instead of the income flowing to investors, it goes right back in the ground, obviously with the hopes of producing even bigger returns in the long run.

A CHECKLIST OF RISKS

To help you communicate with your financial planner in selecting an oil and gas investment, I have prepared the following checklist of risks. In almost every case, the risk is highest for exploratory programs, slightly less for developmental programs, and even less for income programs.

Risk 1: The partnership is not able to locate suitable prospects. This is one of the most overlooked areas of risk in oil and gas. Investors assume that once the partnership has money in hand it can always obtain leases on land likely to produce oil and gas. (Oil and gas partnerships are blindpools, in which the investor does not know specifically where his money will be invested.) In fact, experienced general partners evaluate sixteen prospects for every one they decide to explore, and a single prospect can take a full day to inspect and evaluate. Few geologists can locate more than a dozen quality prospects each year.

The risks are qualitatively different for exploratory and income programs. In exploratory programs, the risk in finding a good prospect is closely tied in with the competence of the geologists and the quality of the geological data they produce. (Geological data comes in two forms: subsurface information, from wells in the surrounding area; and seismic data, from recordings of sound waves bouncing off subsurface formations.) In income programs, the quantity and quality of reserves are often known, and finding good prospects generally depends more on the asking price of leases than any other factor.

Risk 2: A partnership may not achieve adequate diversification. A key advantage partnerships have over single-investor financing is that they can raise enough capital to spread the risk over many wells. No investor owns any one well. Each investor owns a fractional working interest in the total.

The higher the level of speculation, the greater the need for diversification. In income programs, where 90 percent of the wells are producers, a handful of wells in a partnership might be sufficient. In wildcat drilling, where a success ratio of 10%-17% is common, one big hit can pay for the dry holes, but the partnership must drill enough holes to gives investors a chance of finding that winner. Diversification may also be achieved geographically; that is, by investing part of the funds in the Rocky Mountain belt, part in the Mid-Continent, and part in the Gulf Coast.

Risk 3: Not enough of the investor's money goes in the ground. Every general partner is entitled to assess the partnership for certain front-end and maintenance charges, but we still like to see 70 to 75 percent of the limited partner's money invested in drilling or in buying reserves. Management and acquisition fees should be in the range of 4.5 to 9.5 percent, and sales commissions no more than 7 to 8 percent. The offering costs are also passed along to limited partners, and these include registration ($50,000 to $100,000 is typical) and selling ($100,000 to $200,000). The general partner is usually entitled to an overhead reimbursement as well.

Watch out for partnerships in which the general partner has the option to retain prospects for his own account, or in which the sponsor profits from the sale of prospects to the partnership. Exploration and balanced programs will have a more elaborate fee structure than income programs.

Risk 4: Risk of not finding oil. This is the obvious risk area, but in a properly structured program backed by sufficient geological data, it is not always the most prevalent risk. Of course, exploratory programs have the greatest dry hole risk; the success ratios range from 10 percent + in wildcat drilling to 30 to 50 percent in controlled exploratory (tame cat) drilling. Developmental programs — drilling in areas that already have a track record of production — have a nationwide success ratio of about 66 percent.

Risk 5: Risk of not being able to complete a well. Once you've found oil, it's automatically yours, right? Not necessarily. The whole process of casing a well and bringing oil and gas to the surface is a technology-intensive art, and it seems that the equipment to do it is always in short supply. Without completion delays or problems, a well should begin producing oil and income within 18 to 24 months. In an inflationary economy, a well that takes longer than that to pay off is returning dollars that are worth much less than those originally invested.

Risk 6: The disillusionment factor. "Emotional" risks are not listed on any prospectus, but they are very real. Often, after a year or two, with little to show for the investment except tax write-off, the investor begins to have "buyer's remorse." The remorse is intensified if the general partner does not communicate with his limited partner investors. Reports should be accurate, frequent, and of three types: status reports on how the drilling, completion or production is going; financial and tax reports; and reserve reports (independently appraised).

Another cause of disillusionment is any kind of surprise for which the investor is not prepared. If the investor knows he may have to meet an additional assessment, a request for one will usually not increase the disillusionment factor. But if income is lower or comes later than expected, or if the additional assessment comes without warning, investors have a way of turning their backs on an otherwise good partnership.

Risk 7: Fraud. Beware of the take-the-money-and-run promoter. Is there much more fraud in oil and gas than in other tax shelters? The answer is no, for a simple reason. As more and more investors turn to financial planners for help in selecting oil and gas partnerships, the oil and gas con artists of yesterday are packing up and moving to other investment games. They cannot operate under the present requirements of trust and disclosure.

WHAT TO LOOK FOR IN AN OIL AND GAS PARTNERSHIP

I prefer to build a relationship step-by-step with an oil and gas program sponsor, getting independent appraisals of his track record and recommendations from other financial planners before I sink any money into his partnerships. I go slowly, sticking with the less risky income and developmental programs until I know the sponsor very well. If the sponsor's background is primarily in finance or investment, I always check the quality of the geologists and technical people who work for him. If he is a geologist or petroleum engineer, I double-check his financial structure.

I look for programs that are large enough to distribute the front-end fees evenly and painlessly among many investors, and to drill enough holes to achieve diversification. I regard 20 holes as the minimum needed to achieve diversification in an exploratory program. However, I don't care much for the giant programs sold by many stockbrokers because I don't think any program can find $70 million or $80 million worth of quality prospects in one year. I think $10 to $30 million is a good program size for most investors' purposes.

Because our investors do not understand the fossil-fuel excavation business, they place more trust in us in this area than any other, and for that reason we exercise more "due diligence" in oil and gas than in any other investment. We have one last safety check before committing money, and that is the "comfort test." Even if all the numbers and geology reports look promising, if we and our investors do not feel comfortable with a particular program or general partner, we pass. We especially don't like deals in which "the last unit is going tomorrow."

The oil and gas has waited in the ground a million years or more. If it can't wait for that particle of eternity we need to exercise due diligence, we are content to leave it for other investors.

CHAPTER   EIGHT

OIL AND GAS: THE REWARDS

In most kinds of tax-sheltered investments, we try to balance risk and reward. But, in oil and gas, the risk factors are so unique — and so disturbing to many investors — that we need to put all our risk cards on the table early in the game. That is why we discussed the risks in oil and gas investing before we discussed the rewards.

If you are still with us then, it's time to look at the rewards of oil and gas investing, and they are considerable. As we have already mentioned, most successful investing in oil and gas is done through a financial planner who can monitor risk elements. So it is with reward. Ultimately, your success on the "upside" in oil and gas will depend upon a financial planner who can match your needs for income and tax deductions — the two main elements of reward — to an investment that will provide both. In this chapter, then, we will give you an overview of how and why people succeed in oil and gas. You should then have enough information to talk intelligently with your financial planner about investing in the field.

THE RANGE OF NORMAL EXPECTATIONS

Most investments have a "range of normal expectations." If you buy a one-year certificate of deposit that yields 12%, the range of expectations is very narrow. The most it can produce is 12%. The least it can produce is 12% minus whatever penalties you might be charged if forced to redeem it early. Stocks have a wider range of expectations, but perhaps not as wide as many investors think. Historically, stocks held for a period of 10 years or more return (yield plus appreciation) 2 to 6% above the rate of inflation. Of course, you can increase the range of expectations by buying speculative stocks or trading frequently.

The ultimate range of expectations, you might think, would be a double-or-nothing flip of a coin. If you lose, you lose everything. If you win, you double your money.

The main reason I am so fond of oil and gas is that it can have an even greater range of expectations than double or nothing, with far less "downside" and far more potential "upside." If you lose, you don't lose everything. If you win, you can do much better than double your money.

I have never felt more confident about the upside range of expectations in oil and gas. In a volatile economy, oil has become a political and economic weapon of great value. Almost any surprises we encounter will be good surprises.

The two main reasons why oil has such a wide range of expectations are (1) the price and (2) the cushion for failure that is built into any exploratory or developmental program. Let's look at each of these separately.

OIL AND GAS PRICES

In any entrepreneurial investment, we calculate an expected price, the price at which we think we will sell the goods we produce. Every good entrepreneur calculates his expected price conservatively. If a baker is selling bread and he thinks he can charge somewhere between 50¢ and 75¢ a loaf, he is wise to build his budget around 50¢. If later he finds he can charge 75¢, the extra 25¢ is a bonus.

We are now in a period of great opportunities for bonus pricing in oil and gas, particularly gas. Let's look briefly at the history of energy prices.

In 1973, a barrel of domestic crude oil sold for between $3 and $5 a barrel. Seven years later, newly discovered oil sold for between $38 and $40 a barrel. In 1973, natural gas sold for 22¢ per 1000 cubic feet. In 1980, controlled natural gas sold for more than $2.60 per 1000 cubic feet, with the price increasing monthly. Beginning in 1985 (if not sooner), gas will be decontrolled, and it is estimated that it will sell for more than $6 per 1000 cubic feet in constant 1980 dollars.

This dramatic surge represents a 1000 percent increase in oil prices and a twelvefold increase in controlled natural gas prices. (We can also project a 2700 percent increase in natural gas prices when gas is decontrolled.) Meanwhile, the cost of finding oil and gas has been pushed up by inflation almost 300%.

Let's look at how spiraling energy prices have affected the profitability of two hypothetical exploratory gas wells drilled nine years apart, one in 1970 and one in 1979. For illustration, assume the wells are identical except for prices. The price at which gas was sold was 17¢ per MCF (thousand cubic feet) in 1970 and $2 per MCF in 1979.

Year	Costs		Revenue		Discovery ratio for break-even	
1970	Drilling cost	$150,000	4,000,000 MCF		Profit	$373,300
	Operating cost	30,000	(17¢ per MCF)		Risk	150,000
	Royalties (12.5%)	85,000			Ratio	3:1
	Prod. taxes (7%)	41,700				
	Total cost	$306,700	Total revenue	$680,000		

Year	Costs		Revenue		Discovery ratio for break-even	
1979	Drilling cost	$430,000	4,000,000 MCF		Profit	$4,773,000
	Operating cost	77,000	($2 per MCF)		Risk	430,000
	Royalties (22%)	1,760,000			Ratio	12:1
	Prod. taxes (12%)	960,000				
	Total costs	$3,227,000	Total revenue	$8,000,000		

The key term to understand in comparing the two wells is "discovery ratio for break-even." It means "how many wells can we afford to drill to find just one that is productive." In 1970, if the partnership found one productive well in three, it broke even. By 1979, rising gas prices had given the same partnership considerably more margin for error — it could drill 11 dry holes to find one productive well (ratio 12:1) and still break even. If the 1979 partnership found gas at the same ratio as the 1970 program, it would be four times as profitable.

"So what?" you ask. "I didn't invest in gas in either 1970 or 1979." No, but the same ratcheting effect is still pushing gas prices up. By 1985, under phased decontrol, prices will surely more than double again. The prices of leases and royalty payments have already begun to move up in anticipation of the coming leap in gas prices, but this increase will have minimal impact on exploratory or developmental programs. (It will have slightly more impact on an income program.)

Before you sink your money in the ground, you should know the estimated break-even ratio. For a developmental well to make economic sense, its ratio should not be higher than 2:1. (That is, you break even if one in every two wells strikes oil or gas.)

Exploratory wells can go as high as 4:1 and still be good investments because even though they are riskier, the rewards are greater.

Here is the normal range of return on investment in each of the three types of drilling programs, with an indication of how long it takes before income begins flowing to the investor in each.

Type Program	Normal time to first cash distribution	Normal range of return on investment ($ return per $ invested)
Developmental	½ – 1½ years	.75 – $1.50
Balanced	1 – 3 years	.50 – $5.00
Exploratory	3 – 10 years	.25 – $10.00

As you can see, the riskier the program, (1) the greater the range of return, (2) the larger the potential profit, and (3) the longer you may have to wait before income starts flowing back to you. This is most important to realize for two reasons: (1) the dollar you receive seven years from now (at 10%) inflation) will be worth only half as much as the dollar you invest today; and (2) because your investment may not pay income for five years or more, you must be sure you can live with the uncertainty (and without the income).

TAX BENEFITS

Why can't you lose all your money in oil and gas? First, as mentioned in the last chapter, you should invest only in diversified programs drilling at least 20 different wells. With competent management, the odds favor at least one or two of those wells becoming eventual producers, even in very speculative programs (which you should try to avoid).

However, the investor's cushion against total loss (and an added benefit in successful programs) is the tax deductions derived from oil and gas partnerships. They include some of the same tax benefits we have already encountered in real estate, plus some special incentives that apply only to oil and gas.

The tax benefits peculiar to oil and gas investing fall into two main areas: (1) intangible drilling costs and (2) depletion allowances. Intangible drilling costs, or IDC's, provide immediate tax write-offs in the first year or two of the investment. Depletion allowance, which is a variation on the depreciation allowance we encountered in real estate, provides tax benefits over the life of the investment.

In practice, the depletion allowance often covers all the income generated by an oil and gas program. In other words, the income is tax free. In this respect, it offers the same tax benefits as municipal bonds.

Both the IDC and depletion allowances are greater in exploratory and developmental programs than in income programs, in most cases. Let's look at each of the benefits in greater depth.

IDC's

Have you ever heard the joke about the entrepreneur who started a new bakery business — selling doughnut holes? Drilling for oil is a little like that. You pour an enormous amount of work and money into the ground, and all you have to show for it is a hole. Even if you are lucky enough to strike oil, it probably will not spew forth from the ground the way it does in the movies. Instead, you will spend more money to case the well and set the pumps in motion.* In a typical exploratory well, about two-thirds of the total costs are incurred before the case point. These costs produce nothing tangible or salvageable, which is why they are called intangible drilling costs. For every 100 dollars a limited partner sinks into a typical exploration program, 50 to 75 will usually be for IDC's — labor, wages, fuel, and the like. Let's compare IDC's to what we might call "intangible construction costs" in a real estate program.

The money that a builder pours into labor, fuel, and so on, during the construction phase is an out-of-pocket cost, but the builder can't claim most of this cost as a tax deduction in the year it is paid. It becomes a capitalized cost added to the basis (which also includes the price of bricks and mortar.) The builder depreciates all these costs over the life of the building.

In oil drilling, IDC's are written off the year they are incurred, even if the well is successful. This special tax incentive is probably the main reason investors who need instant write-offs buy into exploratory and developmental programs. If either the program or its investors borrow money and if the investors are personally at risk to repay the loan, the IDC tax benefits can be much higher than 75 percent of the investment. Some expenses that are not technically IDC's can also be written off as they are paid; these include the administration costs of starting up the partnership. (Brokerage, leasing, and acquisition fees cannot be written off immediately; they must be added to the basis and capitalized.)

---

*The point at which a well driller stops drilling (because he has found oil) and starts putting the well structure (the case) in place is called the "case point." The rest of the construction phase — setting up the equipment to pump oil out of the ground — is called "completion."

Depletion

Depletion, the onetime classic "rich man's tax loophole," has become a middle-class tax incentive. What was once the exclusive property of the Rockefellers and Murchisons now belongs to the little investor. In fact, the big oil companies and producers no longer even qualify for depletion allowances.

Cost depletion is a lot like depreciation. If you own an estimated 100 barrels of oil stored in its natural underground vault, and if those barrels were acquired at a cost of $2 each, your basis is $200. If you produce and sell 5 barrels during the year, you may take a cost depletion deduction of 5 × $2, or $10. Very simple and fair.

Percentage depletion is a real windfall, particularly when energy prices are rising. For example, if you had qualified for percentage depletion in 1981, you could have deducted 20 percent of your yearly gross revenue if that deduction did not exceed half of your enterprise's taxable income. Thus, if you had sold your 5 barrels of oil for $30 per barrel, you would have made $150 in gross revenue. Your percentage depletion allowance would have been $150 × 20%, or $30, if the taxable income from the property is at least $60.

The difference between the $10 cost depletion write-off and the $30 percentage depletion write-off is dramatic enough, but there are still more benefits available if you qualify for percentage depletion. In cost depletion, you cannot deduct more than the estimated value of the oil and gas reserves. In legal terms, the amount of total cost depletion taken on a property can't exceed the adjusted tax basis of the property. In plain English, once a property is worth nothing, it can't be worth less than nothing.

In percentage depletion, however, you can keep on taking your percentage write-off year after year, as long as the well keeps producing revenues.

You can conceivably write off two or three times the amount of oil or gas you have. The Mobils and Essos did this for years, until the little loophole became so obvious that Congress closed it. Congress mandated a phased-in decrease in the traditional rate of 22% as follows: 20% in 1981, 18% in 1982, 16% in 1983, 15% in 1984 and thereafter. This rate decrease applies only to small producers. Percentage depletion has been eliminated altogether for the onetime giants. Most exploratory and developmental tax shelters still qualify for percentage depletion, so in effect the tables have been reversed. Through partnerships, middle-income taxpayers now have the tax benefits.

TAX TRAPS

Oil and gas has unique tax advantages — and also unique tax traps. (The tax traps are so unique that you should never invest in an oil partnership without reviewing your present and projected tax situation with an accountant or financial planner.) We can't possibly cover them in depth, but we will mention them briefly in the hope that forewarned is forearmed. Two of the tax traps relate to IDC's and one to depletion. Here they are.

First, if you sell an oil and gas tax shelter, the IDC's deducted for successful wells must be "recaptured" to the extent that they exceed the amount you could have deducted had you capitalized these costs. This ruling penalizes particularly the limited partners who take advantage of their rights of presentment and sell out early in a drilling partnership. *Moral: Don't go into oil and gas with short-term expectations.*

Second, IDC's on successful wells can trigger a "tax preference item," which can increase your tax bill, especially (1) if you have not yet received income from this partnership, or (2) if you have a very high earned income. Again, check with your financial planner before buying an oil and gas partnership to make sure.

Third, if you do take advantage of the "something can be worth less than nothing" opportunity of percentage depletion, the amount that you write off in excess of your adjusted basis can also be a tax preference item and add to your tax bill. *Moral: For people who do not plan ahead, a loophole can become a noose.*

REAL ESTATE:
WHERE IT'S BEEN
WHERE IT'S GOING

As anyone who has ever bought a home knows, real estate is America's favorite tax shelter. Few taxpayers who do not own real estate find it worthwhile to claim itemized deductions. But buy a home and you immediately enter the rarefied world of the itemizing affluent, who make tax-favored charitable contributions, take out installment loans to leverage tax advantages, and save every medical receipt in sight. In fact, the entire tax system of this great democracy seems to have been written by and for the King of the Castle.

The interest an American pays on indebtness is a deductible expense (up to a limit), which would seem to encourage massive borrowing. Yet, Americans are still a people who fear and avoid indebtedness — except in real estate mortgages. According to a recent study, about 80 percent of affluent Americans have home-related mortgage loans, but only 45 percent have outstanding personal loans and only 26 percent are carrying cash value loans on insurance policies. The home is by far the biggest generator of interest-expense write-offs.

Similarly, the amount paid on property taxes is a legitimate write-off. Then, there are the new investment tax credits for installing energy-saving equipment in the home. For investment or business real estate (not counting one's own home), there are the advantages of straight-line and accelerated depreciation. In short, you might say that the little vine-covered cottage is America's education in tax avoidance.

When the syndication industry began to market tax-avoidance tools to the general public, it was not surprising that real estate packages found the greatest consumer acceptance. In 1980, public real estate syndicators went over the one billion dollar mark in product offerings; private real estate offerings are estimated to be as high as 10 billion dollars annually. While oil and gas and other shelter areas are just beginning to be accepted by middle-income investors, real estate syndications have had a mass following since their inception. Huge apartment complexes and office buildings have been built with the savings of schoolteachers, middle managers, and civil servants.

We can identify four reasons why real estate has become America's favorite tax shelter.

First, the federal government has bent over backward to provide tax breaks for real estate.

Second, real estate is familiar to most investors. It is tangible, and its ownership conveys status.

Third, real estate syndications have been led by many creative and financially responsible entrepreneurs. The real estate depression of 1974-75 did cause some partnerships to fail, but more headlines were created by busts in real estate corporations and Real Estate Investment Trusts.

Finally, the industry was fortunate to emerge at the right place and time. In the late seventies, the greatest activity was in California and the Sunbelt, where several public programs got in on the groundfloor of the great run-up in real estate prices.

During the seventies, a quarter of a million Americans invested almost three billion dollars in publicly registered real estate tax shelters. The average economic gain on all properties sold by public syndications during this decade was 25 percent annually, according to Questor Associates, a research firm. What created this remarkable growth? Let's identify a few of the elements.

Much of the most successful activity was in apartments that catered to the young and newly independent. The children of the baby boom, now grown up, came to the cities, seeking careers and shelter. Demand was great and apartments were scarce.

Money was not exactly cheap, but there was a "window in time" when interest rates did come down — during 1978 and much of 1979. In buying properties, some syndicators were able to take advantage of the distress sales caused by the real estate depression of 1974-75 to buy property cheap or to assume low-interest mortgages. Despite the cost of money, long-term mortgages were available.

Huge new pools of institutional money began trickling into American real estate, most of it from pension funds or from abroad. Syndications could liquidate for cash virtually at will, and often at a very large profit.

Investors were content to leave their funds in low-yield (but tax-advantaged) real estate. During most of the seventies, they were not aware of such high-yield alternatives as money market funds.

Most of the conditions that made real estate such an attractive investment in the seventies no longer exist. Real estate syndication is now a whole new ballgame. Perhaps, Americans who invested in real estate have had too much of a good thing. In California, where I live and work, and where many of my clients' real estate investments are located, I see the extreme examples of real estate frenzy — investors who are overloaded with second, third, and even fourth mortgages; people buying properties that can't possibly yield a positive cash flow; commercial rents sky-rocketing beyond the reach of merchants; "creative financing" in which real estate brokers become investment bankers in order to move sluggish properties; mortgage terms which run a maximum of five years for people buying the home-of-a-lifetime at prices they would never have considered five years ago. Where will it end?

I think it is inevitable that we in California are heading for a shakeout that could rival that of 1974-75 and which almost certainly will affect a greater number of homeowners and investors. When this shakeout occurs, properties will once again appear on the market at distressed prices, and smart investors who have conserved cash will be able to find bargains galore.

Meanwhile, until a shakeout cools the ardor of investors for real estate, we are flirting with destroying the advantages that have made real estate so attractive. An example: You can now buy highly leveraged partnerships in which the property is almost guaranteed to produce a negative cash flow. This means that rents cover neither expenses nor mortgage payments. Someone must make up the shortfall when this happens, and to lure investors into these deals, some general partners are promising to tide the partnership through the negative cash flow years. We feel that the IRS may question the whole debt structure of such arrangements and the interest-expense write-off, which makes the deal attractive in the first place.

In short, much that we see in real estate tax shelters has become unreal estate, paper transactions designed to take advantage of the government's generous tax treatment of real estate.

TAX ADVANTAGES

Let's look at some of the unique tax advantages of real estate. In the Tax Reform Act of 1976, the government took a major step to curtail tax-shelter excesses by instituting at-risk provisions. Only real estate was exempted.

If, for example, you buy into an oil and gas partnership and put only 10 percent of the purchase price down in cash, you are at risk for that 10 percent. You could lose it all. But what about the 90 percent that you borrow? You could sign a "recourse note" for the 90 percent, which means that whatever happens you are liable for the debt. In this case, you are also at risk for the 90 percent and may deduct the entire amount of interest you pay on it. If, however, the borrowed 90 percent is in the form of an unsecured loan, or a loan backed only by the profits or property of the partnerhsip, you are not at risk. You may not deduct the interest paid on the money you borrowed.

Only in real estate can you be not at risk and still deduct all interest. Most people assume that Congress gave special benefits to real estate investors because it had a soft spot in its heart for real estate, and that is partly true. But it is also true that real estate has a powerful lobby, led by the National Association of Realtors. Even more important, real estate is an almost universally acceptable collateral for a loan. The property itself is the security of last resort.

The Tax Reform Act drastically reduced the number of multiple write-off shelters in all areas except real estate. In real estate you could still theoretically buy into a $1000 property with $100 down and $900 financed. At 20% interest on the $900, total annual interest payments would be $180, or almost twice the amount of cash invested in the deal, not counting other deductions such as depreciation or investment tax credit.

A funny thing happened on the way to multiple write-off real estate deals. Mortgage money became expensive and scarce, and the economics of buying property began to work against highly mortgaged deals. The more money you put down in cash, the lower your mortgage payments and the higher your cash flow. In some parts of California, you must now put down 30 to 40 percent of the purchase price just to produce the first penny of cash flow. If rents go up or interest rates down, that may change, but in effect the economy took away some of the advantages Congress had granted real estate by exempting it from the at-risk rules. We see some new real estate shelters with 80 to 90 percent financing, but in most cases these are highly speculative. The mainstream real estate shelters generally have 30 to 50 percent cash in the deal, which limits most write-offs to less than 1:1 despite the at-risk benefits.

The other great tax benefit of real estate is depreciation, which we have discussed previously, and which applies only to business property, not to your primary residence. Real estate qualifies for accelerated depreciation, which allows the taxpayer to write off property faster in the earlier years of its life than in later years. Today, most real estate can be written off over 15 years. This will give a needed boost to real estate as a tax-sheltering device.

Incidentally, since 1978, buildings classified as Certified Historic Structures have been granted a special five-year full depreciation schedule. A $100,000 building could generate $20,000 in depreciation write-offs each year, and this has led to the creation of at least one tax shelter using only Certified Historic Structures in California.

Perhaps the biggest tax advantage of real estate is in converting dollars that would be taxed as ordinary income into long-term capital gains, upon sale of a building at a profit. While you are *depreciating* real estate every year, it is often *appreciating* in value. The following illustration shows the tax advantages: A $100,000 building is written off over 15 years, producing roughly $6666 per year in depreciation deductions. You can depreciate a building without regard for salvage value; so assuming the building has no salvage value after 15 years, it produces $100,000 in depreciation deductions, or $50,000 in tax savings for a 50 percent bracket taxpayer. Now, upon resale, the property has no basis remaining, so the total sale price must be calculated as a capital gain. The current maximum capital gain rate is 20 percent, so the tax bill for the original investment of $100,000 is only $20,000, or less than half of the tax savings. If the taxpayer has retired and fallen into a lower tax bracket, the tax-upon-sale would be even less.

This works great on paper, but in recent years it has not worked well in practice. Partnerships have not had much trouble selling their properties at a gain, but in a period of tight money they have not always been able to sell for cash. In a typical arrangement, a partnership will sell a building it bought for $100,000 at $150,000, but take back "paper" (issue a loan) equal to $40,000 or so. After paying off its own mortgage, the partnership may have only minimal cash to distribute immediately to investors as profit.

Instead, the partnership and the investors earn regular interest on the paper they receive from the buyer. This practice forces limited partners into "reverse leverage." Instead of borrowing to free up money and create tax advantages, they are lending, with the result that their money is tied up and the interest payments they receive are fully taxable as ordinary income. Furthermore, in the event of a default, the partnership will be forced to take back the property it sold. The problems associated with taking back "paper" are some of the reasons we are so cautious about real estate tax shelters at this time.

The final tax benefit available to real estate is the investment tax credit, also discussed previously. The ITC has never been much of a boon to real estate because it applies only to certain property used to furnish or equip buildings. However, the Revenue Act of 1978 created a major opportunity for rehabilitating older commercial structures (not counting apartments) by extending the investment tax credit to cover rehabilitation expenses. (The amount of the investment tax credit was increased in the 1981 Economic Recovery Tax Act.) This represents a major opportunity for tax savings that has not yet been exploited by syndicators. I would expect to see very shortly attractive shelters designed to benefit from this incentive.

REAL AND UNREAL ESTATE

You've probably heard of tax evaders who keep two sets of books to foil the IRS. One set (perfectly legitimate looking, only very fictional) is kept handy in case the IRS should inspect. The other, kept hidden away, is the real book reflecting profits or losses. In a way, real estate works as a tax shelter because the government permits "double bookkeeping." You can show a loss for tax purposes while generating a real cash profit. (Of course, today this is rarely the case because of high interest rates and high prices.)

The key to this creative accounting is depreciation, which is an unreal loss on real property. Let's use the following example to show how it works (or rather, worked before high prices and high interest rates turned many paper losses into real losses).

You buy a building for $100,000, paying 20% down and financing the rest over 20 years at 14%. Your loan value is $80,000, and on the little table of amortization rates that all real estate people keep handy, you find that right off the bat you are out of pocket $11,938 in annual mortgage payments. Now, let's assume that your annual expense for upkeep and maintenance of the building is

$5000. Your total outflow, mortgage payment plus expense, is $11,938 + $5000 = $16,938. If your total receipts from renting the building are $18,000, you have a positive cash flow of $1062 or about 5.3% of the $20,000 cash investment.

Now, let's look at the other set of books, the ones you use for figuring taxes. In the first year almost all the mortgage payment is interest expense, so you have an interest-expense write-off slightly under $12,000. If you depreciate the building on a straight-line basis over 15 years, you have a depreciation write-off of $6666 ($100,000 ÷ 15). Your expenses for operating the building, $5000, are also deductible, so you have a total deduction of $12,000 + $6666 + $5000 = $23,666. With receipts of $18,000, you show a paper loss of $5,666. In your 50 percent tax bracket, this equals a tax savings of $2833.

Let's recap: On the "real" books, you pocket $1072. On the "unreal" books, you have gained $2833 in tax benefits without losing a dime out of your pocket. Your total benefit is $3905 on an investment of $20,000, or a return equal to 19.5% of the original $20,000 investment.

In real estate partnerships with appreciation potential, we sometimes say that we aim for a tax-sheltered return of 7 to 8 percent. In other words, we are satisfied to have that return if it is completely sheltered from taxes by the "unreal" losses, because we believe that we will also have a large capital gain when the property is sold somewhere between the fifth and tenth year of the partnership.

The preceding example would yield a 5.3 percent sheltered return with some tax benefits left over. This is the kind of economics that made real estate so attractive, but in today's real estate market (particularly in California) you will be lucky to find a highly leveraged property that yields any cash return. Second, the tax benefits may be questioned. Most of the well-structured public tax-shelter programs are by now well known to the IRS. In general, conservatively structured public real estate programs are rarely challenged. But it is still better to have a dollar of cash in hand than a dollar of tax benefits vulnerable to audit. Third, you should be aware that when a real estate program used accelerated depreciation (which we discuss later), there are two tax traps: (1) the amount of accelerated depreciation may trigger a tax preference item, and (2) if the property is sold (particularly in the early years of the partnership life), the sale may lead to "recapture," which can be a very costly tax item.

Finally, it is not inconceivable in today's highly speculative market that the value of your real estate holdings could decline, particularly over the short term. You are always better off investing in real estate partnerships with long-term dollars. Real estate itself is not liquid, and the partnership only increases inflexibility.

THE OUTLOOK

We will have to be smarter and more selective to make money in real estate in the eighties. For instance, smart money is betting that, despite consumer outcries against condominium converters, the average American family still wants to own its own home, even if that home is joined to someone else's by a wall. Now, in buying into apartment syndications, we look for partnerships that are buying properties which have the potential for conversion to condominiums, because this increases the chance of reselling for cash later, at a higher price than apartments would command.

It is simply a fact that not all aspiring homeowners will be able to afford traditional homes, and so we are keeping our eyes open for investment opportunities in prefabricated housing and high quality mobile home parks.

As Will Rogers noted, they aren't making any more land, and they especially aren't making any more prime locations for commercial real estate. Some of the mini-warehouse partnerships have done well as storage units, but because of their excellent locations near freeway offramps, their land may one day be worth more than the warehouses. This attracts our attention.

Since heavy financing lowers the cash return on properties, we are looking for ways to use real estate partnerships which pay almost all cash and which can be used inside IRA and Keogh plans. We are also very interested in several of the emerging vehicles for making real estate partnership units more liquid, including a liquidity fund pioneered here in San Francisco, which buys units from the original owner at a discount from asset value.

Above all, we are conserving our cash, looking for opportunities to join in partnerships that buy up distressed properties when the debt crunch worsens. The eighties will be a very cyclical decade in real estate, with two or three ups and downs for every one we experienced in previous decades. Timing and expert selection of partnerships and properties will be everything. For the amateur real estate investor, the days of wine and roses appear to be over, at least for the next few years.

REAL ESTATE: LIMITED PARTNERSHIPS

Basically, there are two avenues we can pursue in real estate investment. The first is individual ownership, which we'll look at in the next chapter. The other avenue is the real estate limited partnership.

Real estate partnerships are the most diverse of all tax shelters; some handle properties that are valued at more than $100 million; others have only a few thousand dollars invested in three or four properties. By last count, 40 public programs were on the market, offering a choice of apartments, suburban office parks, industrial properties, mini-warehouses and the like.

Why go into partnerships instead of investing directly (as so many did successfully during the last decade)? The first question you should always ask yourself is, "Can I afford the time and expense to buy property directly"? Certainly, during the sixties and seventies, many weekend landlords were able to fatten their pocketbooks by buying apartment houses or duplexes directly, perhaps renovating them, and then selling them for huge profits in a bull market. Some people have a knack (and the time) for taking a rundown property and restoring it, and these people should not be discouraged from entering real estate on their own. But not everyone is by nature a potential landlord. For example, consider the following. (1) What do you do when a hot water pipe bursts at three in the morning, ruining the carpets? (2) Can you sleep at nights knowing that your five-year balloon mortgage payment is next month? (3) Do you like to spend long afternoons in the tax assessor's office, waiting to protest a 30 percent increase in your property taxes? (4) What about eviction? Are you willing to put up with screaming matches, followed by visits to the sheriff's office, followed by threatening telephone calls?

I do not mean to paint too dark a picture of the honorable profession of landlord. I do want you to know what you are getting into.

Single owners made large profits in multiple-housing real estate in the sixties and seventies because they had easy access to financing, could buy property cheaply, raised rents almost at will, and rode the big upward surge in property values. It was not uncommon to see properties change hands three or four times in a five-year period, each time at a higher price.

The eighties are already squeezing the amateurs out of the big real estate ownership game. The keys to success in this decade will be expertly negotiated financing, access to hard cash (as opposed to borrowed money), patience, and professional property management.

Let me give you an idea of how things have changed. One of the largest real estate syndicators is Consolidated Capital, head-quartered in the San Francisco Bay area. ConCap, as it is called, is best known to its more than 30,000 limited partner investors (plus another 40,000 investors in the REIT) as an investment company. Yet, to keep its properties full and fit, ConCap employs (through a subsidiary) no less than 1800 people to manage them. It sponsors special night showings to let prospective tenants inspect apartments after working hours. It buys carpet by the boxcar, at less than half the retail price. In Houston, where the apartment market has been sluggish lately, ConCap's aggressive management techniques have reduced vacancies to less than 4 percent in all apartments it manages there, compared to 5 to 10 percent in similar complexes. Unless you can compete with that kind of expertise, think twice about going into the apartment business as a private investor.

PUBLIC VS. PRIVATE PARTNERSHIPS

The next major choice you must make is between a public and a private syndication program. The public business is well established, you might even say "institutionalized." Six major syndicators have raised well over half the dollars in the public real estate industry in recent years. (The six are Consolidated Capital, Balcor, Integrated Resources, JMB Realy, McNeil, and Fox & Carskadon.) Their programs are sold both through Merrill Lynch and E.F. Hutton and through smaller independent brokers and financial planning firms.

The largest public programs offer a solid reputation in the business, an expert staff, and a demonstrated track record. They are also very accessible to the average investor. You can usually buy into their partnerships with $5000. The pools that these companies raise are so large — typically $30 to $100 million — that they may include a dozen or more properties. This gives the investor the benefits of great diversification, but there is a drawback: The properties are usually purchased in a blindpool. The investor has no idea what properties his money is invested in. In recent offerings, the big public partnerships have used their main weapon — access to cash in a cash-short economy — to make attractive deals. This also has its drawback: Although large cash down payments increase cash flow to the limited partners, they decrease tax write-offs. Most of the large public programs provide no more than a 6 percent tax-sheltered cash flow.

Some of the large public sponsors also offer private real estate programs. (In fact, one of the Big Six, Integrated Resources, is the largest private real estate deal-maker in the United States.) Most of the private deals are small; they are usually put together by local attorneys, accountants, financial planners, or real estate brokers to buy local properties. These private partnerships typically pool the investment dollars of a few high bracket taxpayers to buy one property, or perhaps a chain of related properties. Although abuses do exist, private real estate syndication has come into its own as an important source of capital for real estate. Investors have the advantage of being able to see and inspect the property they are buying, and tax benefits may be tailored to their needs. The problems are limited access — the average ticket for getting into one of these deals is now over $50,000 — and lack of diversification. As with other private tax deals, the burden is on the seller of the offering to disclose all the particulars. This is done through an offering circular in lieu of an SEC-registered prospectus. The seller must also make sure that the investor is either financially sophisticated or has the benefit of an adviser who is.

Some of the major real estate syndicators have raised so much money in recent years that I have begun to ask, "Can a partnership be too large, too diversified?" I think so. Certainly, the quantity of choice real estate available at a reasonable price is limited. When a syndication is raising more than $100 million in a single partnership, as one major sponsor is doing, I question whether all that money will be spent with the same wisdom a partnership would normally exercise in spending $20 million.

Another criterion for investment is how much tax shelter does the investor need. Private deals and highly leveraged deals spin off more shelter in the early years of the partnership. Some taxpayers go into real estate partnerships not because they want tax benefits but because they love real estate and believe it is the best road to long-term appreciation. Low-leveraged and net-leased partnerships work well for these investors. A recent innovation in this industry is the partnership designed specifically for pension and Keogh accounts. These partnerships use no leverage and create few (if any) tax benefits. (Such benefits would be useless anyway in a tax-sheltered retirement plan.) Another innovation is the so-called A-B partnership, which allows some investors (the A group) to take the income and others (the B group) to take the capital gain appreciation. Some partnerships, mainly highly leveraged ones, look for the quick turnaround — a sale in 3 to 5 years — to produce a capital gain. Some hotel and mini-warehouse partnerships have excellent potential for income, because they can raise rent rates easily.

The following is a list of your major choices in the syndicated real estate "supermarket." After a description of each type of property, I have listed one or more programs of this type which, at the time of this writing, were new on the market.

GARDEN APARTMENTS

When Americans fled from the cities in the sixties and seventies, the garden apartment was waiting for them. Garden apartments are grouped in large complexes of 100 units or more and are not higher than two or three stories, with plenty of patios and green space. They particularly appealed to young singles and newly-weds. In the mid-eighties, when the housing shortage becomes more acute, garden apartments should once again be in demand, and they will attract a new type of tenant: growing families that simply can't afford a home of their own.

A partnership of this type ordinarily buys two or more apartment complexes. The ideal apartment property is near a metropolitan area where vacancies are scarce and rents can be raised. The property should have a lower vacancy factor than similar properties nearby, and even more importantly, its turnover rate should be low. (If half the apartments change hands each year, turnover is 50 percent.) The apartment complexes that appeal to "swinging singles" have good locations, high rents, and attractive extras (pools, saunas, party rooms) but they are not good partnership properties, because "swinging singles" tend to move frequently.

The key to a successful garden apartment partnership is good property management. Maintenance should be done on a regular schedule, especially such chores as reroofing, installing new carpeting, and painting. Maintenance, of course, costs money and can cut into the limited partner's cash flow. But, when the apartments are eventually sold, the partners should more than recoup the cash in capital gains.

Garden apartments once followed pretty much the same economic cycle all across the country. No longer is that so. At the time of this writing, apartment rents are booming in Phoenix, beginning to show signs of life in Houston, and lagging in Atlanta. When the vacancy rate is below 5 percent, it is a landlord's market: rents can be raised; tenants selected more carefully; and lease terms made more restrictive. When the vacancy rate is above 10 percent it is a renter's market: landlords must spend more money on marketing vacant units; and rents can't be increased because if they are, tenants will skip to the complex down the road offering three months of free rent.

The ideal time to buy into a garden apartment partnership is when a renter's market is just turning into a landlord's market. With luck, you will receive a 7 to 8% tax-sheltered return on your money and a nice capital gain in 5 to 10 years when the partnership is liquidated.

Your tax benefits will be determined by the way the property is financed. The more cash your partnership puts down, the lower the write-offs will be. For a partnership paying 40 percent cash and financing the rest, expect a 20 to 30 percent write-off on dollars invested in the first year, and slightly less in later years.

Important note: As I mentioned in the previous chapter, one new key to successful apartment investing is the potential to turn apartments into condominiums or cooperatives at some point in the future. In this regard, the best properties are in jurisdictions that do not have rigid ordinances against conversion. The best tenants are young, upwardly mobile professionals. The worst tenants for conversion purposes are elderly people living on fixed incomes, because they can't afford to buy the unit and they have few choices for relocation.

Examples of garden apartment partnerships: National Property Investors (Integrated Resources), Shelter Properties (E.F. Hutton), and Balcor Realty Investors.

COMMERCIAL PROPERTIES

If garden apartments have begun to decrease a bit in popularity, commercial properties (mainly office buildings, shopping centers, and hotels) have more than taken up the slack. Major advantages of these properties are: (1) the ability to keep rents increasing at or above the rate of inflation; and (2) the intrinsic value of the prime locations occupied by these properties. In many cases, there is a third advantage: the partnership may, under some arrangements, share in the gross receipts of the property's merchants or tenants.

The outlook for these properties is excellent. In the eighties, millions of new jobs will be created in the white-collar service industries. An average of 100 square feet of office space must be constructed for each new worker. As the baby boom children grow to maturity, they will need new retail facilities, restaurants, hotels, and hospitals. And this growth wave is not, as was the case with garden apartments, a Sunbelt phenomenon. While office rents still average $10 or so per square foot in the Sunbelt, they have climbed to $25 a square foot in Chicago's Loop, and as high as $35 to $40 along New York's Madison Avenue.

Commercial tenants, anxious to find any space, now sign escalation clauses which give the owner the power to raise rents to keep pace with inflation. As it is with garden apartments, the key to successful commercial partnerships is good management. Cash return may not be much higher than the 7 to 8 percent for apartment partnerships, but tax benefits can be 1:1 or even higher, for highly leveraged properties.

Examples of commercial partnerships: Shearson/Murray Real Estate Fund, Koger Partnership, JMB Income Properties.

BALANCED PARTNERSHIPS

These partnerships buy mixed residential and commercial properties. Examples: McNeil Real Estate Fund XII, Consolidated Capital Properties, Carlyle Real Estate Limited Partnership, and Angeles Partners.

TRIPLE-NET LEASED REAL ESTATE

A sound "net-net-net" partnership may be the most conservative buy in real estate. It is virtually equivalent to owning a high-yield bond. Here's how it works: A partnership buys office or industrial space and then immediately leases it long-term to a "top credit" — usually a Fortune 500 company. The company which leases the property agrees to pay (1) operating expenses, (2) maintenance, and (3) taxes. The partnership's responsibility is to pay expenses net of all three areas, thus the term triple-net lease. Usually, the only expense left for the partnership is debt service on the loan, which is constant, so the risk is minimal. The partnership may qualify for tax deductions in depreciation and interest-expense, however.

A partnership of this type can return cash flow, partially sheltered, of 12–14% per year. One company has dominated this field, and that is Integrated Resources, with its very successful series of American Property Investors partnerships.

WRAPAROUND MORTGAGES

In recent years, a new kind of real estate partnership has emerged, much like the triple-net lease partnerships in offering high yields without great risk. This type of partnership invests in "wraparound" mortgages, a financial vehicle designed to help with purchases and sales of real estate in times of tight money. (It's getting hard to remember when money wasn't tight.) "Wraps" work a lot like the "taking back paper" example in the previous chapter. While continuing to pay off a first mortgage, a seller or middle man issues a new "wraparound" second mortgage on the property which the buyer must pay off. In practice, a limited partnership would use cash from investors to simply pay off the first mortgage. Since the wrap is usually issued at a higher rate than the original mortgage, the investor can have the advantage of a leveraging effect, which has produced cash flows as high as 15 to 16 percent. Tax benefits are not significant in this type of partnership. The pioneering companies in this area were Consolidated Capital with its Income Trust and Balcor with its Pension Investors.

MINI-WAREHOUSES

A mini-warehouse is a recent creation, the product of a mobile, convenience-oriented consumer society. When you run out of closet or garage space, or when you are simply in between permanent accommodations, you shell out $50 to $100 per month to buy a bare-bones "home away from home" for your possessions. A mini-warehouse is the simplest of all real estate structures. All you need is a good location near a freeway offramp, a sturdy fence (to keep vandals away), and a series of concrete or metal structures with padlocked doors. From a financial point of view, these properties have an excellent cash flow — usually 12 to 24 percent in the early years, going even higher as rents rise — and very little worry or overhead. Mini-warehouses are not usually financed, and there is not much to depreciate, so tax deductions are not significant. After 10 years or so, the partnership may have a choice: Sell the warehouse as is or sell the site for further development. (After all, how many choice sites are left near freeway offramps?) With high returns and low leverage, mini-warehouse partnerships work well in pension plans. *One caution:* In a major recession, mini-warehouse storage would probably be one of the first expenses people would cut back on.

Leaders in this field are Public Storage and McCombs Properties.

LOW-RENT HOUSING

Who would want to join a partnership that buys properties in such a high-risk market? Only some very smart investors who need deep tax shelter. The government has provided a variety of incentives, including accelerated depreciation without recapture, rental subsidies, and a very lenient audit "oversight" for government-assisted housing deals. Good management is paramount, and it helps to buy in a transition neighborhood, where tenants are hard-working people who simply can't afford any better housing. Often, these are cashless deals. Write-offs are 2:1 or higher, meaning that a 50 percent bracket taxpayer pays for the entire investment with dollars that otherwise would have gone to taxes. The other side of "cashless," of course, is that these deals often do not return significant cash income for years, if ever. Tax benefits can be as high as four or five times the cost of the initial investment over the life of the deal. Most subsidized housing partnerships are private. One public partnership recently on the market is Winthrop Residential Associates. (Subsidized housing will be discussed in detail in chapters 12-14.)

REHAB COMMERCIAL REAL ESTATE

This is the sleeper in real estate shelters. Since 1978, a big tax break has been on the books for investors who restore older buildings to commercial (but not residential) use. America's great fortunes were built on a foundation of real estate. Perhaps more fortunes will be built in this decade. In any case, the eighties will be a volatile, dynamic, exciting decade for American real estate.

The Saudis will want to own some, and so will the French, the British, and the South Africans. This may be reason enough for more Americans to invest at least part of their disposable income in what may soon become an endangered species — American real estate.

QUESTIONS TO ASK A FINANCIAL ADVISER ABOUT REAL ESTATE

I do not say this about any other area of investment, but I will say it about real estate: If you need tax help, you need a financial adviser who has a great deal of experience in real estate partnerships. To help you determine your adviser's experience in this area, I have included a checklist of questions that he or she should be able to answer.

1. What real estate partnerships have you recommended in the past year? (A good adviser will have recommended at least two.)

2. What real estate properties have you personally inspected? (You can't expect an adviser to inspect every property he or she recommends, but a good adviser will keep informed by visiting at least a property or two a year.)

3. What general partners do you know well? (Don't you want your adviser to know the person who is getting your money?)

4. What do you consider an acceptable cash-on-cash return for your investors? (Cash-on-cash means the cash you get back annually as a percentage of cash you invest. Beware of advisers who promise too much.)

5. What is the most attractive area you are now studying in real estate? What is the least attractive?

6. Have you ever done, or hired someone else to do, an independent analysis of a real estate partnership's economics? Does your broker-dealer provide any help in this area? (Your adviser must rely, to a certain extent, on numbers supplied by the partnership, but advisers who work extensively in real estate also obtain independent reports. Broker-dealers, the securities dealers who supervise most advisers, can be a big help in this area.)

CHAPTER ELEVEN

RESIDENTIAL REAL ESTATE: INDIVIDUAL INVESTORS

The real estate market is currently in a crisis situation. High interest rates and high prices have cut sales volume. Foreclosures are on the rise. The new adjustable-rate mortgages have replaced the older fixed-rate mortgages, making buying a home even more difficult. In general, the housing market looks very dismal. Why, then, would anyone consider getting into residential real estate as an individual investor?

The answer is that the long term outlook for residential real estate is outstanding. In addition, the 1981 Economic Recovery Tax Act has given residential real estate an enormous shot in the arm in terms of increasing tax-shelter benefits. Finally, there are ways to avoid the management headaches usually associated with individual ownership.

Let's begin by taking a closer look at the housing market, the traditional starting point for individual real estate investors.

THE HOUSING MARKET

Housing prices have risen every year except two for the past 70 years. During the late 1970's they rose at an astonishingly fast pace. The small investor looked at the increasing prices and decided that residential housing was the best investment vehicle going. All he had to do was buy a house or other piece of residential property, wait six months or a year, then sell it for a handsome profit.

The problems started in 1980 with the advent of high interest rates. This was soon followed by the adjustable-rate mortgage, which meant that home buyers getting new loans from lending institutions couldn't borrow money at a fixed rate of interest. The rate would vary according to other interest rates. The result was twofold: buyers found it more difficult to purchase property, and sellers were forced to finance at least a part of the property they sold. Sales involving second mortgages with balloon payments due in three to five years became increasingly common.

Investors coming into this market found other problems. Whereas in 1975 it was possible to buy a house for investment purposes, rent it out, and cover basic expenses with the rental income, by 1982 rental income in many cases covered only one-half to two-thirds of expenses. In order to maintain the property, the investor had to come up with additional cash each month. Negative cash flow real estate became the rule. Nevertheless, investors were still willing to buy property even if it produced a large negative cash flow, because of: (1) their need for tax shelter and (2) their conviction that the value of the property would continue to increase so much that the ultimate appreciation would more than cover the negative cash flow.

By the recession of 1981-82, however, many individual investors were rethinking their positions. Housing resale volume dropped dramatically. Single family homes waited six to nine months to be sold. There was no market for some apartment buildings. Auctions were being held to promote the sale of condominiums. Although there appeared to be continued price appreciation, it was of little benefit to sellers, who were now receiving paper instead of cash. When that paper was discounted to its present cash value, it became obvious that property values were actually declining.

Investors who already owned many properties were often in real trouble. They had large negative cash flows; they had balloon-payment seconds coming due with no cash to pay them off; and the price appreciation they had counted on wasn't really there. Investors began to shy away from real estate. They felt that the parade had passed them by. They believed that there was no way for them to get into real estate now. Besides, with the way the market was going, they wondered if they really wanted to.

I've painted a pretty dim picture of the residential real estate market, but, I believe, it is an accurate one. I also believe that a turnaround is on its way.

WHY THERE WILL BE A RESIDENTIAL REAL ESTATE TURNAROUND

1. The supply of available residences is shrinking in most parts of the country. Back during the recession of 1974-75, there was a housing surplus. Then, when people stopped buying during the recession, builders stopped putting up new homes. The result was that at the end of the recession, when buyers came back into the

market, there was very little to buy. This shortage started the price spiral of the last decade, and the same thing is happening again today.

Robert Irwin, in his book *Riches in Real Estate,* points out that we are at the lowest level of new home production since the 1950's. The number of new apartment units being constructed today is almost equal to the number being lost to old age. We really aren't adding any new apartments to our housing inventories. The reason is obvious — residential property isn't selling, so builders aren't building. Our silent shortage of housing is reflected in rental vacancy rates of below 5 percent (a national average). Try to rent a house or apartment anywhere today. Even if you can find one, chances are you'll have to pay enormous rent. We are rapidly reaching the stage where there just won't be enough housing to go around.

2. Demand is staggering. The baby boom children are now grown up, married, and looking for new homes. High divorce rates create a need for additional residences. Older citizens live longer. The need for housing has never been greater. And it's increasing at a fast pace. Hal Morris, in his book *Crisis Real Estate Investing,* points out that during the 1970's, 32 million Americans reached the age of 30 — the prime buying age for a first home. Guess how many are expected to reach that age during the 1980's? The answer is a staggering 42 million. And they all will need a place to live.

3. Overseas investors are plunging into the American market, attracted by our stable government, (relatively) low inflation rate, and comparatively cheap housing prices. In Hong Kong, for example, a modest three bedroom house sells for $300,000. In Switzerland, the price is $200,000. In parts of the United States, only $100,000. It's no wonder that foreign visitors are eager to buy our real estate.

Perhaps the most important reason to be optimistic about the residential real estate market is the 1981 Economy Recovery Tax Act. It makes buying residential real estate a more attractive possibility than it has been in the last few years.

THE 1981 ECONOMIC RECOVERY TAX ACT AND RESIDENTIAL REAL ESTATE

Real estate has always been a major tax shelter because of its possibilities for leveraging and depreciation. Let's quickly review how real estate tax shelters worked in the past and then take a look at how they work today.

Assume that you buy an investment home for $100,000. Typically, you might put 20 percent down, or $20,000, and carry a mortgage of $80,000. (We won't consider the nature of the mortgage now; we're just looking at the property from the viewpoint of leveraging and taxation.)

$80,000	Mortgage
20,000	Cash down
$100,000	Purchase price

Let's further assume that your mortgage payment is based on a 30 year, 14 percent fixed-rate mortgage. Your monthly payment is roughly $950 a month; taxes and insurance will increase your monthly outlay to $1100.

You find, however, that you can only rent the property for $800 a month, meaning that each month you own the property, you have a $300 negative cash flow. Before you panic, remember that you can enter most of your negative cash flow (almost dollar for dollar) in the write-off column of your tax return. So to begin with, you show $3600 (12 × 300) in the write-off column. And you have yet to figure in depreciation.

Depreciation — The Old Rules

The house you bought was a resale. Therefore, the shortest term you can depreciate it for is 20 years and the highest rate of depreciation is 125 percent. (Remember, you can only depreciate the house, not the land.)

$100,000	Property
− 20,000	Land
$80,000	House value

Now let's see what your first year's depreciation will be.

$80,000	Value of house
÷20 years	Term of depreciation
$4,000	Per year (straight line)
×125%	Rate of depreciation
$5,000	First year's depreciation

When you add the $5000 in depreciation to the $3600 in negative cash flow, you end up with a total write-off of $8600. (Not all the negative cash flow is a write-off since some of it goes to repay mortgage principal. But, since only a negligible amount of the principal is paid back in the early years of a mortgage, you can ignore it here.)

$8,600	First year write-off
×50%	Tax bracket
$4,300	Tax savings
−3,600	Negative cash flow
$ 700	Cash in hand after tax considerations

Assuming you're in the 50 percent tax bracket, the tax shelter aspect of the property will cover your negative cash flow and produce a very small income. But when vacancies, repairs and maintenance and management are thrown in, you will probably show a mild loss.

Remember, this is the way it was. Now let's consider your property under the new tax law.

DEPRECIATION — THE PRESENT RULES

The 1981 Economy Recovery Tax Act reduced the term of depreciation for used real estate purchased after January 1, 1981, to 15 years and increased the rate of depreciation to 175 percent. Note the difference it makes.

$80,000	Value
÷15 years	Term of depreciation
$ 5,333	Per year (straight-line)
×175%	Rate of depreciation
$ 9,333	First year's depreciation

Under the new law, you can write off $9333 in depreciation. When you add this to your negative cash flow, you have a write-off of almost $13,000.

$13,000	First year write-off
×50%	Tax bracket
$ 6,500	Tax savings
−3,600	Negative cash flow
$ 2,900	Cash in hand after tax considerations

Now you have money coming in after taxes to cover your negative cash flow and maintenance expenses. If you can keep maintenance expenses down to $900, you will make a profit of about $2000. Since you initially invested $20,000 in the property, you are getting a 10 percent return on investment dollars.

RECAPTURE

Your investment gives you a tax shelter by permitting you to defer taxes on ordinary income to the future. When you sell your property (assuming you've held it for more than one year and otherwise qualify), you can declare a capital gain. You'll pay taxes on your gain at the lower capital gains rate.

However, there is a recapture of accelerated depreciation in real estate. That portion above straight-line is recaptured at the ordinary income rate, not capital gains rate. For example, here again is our first year's depreciation, using the straight line and 175% accelerated methods.

$5,333	Straight-line (capital gains rate)
$9,333	Accelerated depreciation (175%)
$4,000	Recapture

If you want to avoid recapture of accelerated depreciation on residential property you must hold it for 15 years. At that time the building is completely depreciated whether straight-line or accelerated depreciation is used.

HOW TO GET INTO TODAY'S MARKET
AS AN INDIVIDUAL INVESTOR

It is not easy for the individual investor to buy residential real estate today. Yet, now is perhaps one of the best times to buy. How, then, can the small investor overcome the obstacles of high interest rates and "creative" financing to take advantage of the situation?

Equity Sharing

Equity sharing helps the investor who has money, but who doesn't want to get involved in the management of real estate. Equity sharing also helps the investor who wants to get into today's market, but doesn't have the capital to get started. Equity sharing is a way to invest in real estate, either actively or passively, either with capital or without. It is the coming form of real estate investment.

Equity sharing permits two (or more) people who have different resources but the same goal to combine those resources to buy a house, condominium, or apartment building to make a profit. It is the same way that young couples who are short on cash finance the purchase of their first home. They borrow from their parents.

Their mothers and fathers give them enough money to get started. In return, they promise to pay back their parents when they sell the property.

In today's market, there are also two parties. One is the investor with capital. Usually this person is in the 50 percent tax bracket with some disposable income. He would like to invest in real estate, but doesn't want to bother with management. The second person is the investor who has little capital and virtually no disposable income. Yet, this person too wants to get involved in real estate. And because he has no capital to invest, he is willing to make up for it with hard work.

In its simplest form, the investor with capital pays the down payment on a house. The amount could be anywhere from 10 to 50 percent of the price. The investor with no money moves into the house as the occupant, maintains the property, and makes the mortgage payment. At the end of an agreed-upon period of time, often five years, the house is sold. The investor takes his money out first; then the balance is split as profit between the two parties. Each party gets half the profit, and each receives some of the benefits of owning a house. The investor with capital doesn't have to worry about negative cash flow or management. The investor with no money is able to buy a house even though he has no down payment.

There are many variations on this theme. One investor does not have to occupy the house; both could decide to rent it out, making up out of their pockets any negative cash flow. Similarly, an investor with capital can continue to buy property in this fashion for as long as his money holds out. Equity investing offers a method to get into real estate at a time when the market is down. (This method is discussed in great detail in Morris's *Crisis in Real Estate Investing*.)

Although I do believe there will be a turnaround in the real estate market, I generally advise my clients to stick with limited partnerships for now. They are probably safer. Nevertheless, I do understand that there will always be risk-takers who want to go it alone. Fortunately for them, there are still opportunities in residential real estate.

CHAPTER TWELVE

GOVERNMENT HOUSING: A DEEP SHELTER FOR INCOME

Government housing programs are some of the most conservative, yet financially rewarding deep shelter programs. Write-offs can approach 300 percent, and risks are often minimal. Of course, government programs do have constraints, drawbacks, and risks (in some cases). In other words, they aren't for everyone. But every taxpayer should be aware of these programs and what they can provide in the way of tax relief.

In this chapter we'll examine the tax write-off benefits. In subsequent chapters we'll look at potential problems and risks.

WHAT ARE GOVERNMENT HOUSING PROGRAMS?

All the programs involve either building new apartment buildings or rehabilitating old ones. The philosophy behind the programs appears to be a genuine desire to provide reasonably priced rental housing for low- and moderate-income Americans. There are three major types of housing programs. The first is a *non-subsidized program* (often under FHA Section 221(d)(4)) in which a builder or developer is offered a mortgage at far below the current market rates (at the time of this writing, 7½%).

The second method is a *subsidized program* under Section 8 of the U.S. Housing Act of 1937. Under Section 8, the government actually subsidizes the rent of low-income tenants. The subsidy, which is paid directly to the building owner, can be significant, often as much as 75 percent of the total monthly rent payment. Subsidized programs provide quality housing for people who otherwise couldn't afford it. Usually the rehabilitation program is used in conjunction with the rent subsidy plan.

All these programs are administered by the FHA and all are financed in the usual way. Often up to 90 percent of the value is raised by mortgages; the remaining capital is provided by investors. In this sense, these FHA programs appear to be like any other real estate limited partnership. You pool your money with others and buy (or in this case, build or rehabilitate) a piece of real estate. An investor might reasonably ask, what's the big difference?

There are many differences, and they vary from program to program (we'll cover these in the next chapter), but essentially, the big difference has to do with the economics of the return of the investment involved. Normally, in real estate you are concerned first with profit. Either you want some profit on an annual basis in terms of strong positive cash flow, or you want to sell your building and realize a hefty profit from the anticipated appreciation.

These are not likely to be your immediate goals in a government housing investment, however. Low-income housing, in particular, rarely produces significant cash distributions. In all the programs, in fact, there are constraints placed on the owners that prevent the buildings from producing large positive cash flows.

The goal of selling at a profit is almost as unrealistic in some government programs. Although appreciation in the Section 221's (d)(4)'s can be strong, it is weak in other programs. Most of the programs (for reasons that will be evident in a moment) are set up to run for at least 15 years. In the case of the subsidy plans (Section 8), it is difficult to predict what the building's market value will be at the end of that period. However, because the property generates only a limited cash flow, it is fairly certain that it won't be large in the short term.

Well then, if you're not likely to realize any real income from these programs, why go into them at all? At this stage, it certainly sounds like a no-win situation.

TAX ADVANTAGES — DEEP SHELTER

The advantages come from the tax write-off. Investors buy into these programs almost exclusively for the tax benefits they offer over a 15- or 20-year period. Government programs are deep tax shelters. Therefore, they are wise investments only for investors who remain in a high tax bracket (45 to 50 percent) for the best part of 10 years. Investors who drop into a lower tax bracket will probably not benefit from the program.

In the initial years of the program tax write-offs are as high as 300 percent of amount invested. Over the life of the investment, write-offs tend to range from 300 to 400 percent of the total money invested. The write-off under these programs comes basically from depreciation. In the vast majority of cases, the amount of money that is received from rents just about matches the amount that is paid out in operating expenses and mortgage payments. As an income-producing investment, then, most HUD programs are a wash.

Depreciation

When depreciation is thrown into the expense column, these properties suddenly become very attractive. Since most programs involve apartment buildings with market values in the range of 5 to 15 million dollars, the dollar value of depreciation can be staggering. If the building alone is worth, say, 15 million dollars and it is depreciated over 15 years (the current term allowed), depreciation is a million dollars a year.

Keep that million dollar a year depreciation figure in the back of your mind while we look at the financing. Let's assume that the total value of the project is $18 million ($15 million for the building and $3 million for the land) and that mortgages are taken out for 70 percent of the value, or 12.6 million. That means that the total investor capital raised was 5.4 million dollars.

5.4 million	Investor capital
12.6	Financing
18 million	Total cost

Now let's take the depreciation figure, one million dollars, and compare it with the total capital raised, 5.4 million dollars.

1 million	Annual depreciation (straight-line)
5.4 million	Total capital raised

Right away we can see that the first year's write-off for the investor is going to be about 20 percent. These buildings, however, are eligible for accelerated depreciation. Currently, the rate is 200 percent. That means that in the first year, the one million annual depreciation figure becomes two million.

1 million	(Straight-line)
×200%	Accelerated rate
2 million	Total depreciation taken

We are rapidly approaching a 40 percent write-off. But (if you are still with us), there is more to come.

In most HUD programs, capital is raised not all in one year but over a period of four to five years. Typically, an offering in a HUD limited partnership will cost the investor between $25,000 and

$75,000. But, the investor does not have to come up with the money all at one time. Rather, he invests $5000 to $20,000 per year over four to six years.

This time frame covers both the construction period and the time when the building is finished, but not yet occupied. Construction period costs are generally capitalized. But, full depreciation is taken during the first year of operation, when the building is probably producing little income because it is only partly filled. Therefore, although the investor may have put in only a portion of the money to be invested (one million of the 5.4 million) a full year's depreciation may be claimed. This gives multiple write-offs in the early years. In the example, even though the total capital to be raised is 5.4 million, at the end of the second year perhaps only one or two million will have been raised. Yet, nearly two million in depreciation may be claimed. And if the building is not yet filled up, there may be operating losses to add to the write-off.

A typical tax structure on a HUD program is shown in the chart on the following page.

Year	Minimum investment	Write-off	Write-off per year as a percent of $ invested per year	Cumulative write-off	Cumulative write-off as a % of $ invested
1982	$ 7,629	$ 3,476	45.5%	$ 3,476	45.5%
1983	5,399	17,306	320.5	20,786	159.5
1984	4,616	12,977	281.1	33,159	187.9
1985	8,640	9,529	110.2	43,288	164.7
1986	— 0 —	8,423	—	51,711	196.7
1987	— 0 —	7,527	—	59,238	225.3
1988	— 0 —	6,463	—	65,701	249.9
1989	— 0 —	6,124	—	71,825	273.2
1990	— 0 —	5,794	—	77,619	295.3
1991	— 0 —	5,474	—	83,093	316.1
1992	— 0 —	4,721	—	87,814	334.0
1993	— 0 —	3,118	—	90,932	345.9
1994	— 0 —	2,754	—	93,686	356.4
1995	— 0 —	2,416	—	96,102	365.6
1996	— 0 —	2,052	—	98,154	373.4
1997	— 0 —	981	—	99,135	377.0
Totals	$26,284	$99,135			377%

SALE OF THE BUILDING

As we noted earlier, if the building is held for the full depreciation period, accelerated depreciation does not have to be recaptured. When the building is sold, all gain will be taxed as capital gains. The building will be sold for enough money both to pay the entire capital gains tax and to repay the original investors. (Remember, the mortgage debt has been reduced during the 15-year period. Even if the building sells for no more than what it cost, it should return enough money to cover tax liability.)

It should be expected that the normal holding period for a subsidized (Section 8) building is 20 years. The expected holding period for a nonsubsidized (Section 221(d)(4)) will be 5 years.

If the building is held for 15 years or more, the total gain will be taxed as long term capital gains. If held for less than 15 years a portion of the gain will be taxed as ordinary income.

Recapture in the Event of Foreclosure or Early Sale

The great danger is that the building will be sold or lost prematurely. If that happens, then the investors would have to bring their capital accounts back to zero. Some of the gain to be reported would probably be ordinary income and the balance capital gains. The HUD programs only work if they are used as deep tax shelters. Untimely sale can destroy the benefits. (It is unlikely, however, that a partnership would sell without making a profit; foreclosure is probably the only real danger.)

The relative risk in investing in a government assisted building is very low. There has never been a foreclosure on a Section 8 building. With a non-subsidized building there is a bona fide business risk of renting the apartment. Rents charged have to be competitive with other buildings in the area that may have been built in years past at lower costs. However, when and if a building does run into trouble, FHA does everything in its power to help make the building a success.

GOVERNMENT HOUSING IN THE 1980's

Currently, due to federal administration budget cut back, there will be fewer government-assisted housing constructions. There will be few buildings constructed under the 221(d)(4) program as no 7½% money is included in the fiscal budget for 1983, nor is there any money included in the fiscal budget for the Section 8 program.

Consequently, there will be a rapidly decreasing supply of buildings to syndicate. However, a rapidly developing area within the government-assisted housing limited partnerships is that of re-syndication. That is re-syndication of existing buildings constructed under a government-assisted program some 5 to 10 years ago. These buildings are called 'second users' in the trade. The reason they are more attractive is that under the new tax law (ERTA), these buildings can now be depreciated over a 15-year period. Why should we consider re-syndicating old buildings? One reason is that the prices are very good. Cost of construction ten years ago was $10,000 to $12,000 per unit. Even allowing the sellers a nice profit, there is enough room for an excellent profit potential for the new owners and they will only have to wait another ten years to refinance a conventional loan or sell when the 20 year government restriction clock runs out.

For the person in the 45 or 50 percent tax bracket, the government programs can make a great deal of sense.

NEW TAX LAW PROVISIONS
AFFECTING SUBSIDIZED HOUSING ∗

Property Type	Expenditure	Old Law	New Law
New Construction. ∗	All Construction Costs.	200% D.B. over asset's useful life. Useful lives ranged from 5 to 45 years. Composite useful lives were from 23 to 33 years depending upon construction type.	200% D.B. over 15 years.
Rehabilitation of a nonhistoric property (I.R.C. 167 (k)). ∗	Purchase of existing building.	125% D.B. over useful life (normally 45 years).	200% D.B. over 15 years.
	Rehabilitation expenditures.	60-month write-off up to $20,000 per apartment unit.	Option to increase 60-month write-off up to $40,000 per unit.
	Treatment of excess over $20,000 or $40,000 limit.	Accelerated depreciation over useful life, normally 6 to 45 years.	200% D.B. over 15 years.
	Profit limitation on sale.	No legal restriction.	Essentially restricted to recovery of original investment if more than $20,000 per unit is written off over 60 months.
Rehabilitation of certified historic structures. ∗∗	Purchase of existing building.	125% D.B. over useful life (normally 45 years).	200% D.B. over 15 years.
	Rehabilitation expenditures.	60-month write-off (I.R.C. 191 - repealed effective 1/1/82).	15-year straight line depreciation. 25% investment credit of rehabilitation expenditures (I.R.C. 48 and 168).

∗ New laws effective 1/1/81
∗∗ New laws effective 1/1/82

Abbreviations:
D.B. - Declining Balance Depreciation
I.R.C. - Internal Revenue Code Section

NEW LAW TAX SAVINGS
50% TAXPAYER *
(000's)

Year	Investment	New Construction Section 8 (High-rise Building)	Rehab 167 (k) $20,000*	Rehab 167 (k) $40,000**	Certified Historic Rehab
1981	$ 8	$ 3	$ 3	$ 3	$ 3
1982	11	11	14	16	35 (1)
1983	10	12	13	16	6
1984	9	12	12	13	5
1985	7	9	8	12	5
1986	-	6	7	10	4
1987	-	4	6	5	4
1988-97		22	12	-	26
	$45	$79	$75	$75	$88

(1) Includes Investment tax credits of $28,000.
* Rehabilitation costs up to $20,000 per apartment unit amortized over 5 years. Remainder of expense depreciated over 15 years.
** Rehabilitation costs up to $40,000 per unit amortized over 5 years.
Note - This table does not include taxes that would be due upon foreclosure in 1997 of $23,000, $28,000, $28,000 and $25,000, respectively, for each investment shown above.

SUBSIDIZED HOUSING
RATES OF RETURN *

	Adjusted Rate of Return For 1984 Tax Bracket of*			Internal Rate of Return For 1984 Tax Bracket of**		
	42%	45%	50%	42%	45%	50%
Section 8 - New Construction	6.5%	6.9%	7.3%	9.7%	12.1%	14.6%
Section 167(k) Rehab - Amortization of $20,000 per unit over 5 years	6.2	6.7	7.2	7.8	10.3	14.1
Section 167 (k) Rehab - Amortization of $40,000 per unit over 5 years	6.7	7.1	7.6	10.8	13.4	18.7
Certified Historic Rehabilitation	8.1	8.3	8.7	21.1	22.3	23.9

Note: Calculations are for a 1981 investment with the building placed in service in July 1982. Assumes all properties are foreclosed in seventeenth year of ownership. Rates of return are after tax per annum. Tax savings for a married individual were calculated using current tax rates phased into the indicated bracket in 1984.

* Assumes constant after tax reinvestment of 6% over the life of the investment.
** Represents the rate of return on principal plus the rate of return of principal. The sinking fund method was used at 6% to pay the tax cost of foreclosure.

CHAPTER THIRTEEN

HUD PROGRAMS: A BRIEF BACKGROUND

The HUD programs discussed in the last chapter are designed to build apartment houses or, to be more precise, large apartment complexes. Their purpose, as noted, is to provide housing that would not otherwise be available to low- and moderate-income families.

THE PROJECTS

The first low-income apartment complexes were the "projects" — the public housing put up by local authorities after the Second World War. The projects were built with direct subsidies from the federal government. Local housing authorities raised money for these projects by the sale of tax-exempt (municipal) bonds. Under the terms of the bond, the bearer did not have to pay federal income tax on the interest.

These first projects did not turn out well — in fact, many became ghettos and slums. At first, poor design and cheap construction was blamed for their failure. Therefore, a "turnkey" program, which allowed private developers to design and construct the projects, was established. The private sector was given its chance to design and construct what everyone hoped would be high quality low-income housing. A local developer or builder handled the whole project from design to development. When it was finished and ready for the new tenants to turn their keys in the locks, the local housing authority bought the project, usually with funds advanced by the federal government.

These early projects were primarily designed for people who were at the bottom of the income scale, often on welfare. But, in the 1960's it became apparent that there were also many families not on welfare who could not afford adequate housing. Low-income rental housing was needed, but the projects did not seem to be the answer. By then, they had an extremely negative image.

THE FHA 236 PROGRAM — AN ALTERNATIVE TO THE PROJECTS

The FHA 236 program was designed to encourage development of low-income rental housing by offering developers a subsidized mortgage. (In those days, mortgage interest rates were under 6 percent.) The subsidy worked in this fashion. The builder obtained a mortgage in the normal manner. Then, the FHA made up the difference between the cost of mortgage payments at that interest rate and the cost of payments at an interest rate of roughly one percent.

The catch in these programs was that the owners of the building were required to offer apartments at rental rates that reflected the lower mortgage payment. The owners were not free to raise rents as they desired.

In the 1970's the FHA programs ran into deep trouble when costs skyrocketed. Heating, taxes, maintenance, and other costs of operation rose dramatically. Yet, building owners frequently were not able to raise rents sufficiently to cover these unexpected expenses. The problem that plagued the 236's was the inability to get needed rent increases approved fast enough by the FHA. When the owners could not increase rents, they could not pay their expenses, and they lost their buildings by foreclosures. (It should be noted that almost all of these foreclosures were sponsored and managed by nonprofit organizations.)

After some owners started giving their buildings back to the FHA, the FHA improved and streamlined its procedures and, more importantly, changed its attitude toward rent increases.

SECTION 8 PROGRAM

In the 1970's in response to the problems that surfaced in the 236 program, a new Section 8 program was created. Under Section 8, HUD agreed to subsidize the owner of the building for the difference between what it considered fair market rent and what it determined the tenant could actually afford. In general, HUD has been fair to generous in its determinations of "fair market rent" and "tenant affordability." To determine fair market rent, HUD surveys the rents for comparable buildings in the community. It then creates a comparable rent structure for the investor's building. Depending on the building's amenities, the fair market rent can be, in some cases, as much as 125 percent of the average rent in the surrounding market.

How does HUD determine "tenant affordability"? Generally speaking, in order to qualify, a tenant must be making no more than 80 percent of the median income for the community. Family size is also taken into consideration. Once it qualifies for the subsidy, the family is required to pay only 15 to 25 percent of its total income in rent. The remainder is paid directly to the owner by HUD.

If, for example, a tenant's income is $10,000 a year, he or she might have to pay 25 percent of that amount in rent — $2500 a year. This is not a great deal to pay for an apartment that would normally rent for $700 a month.

The difference between the amount the subsidized tenant pays and the "fair market rent" of the unit is paid by HUD directly to the building's owner.

$700	Rental rate (fair market rent)
−208	Tenant's contribution
$492	HUD's subsidy per month

What should be obvious from these figures is that (1) HUD is going to have to spend a lot of money; (2) subsidized housing is a terrific boon for the tenants; and (3) the owners will have full occupancy.

DIFFERENCES BETWEEN SECTION 8 AND FHA 236

Did the Section 8 programs eliminate all the problems that plagued the 236 programs? For example, what did the owner do when there was a sudden increase in utility costs? The answer is built right into the program. Increases in operating costs are automatically added to rent rates. HUD does not even have to give specific permission for this. In addition, the owner may petition HUD for a subsidy increase if there should be a special need. HUD is obligated to investigate the special need situation, and if it finds that raising rents is warranted, it must do so.

In addition, HUD will pay 80 percent of the regular rental rate for a full two months in the case of a vacancy. It will also pay that unit's contribution to the debt service (mortgage interest rate) for up to a full year. (However, vacancy insurance hasn't been necessary. Typically, units built under the Section 8 program are filled on the day they open. It is not unusual to find 100-unit buildings with waiting lists that contain 400 names.)

SECTION 8 LOCK-IN

Thus far, it would seem that there are only pluses to the HUD Section 8 program. There are a few minuses but only for the investor. Perhaps the most important to remember is the mandatory 20-year lock-in feature. As soon as the building is constructed, the owners enter into a Housing Assistance Payments Contract (HAP) with HUD. Once entered into, the owners cannot withdraw from the contract for the specified period of time, even if by selling. At the end of 20 years, the building can be sold, and the profits split up.

REDUCED MORTGAGE RATE PROGRAMS (NON-SECTION-8 SUBSIDIZED)

There are two kinds of reduced mortgage rate programs: an insured program, Section 221(d)(4), which we discussed earlier, and is an uninsured program, which we'll go into in a few moments.

FHA Insured Programs

The insured programs under Section 221(d)(4) require a mortgage loan of 90 percent. (Because of the highly technical way the actual mortgage is determined, it may be close to, but not actually 90 percent.) The mortgage is for 40 years, and it is insured by the FHA up to a maximum interest rate (roughly 11 percent).

Insured GNMA Tandems

Most of these mortgages are actually held in "tandem" by the FHA and the Government National Mortgage Association (GNMA, commonly called "Ginnie Mae"). Ginnie Mae under its Program 23 funds the money for the mortgage at a lower than market interest rate if that mortgage is going to be insured by FHA. At the present time, Ginnie Mae is offering these mortgages at an interest rate of 7.5 percent.

The way it works is quite simple: After the construction period (financed by a private construction loan obtained by the developer), Ginnie Mae funds the permanent loan on the building. At the same time FHA insures it for a cost of one-half percentage point over the interest rate of the loan. The FHA insurance means that in the event the building gets into financial trouble, the FHA will guarantee up to 99 percent of the loan. What it means to Ginnie Mae is that if the owners can't make the payments, the FHA will.

As we'll see in the next chapter, the FHA/GNMA tandem plan requires developers to meet certain criteria, including establish reserve funds for various contingencies. For example, there is a 2 percent working capital reserve that the builder must set aside as a capital reserve. It is to be used in the event that there is an unexpected need in the initial stages of the project's development. In addition, a special replacement reserve must be kept to finance the replacement of personal property, such as stoves, refrigerators, carpeting, and drapes, in the unit.

There is also a very precise formula used for determining how much the land can cost, how much the building should cost, and how much the financing should cost. Further, the FHA is very careful to see that estimates of potential rent income are based on investigation, rather than on fantasy.

In other words, the properties developed under this program have every chance of succeeding. This is important since we're speaking here of apartments to be rented in the open market without a rental subsidy. Perhaps it's the fact that the government has put its name on the line that makes them economically viable.

NONINSURED PROGRAMS (SECTION 8 SUBSIDIZED)

You'll recall that I noted that the very first government programs involved local housing authorities putting up the money for buildings. To some extent this is still occurring.

Municipal Bond Programs

Some municipalities (cities, townships, counties), seeing the need for low- to moderate-income housing, have undertaken such projects themselves. (These are usually Section 8 HUD programs.) The agency handling the project is normally part of a local housing authority and is created specifically for the purpose of organizing and overseeing new building projects.

Under these plans, the money for the program is raised by using the municipality's ability to offer tax-free bonds — municipal bonds that are frequently offered by securities dealers.

The result is that the housing authority borrows money at far lower than market rates. It then offers this money to developers, usually adding on a small percentage to cover its operating costs. For the developer, it's very much like the Section 221(d)(4) program. The advantage is the lower mortgage cost.

For the HUD investor, however, there are other considerations. As noted earlier, the FHA has very strict requirements for calculating the suitability of a new apartment building in the local market, the actual rents likely to be obtained, and the actual maintenance expenses. The FHA also requires that strong reserves be put aside.

Under the municipal bond program (also sometimes called an 11(b), program), this same sort of thoroughness may be required if the mortgage is eventually to be covered by FHA insurance. (It is possible to obtain FHA mortgage insurance on municipal projects that meets requirements. However, FHA insurance is not mandatory.)

Uninsured Municipal Programs

Some of the municipal programs are not FHA insured. In these programs sometimes have optimistic projections of income expenses are used than in the FHA programs. For example, in the noninsured programs, vacancies as a cost factor are sometimes not included or are given a nominal figure (1 or 2%). In an FHA insured building, the vacancy rate is automatically given as 5 percent. This provides an economic cushion should the FHA building run into hard times.

In addition, in uninsured programs, replacement reserves may not be required. (However, a reserve for mortgage debt is often included, and it may be higher than that required for insured programs.)

It should not be assumed, however, that uninsured programs are automatically more risky than insured programs. In a Section 8 (rent subsidies) program, for example, the chances for either an insured or uninsured program running into trouble are slim. But as far as the investor is concerned, even a slight increase in risk should be taken into account. Sometimes, the risk balance is in favor of the uninsured program. For example, uninsured buildings are often in far better locations than insured buildings. Then, even without insurance, the former program may turn out to be a better investment than the latter.

REHABILITATION PROGRAMS

Rehabilitation programs are generally Section 8 programs. The big advantage for the investor/owner is the short write-off period — just five years. This allows for enormous early tax write-offs, often in the area of 300 percent.

The rehabilitation programs are handled and financed in a fashion similar to the programs we've just described. There is one drawback, however, that must be carefully considered.

Often Rehabs are located in the older, less desirable sections of cities. If they are built under Section 221(d)(4) without Section 8 subsidies, there may be an occupancy problem. Tenants who can

114

afford competitive rents (which are what these programs offer) often don't want to live in the older city neighborhoods. This problem can be solved by a Section 8 subsidized program. With the rent subsidy, there should be virtually no problem in renting the building. There will, however, be a problem in disposing of the building after the 15 to 20 year holding period. At that time, the building's residual value may be very low. It is difficult to determine or project what the sale price would be because of the changing character of the surrounding area(s).

All in all, the vast majority of HUD programs developed over the past few years have done very well. Unlike the older 236 programs, which ran afoul of escalating costs not recoverable through rent increases, the modern programs have been fortified to survive in the wild economic times of the 1980's. They can offer investors both a strong tax shelter and an economically sound investment.

CHAPTER FOURTEEN

HUD PROGRAMS: RISKS AND REWARDS

If the overall picture of a HUD program is appealing to you, you are then faced with making a choice. Of the numerous HUD programs available, some will offer greater benefits than others. Some will offer greater risks than others. How, then, do you decide which program is best for you?

RISKS

Perhaps the first thing you should do is to evaluate the risk factors common to all HUD programs.

CONSTRUCTION PERIOD RISKS

Generally speaking, HUD programs are put together before ground has been broken on the building site. That means that the investor in a limited partnership has to bear the risks of construction. If there is any place that Murphy's law operates without fail, it is in construction. Whatever can go wrong, will. That does not mean, however, that projects tend not to be completed. Virtually all the HUD apartment buildings that enter the construction phase are successfully completed.

There may, however, be delays and increased costs. In some cases — decreased costs. In a program that is soundly developed, increased costs (and increased time) are largely accounted for in buffered estimates. A contractor who has had a great deal of experience usually knows where the problems will be and anticipates them. To offset potential risks, contractors are frequently bonded or made to sign performance guarantees, so even if the contractor should fold, there will be enough money left to finish the project.

MARKETING RISKS

After the construction period, marketing is the single biggest risk. If the apartment building, for one reason or another, doesn't fill up, there will be a loss of rental income. The end result could be foreclosure and loss of the investor's capital. (In the case of a deep tax shelter, such a loss might show up as a large tax gain that would be taxed as ordinary income.)

Subsidy Program Risks

For all practical purposes, there is no marketing risk in a subsidy program. The reason should be obvious. With the massive rent subsidies offered, tenants are not hard to find. In fact, these buildings usually fill up the day they are opened. Further, in the event that there should be a problem finding tenants, there is vacancy insurance. (Remember that the government will pay the owner 80 percent of the rental rate for two months of vacancy and then will pay enough to equal that unit's portion of mortgage debt for up to a year.) With guarantees like that, the chance of not being able to make mortgage payments out of rent income in virtually nonexistent.

Nonsubsidy Program Risks

In the past, most HUD housing was subsidized. More recently, however, the government, in an attempt to reduce spending, has cut back on subsidy programs. Ginnie Mae funding has also been cut back. As a result, many of the new HUD offerings are nonsubsidy programs using municipal-bond or other forms of financing.

The marketing risks in nonsubsidy programs are far greater than in the subsidy ones. Basically they occur during the rent-up phase of the project.

Fill-up Risks

In the subsidy programs, renting is usually completed the first day. Not so in nonsubsidy programs. These buildings are competing with every other building in the city. And often other units are offering lower rents for the same space. The reason for this is simply that existing apartment units, those three, five or more years old, were built and financed more cheaply. They can charge less and still make a profit. This, of course, is a problem no different from the one any owner of a new apartment building faces. To counter it, the new building is often able to offer more modern features — and newness itself has a certain market appeal. Nevertheless, it is most unlikely that the owner of a nonsubsidized building will fill up in one day. He may have to wait several months or, in the worst possible scenario, several years. He could be stuck with only a partly or even minimally rented building.

Most nonsubsidized building programs are (or should be) prepared for this contingency. The general partner should have set aside funds to cover payment of debt during the fill-up period (2% of the mortgage). These funds should be sufficiently large to cover negative cash flow during fill-up plus all other initial expenses. (Some mortgages, for example, do not cover personal property. That means that furniture for the lobby and other similar items may have to be paid for directly out of investor's capital.)

In the majority of cases the fill-up is handled successfully. Within a reasonable period of time, the property has enough tenants to cover its expenses. But, in some very few cases there are problems, and fill-up is not accomplished as anticipated. Let's look at some of the reasons.

WHEN A BUILDING DOESN'T FILL UP

It could be possible that between the time the project was conceived and the time it was completed, the market changed from a landlord's market to a renter's market. Or the economy in the area could have gone into a decline, reducing the pool of potential tenants able to handle the rental rate.

Bob Christensen of Security Pacific, Inc., who put together many HUD proposals, says that out of the more than 280 programs he has worked on, only one could not eventually be filled up. A few of the others took longer than expected to fill up, but they all made it eventually. There was one building, however, that simply could not be filled at the projected rental rate. What happened to that program and to the investors involved?

The building in question was an FHA-insured nonsubsidized building. After the money set aside for the initial fill-up period was used up, the general partner went to the FHA and explained the difficulty and indicated that the partnership was working hard to correct it. (You have to remember that the FHA doesn't really want to foreclose on the property it insures. If you're having problems renting the building, the FHA will too.) The FHA allowed the general partner to use the 2% of mortgage working capital reserve he had set aside to be used to offset mortgage payments during this difficult period.

When the mortgage working capital reserve was used up, and the project still wasn't filled up, the FHA allowed the general partner to dip into the replacement reserves. (This is the money set aside for the replacement of items such as drapes, carpeting, and stoves.) When this reserve was gone, the FHA gave a moratorium on mortgage payments. The project simply did not have to make any mortgage payments until the building filled up. In addition, the FHA gave the partnership a working capital loan (at 3%) and an allocation of Section 8 elderly units.

The next day it was filled.

The investors, of course, were thrilled. In this worst possible scenario, they had come out heroes rather than villains. During the period when the building could not be rented, the write-offs were enormous because of the negative cash flow. They actually did better, from a tax-shelter standpoint, than if the project had filled up as planned.

It should be pointed out, however, that this was an FHA-insured program. If the building had been developed using, say, municipal bonds without FHA insurance, the result might have been much different.

These then, are the basic risks of any HUD program. An investor considering such a program should consider them carefully. Once again they are:

1. The risks of problems occurring during the construction phase.

2. The risk of the project turning out to be economically unsound and ultimately foreclosed by the mortgage holder.

HOW TO EVALUATE HUD PROPERTIES

An investor who wants to get into a HUD program for its benefits often has to choose between several different programs. What criteria should be used to make the choice? There are many, including the special financial position of the investor. But in general, the investor will want to see whether the program is subsidized or nonsubsidized; and whether it is FHA insured or uninsured. The investor will also want to know how sound the program is economically, who the general partner is, and how soon the property will be sold (and what effect this will have on taxes.) In addition, there is the question of return. Which program will offer the greatest return?

There are two methods of comparing rate of return. One is the "discounted rate of return." Let's see how this works.

If you are given $100 today and must give it back in three years, is there any gain to you? Think before you answer. There is definite gain: You have the use of $100 over a three-year period. Just by sticking it in the bank at 10% interest, you will earn roughly $35. In other words, your return was 35%.

The same principle applies in HUD programs (and in other investments as well). Remember, these are tax-deferral shelters. You take money that you would otherwise give to the government and invest it. At a later date, you get that money back in the form of a gain on which you must pay taxes, hopefully at a lower capital gains rate.

The money you save initially (through write-offs), the time it is invested, and the tax rate eventually paid together produce a figure commonly called the "discounted rate of return." Each HUD program has its own discounted rate of return and by comparing those, you can see which offers you the greatest return. (The partnership offering the program or your financial planner can usually supply this information.)

Another way to evaluate return is to capitalize the cash flow or to make a new present value analysis. This sounds more complicated than it really is. All that you do is compare the after-tax cash flow of different programs. (Note that I said *after tax*. This means the cash you have in hand after all taxes are paid.) Presumably, all other factors being equal, you would want the program that offered you the best after-tax cash flow. (Capitalizing this figure would simply mean giving it a percentage rate of return.)

HUD programs have been around for a long time. They have been successful in providing deep tax shelters at minimum risk to tens of thousands of investors. They can be an excellent investment for the taxpayer who is in a sufficiently high tax bracket to take advantage of the excellent write-off benefits they offer.

CHAPTER FIFTEEN

R & D PARTNERSHIPS: TECHNOLOGY'S TAX SHELTERS

Research and Development is a relatively new area for tax shelters. In fact, prior to the Supreme Court case of *Snow vs. Commissioner* in 1974, there were for all practical purposes no research and development shelters. Although R&D programs have no track record to speak of, they have caught investors' attention, they have been widely distributed, and their offerings have been purchased with largely good results.

The reason so many investors like R&D programs is that they offer a tax shelter and the potential for substantial returns. In addition, depending on the structure of the program, it is possible to get a large write-off in the year of purchase, even if the purchase occurs in late December.

WHY RESEARCH AND DEVELOPMENT?

In the late 1960's and the early 1970's, a large hue and cry was made about the fact that the United States was falling behind other countries, principally Japan and Germany, in applied research and development of new technology. It was widely observed that we were simply no longer the leader in this field. On March 8, 1976, *Business Week* published an article entitled "The Silent Crisis in R&D." The article stated that the United States faced a serious contraction of its long-term growth rate as a result of the slump in spending for research and development. The slowdown in financial support was apparent in private industry and government ventures alike.

Between 1953 and 1961, R&D expenditures, adjusted for inflation, increased at an average annual rate of 13.9 percent. But between 1967 and 1975, the government support to R&D actually shrank by 3 percent per year, according to the National Science Foundation. Why did expenditures in R&D drop so dramatically during this period?

One explanation is inflation. The government simply found that its priorities in an inflationary economy were elsewhere. In terms of private financing, inflation was even more obviously the culprit.

In the early 1970's, inflation hit with such a bang that by 1974 the real dollar value of common stocks had declined more than it declined during the Great Depression of the 1930's (a deflationary period in comparison with the inflation of the 1970's). The small- to medium-size brokerage firms typically responsible for underwriting stock offerings on behalf of start-up technology companies were devastated during this period. In fact, many that had survived the crash of 1929 were driven out of business in the mid-1970's. With the loss of these traditional sources of start-up equity capital, technology companies were unable to attract capital from lending institutions. It was a difficult time indeed.

But help was on the way, both from the industry itself and from private venture capital. In this chapter, we will look at the structure, benefits, and activities of limited partnerships that provide venture capital to fund research and development.

IS R&D A GOOD INVESTMENT?

Although R&D limited partnerships are relatively new, they have already made a significant impact on business.

1. Organized R&D projects account for approximately 40 percent of the total increase in the U.S. productivity rate. Nestor E. Terleckyz of the National Planning Association found a direct productivity return of 30 percent per year on R&D in manufacturing industries during 1948-1966. Some industries that do little of their own R&D, but which buy from R&D intensive industries achieved productivity gains of up to 80 percent per year. Another study, by Edwin Mansfield of the Wharton School, indicated that the high rates of return persisted into the 1970's. Using case studies from projects that spanned two decades (1950-70), he found that when adjusted for unsuccessful R&D efforts, a return between 25 percent and 50 percent was recorded annually.

2. Industry receives an annual 30 percent average return on its R&D expenditures — about twice the return realized from capital investments.

3. *Approximately 80 percent of the commercially viable new product ideas originate from research financed by individual investors and small companies.*

4. Although industry invests ten times as much in plant operations as in R&D, one dollar of R&D has almost four times the impact on growth that one dollar invested in plant and equipment has.

All of which shows that the potential for strong profits in the field of R&D does exist. Investors who become involved in R&D programs are usually looking for a tax shelter immediately and big profits somewhere down the road.

WHAT DOES R&D PRODUCE?

The products can be virtually anything. Usually, they involve the application of new technology. Once a product is developed, it is sold, often directly to consumers in the marketplace. The result of these sales is a profit that goes back to the investor, often in the form of a very large return.

HOW DO R&D PROGRAMS WORK?

It is important to understand that the research and development programs offered to investors are not generally of the "pure" research type. In other words, the money doesn't go to fund an inventor to sit in a workshop and dream up a new product or a new technology. A program to fund pure research would probably be doomed from the onset. Besides the obvious drawback that the inventor might not be able to invent something useful, there is also the problem that even if he did invent a new process, the inventor might not have the wherewithal to develop or market it.

For a program to be successful, there has to be both ends of the knot. There has to be research (so that investors are able to get in on the ground floor at reasonable prices), and there has to be development so that the means are at hand to exploit the product fully in the marketplace.

Generally speaking, a successful R&D program consists of five distinct activities. Each of these is as important as any other and together they form a chain. If there is a weak link anywhere along the line, the program can fail. If, however, all the links are strong, the program can have significant success.

1. After an inventor rushes forward exclaiming Eureka, a considerable amount of preliminary research and development work is required to determine if his idea is brilliant or not. Included in this phase of the program are market studies, design work, product cost analyses, sales projections, and the necessary laboratory and field testing. All this is done to define realistically the

expected return on invested capital, risk/reward ratios, patentability, and other common business formulas used in evaluating an investment.

2. If the new product idea looks commercially viable, more work is done to develop a final product. It's one thing to discover that a strong, tiny flow of water will clean teeth effectively. It's quite another to develop a water spray machine that can be sold at a price consumers will be willing to pay.

This is the stage of R&D where the investor's capital first goes to work. A general partner who regularly handles such programs is approached by the inventor or someone else interested in the ultimate product. The general partner then organizes a limited partnership, following the regulations and criteria set by the IRS. Once the partnership is established, the inventor, who is usually someone working for a high technology company, assigns all rights, title, and interest in the product over to the partnership. The partnership then offers shares to individual investors.

3. The partnership now hires a competent R&D organization to conduct whatever research is necessary to make the product ready for the market. Often, this organization is a subsidiary of the general partner's corporation with a good track record in final product development.

4. At this point the partnership has one of two options. The first option is to begin start-up production activities. The partnership can job out the production, relying on vendors to supply the components of their specific product, the castings, molded plastics, electronic components, and so on. This activity can be conducted piecemeal until the partnership has enough product on hand to supply it to distributors. For a partnership choosing this option, the next phase involves obtaining distributors, dealers, licensees, and other marketing support.

5. Or, as a different option, and the one that is usually chosen, the partnership can assign all its rights of ownership to a corporation that will handle the manufacturing and marketing. In return, the corporation will pay a royalty to the limited partnership which will be received as long-term capital gains by the individual investors.

It should be noted that individual investors normally do not get involved until after an idea for a product has been conceived and its commercial viability determined.

HOW DOES AN R&D PARTNERSHIP SHELTER TAXES?

After reading the preceding step-by-step description of an R&D program, you might reasonably wonder how a tax shelter fits into the scheme of things. Tax shelter benefits are acquired in the following manner.

In actual practice, the inventor of a product idea is usually not an individual but a division or department of a technology company. That company then makes use of a R&D limited partnership to raise funds to develop one or more new product ideas it has conceived or acquired. The partnership may be either a private syndication or a publicly registered (SEC) partnership. The ultimate research and development is normally conducted by the original technology company or by an affiliate under a turnkey contract with the partnership.

What is critical here is to see the nature of the partnership. It acquires rights to the idea from the company, then gives to the company, usually through an affiliate, a contract for all research and development work. This relationship means that the limited partnership is able to consider all the money committed in the final development contract it gave to the company as an expense item.

In addition, if the partnership uses the accrual method of accounting, the entire amount of the R&D final development contract can be expensed *the day the R&D contract is entered into.* It is for this reason that typical partnerships offer full write-off whenever the investor comes on board, even to the December investors. The amount of write-off thus obtained for typical partnerships is in the range of 85 percent, unless recourse notes are used to provide higher write-offs.

Although we've just looked at the basic vehicle for the R&D tax shelter, there are some additional points which should be carefully considered to fully understand its operation.

Deductibility

In the case of *Snow vs. Commissioner*, The Supreme Court held that a new limited partnership, formed for the purpose of undertaking the development of a new product idea, is permitted to deduct all expenses incurred in the development of that product. This allows deductibility of the R&D contract under section 174 of the IRS Code.

"Order and Risk" Requirement

To ensure the deductibility of an R&D expense, it is absolutely essential that the development contract be conducted at the risk of the taxpayers claiming the deduction. In other words, the contract agreement must not in any way imply any guarantee that the research will succeed or that the product will provide economic return. The partnership structure must ensure that the limited partner's entire investment will be lost if the development program proves totally unsuccessful.

Deductible Expenses

In general terms, all expenditures relative to research and experimental laboratory and test activities, as well as the cost of applying for and obtaining a patent, are deductible expenses. (Acquisition cost for obtaining a patent, model, or process owned by another would not be included.) Equipment, tooling, or any other depreciable or depletable property used in connection with the R&D activity, however, is deductible only if such property, acquired or improved, remains the property of the organization conducting the development work on behalf of the partnership.

Among the activities not permissible as deductible expenses are the costs of structuring the partnership, clearing and printing the offering, and commissions. In the R&D contract, quality control, cost analysis, ordinary testing, management studies, consumer surveys, market promotions, and sales literature are not deductible expenses.

Accrual Accounts by Partnership

The partnership *must* use the accrual method of accounting to ensure deductibility of the turnkey R&D contract in the year of the investment. Since the research and experimental expenditures, particularly for year-end investments, will rarely be completed in less than a year, the obligations to pay the entire R&D contract amount must be completely independent of the obligation to perform or successfully complete the R&D contract.

Capital Gains Treatment of Distributions

Sections 1222 and 1235 of the IRS Code provide for capital gains treatment of all profits received from the sales of the products developed after the R&D limited partnership was formed. Section 1235 permits, in the case of patentable products, a transfer of all substantial rights to the product developed to an entity independent of the partnership in return for a royalty based on sales of the product. (This is essentially what happened when a limited partnership assigns its rights to a company to exploit a new product.)

In the event the technology may not be patentable, Section 1222 may be relied upon if the partnership meets the one-year holding period by agreeing to a nonexclusive lease allowing the assignee to evaluate the technology and including an option to purchase after the passage of 12 months.

In summary, it is essential that the partnership transfer all substantial rights to the product for its entire useful life to the assignee (the entity intended to conduct manufacturing and marketing activities for commercialization of the product) for the royalty payments to qualify for capital gains treatment of distributions passed on to the individual limited partners.

What should be further pointed out here is the matter of distributions. Because of the way the partnership is structured in the overall product development, as long as it basically assigns the product to another company for development and receives a *royalty*, or lease, as its return, the money it gets and passes back to the partners is treated as a *capital gain*.

So, investors initially place their money in a limited partnership for research and development and receive an initial tax write-off. Later, assuming the product is successfully developed and marketed, their return is in the form of a capital gain.

At this point, you probably still have some questions to ask. What is the risk/reward ratio? If the product does well, how much can I make? What are the chances of it doing badly? We'll cover these areas in the next chapter.

R & D PARTNERSHIPS:
REWARDS AND TASKS

R&D partnerships come in a variety of forms. While they may appear different, all have many things in common, including the risks and rewards involved. Let's quickly examine the reward structure, and then take a look at the risks and see how they can be minimized.

R&D REWARDS

1. A deduction of about 85 percent of the invested funds against taxable income, even for partners admitted to the partnership as late as December. (With leveraging, higher write-offs are possible, but this is not recommended.)

2. A 25 percent research and development investment tax credit for certain qualifying partnerships (resulting from legislation passed by Congress in the Economic Recovery Tax Act of 1981). Qualification for the investment tax credit is complex and is available to the limited partners only in subsequent years.

3. No recapture of the original 85 percent write-off.

4. No tax preference items. In other words, the limited partner is not subject to the alternate minimum income tax.

5. All distributions to the limited partners receive preferable tax treatment at long-term capital gains rates.

The actual investment in an R&D partnership is usually at least $5000 with the average somewhere between $10,000 and $20,000. The return on any one investment is impossible to predict with certainty, but in general it amounts to 10 percent of the gross sales of the product for as long as 20 years. This is the royalty return that comes to the investor as capital gain.

In terms of return on capital invested, assuming the project is successful, companies typically project a return ratio of between four to one and ten to one. In other words, if the investor puts up $10,000, the return potential is between $40,000 and $100,000, depending on the company, the offering, the structure of the deal, and other factors. It should be clear that R&D programs are money-makers, or at least they are intended to be.

Of course, as with all investments, there are risks. Some R&D programs simply do not succeed. In those cases the investor may lose the original investment, less the taxes originally saved. Before we take a look at the risks in R&D projects, and how to identify and minimize them, let's briefly take a look at leveraging.

Leveraging

Some partnerships offer leveraging as an added inducement. In other words, the investor can borrow a portion of the capital needed to buy into the partnership. The borrowed money can be either in the form of a loan, which the investor obtains personally before entering the partnership, or in the form of an overall partnership loan, which the investor signs for upon joining.

Since 1976, nonrecourse loans cannot be used to develop tax shelters except with real estate. Therefore, if the investor obtains such leveraging, in order to gain tax advantages, he must be committed to repaying the loan regardless of how the project turns out. If the project is successful, there is no problem. The investor can leverage a much higher tax shelter and a much higher profit. But, if the project is not successful, the investor will lose whatever money he originally put up and the money he borrowed. For this reason, investors should be cautious about getting into R&D programs that involve partnership leveraging. (Most offerings today do not.)

R&D RISKS

All investments have risks. Research and development is no different. The following list should help you to identify the risks common to all R&D programs.

1. *Possible failure to complete development work.* In other words, an unforeseen wrinkle during the final research stage might make it impossible to produce a commercially viable product.

2. *Excessive manufacturing costs.* If a commercially viable product is developed, it must be manufactured before it can be sold. If the manufacturing costs turn out to be excessive, the product may be too costly to be competitive in the marketplace.

3. *Market share.* What percentage of the total market will the product need to capture in order to be successful? Ten percent, 50 percent, or more? If it can't appeal to the required amount, it won't earn the desired level of profit.

4. *Insufficient working capital for operations.* Will the limited partnership be sufficiently funded to complete the research and development necessary? Will the company selected for exploiting the product have sufficient resources to manufacture and fully distribute the product?

5. *Technological obsolescence.* We are living in a very fast world. Twenty years ago, a new product could look forward to a life-span of many years. Therefore, if it took many years to develop a product, there was no problem. The market that existed when the idea was conceived would still be there by the time the product emerged. This is not the case today. If the time between conceptualization and commercialization is too long, the market may have moved elsewhere. The product could be obsolete by the time it reaches the consumer.

6. *IRS audit failure.* If the partnership is not properly structured to conform to IRS standards, it could fail an audit. The result could be a denial of some or all of the tax benefits. In addition, distributions that were expected to be capital gains could come back as ordinary income.

These, then, are the basic risks involved in R&D. They are really no different from the risks involved in introducing any new product to the market. They are essentially the same risks that every manufacturer in the country faces in bringing out any of the millions and millions of products that we purchase daily.

How to Minimize Risks

While it is obviously not possible to eliminate the risks in R&D, it is possible to minimize them.

1. In response to concerns about the *inability to develop a marketable product,* risk can be minimized through diversification. If the limited partnership offered to the investor is for a single product and if that product does not reach the marketplace, the program will be a failure. On the other hand, if the program is for multiple products, the program can succeed if only some of the products prove to be commercially successful. By spreading the risk across multiple products and technologies, the chance for success is greatly enhanced.

In general, the large SEC registered public offerings tend to be the ones, because of their size, which cover multiple products.

2. While excessive *manufacturing costs and failure to capture market share* can be a concern, you have to ultimately trust that the company developing the product has made intelligent market projections. There are two important items to look for here. The first and perhaps most important is track record. Has the technology company manufactured a similar item before, and if so, how many times and how successfully? Has the company demonstrated its ability to project accurate manufacturing costs? If the answer is yes, you can feel more comfortable about current predictions. And again, you are better off with a multiple-product offering.

Then, there is the matter of market share. How large a market share must the product have to be successful? The larger the share a product must have in order to be successful, the greater the risk. As a rule of thumb, a product that needs to capture only 5 percent of the market might be considered the least risky. Of course, this is only a generalization. Perhaps the potential for profit would justify a high risk. Nevertheless, market share estimates are sometimes based on unrealistic and overly optimistic assumptions. They often do not justify claims of economic viability. When things do not go well, the investor may be left with only short-term tax benefits, losing the intermediate and long-term distributions that should be an important goal for most.

3. Concerns about *insufficient working capital and IRS audit failure* should be alleviated by the general partners and the technology company making the offering. If the partnership has done its homework, it will know how much capital is needed and where it can be found. In addition, the partnership should have had enough experience to be able to structure the program so that it can withstand an IRS audit. Here, as in all investments where similar concerns surface, the track record of the general partner is probably the best guide.

4. Finally, there is the matter of *technological obsolescence.* What if the product is outdated by the time it reaches the market? If the time frame is long, the risk increases that the market will change. If the time frame is short, the risk decreases. Both market share assumptions and time frame projections become less dependable as time passes. It is preferable, therefore, to invest in R&D partnerships that fund products which can be brought to the market in a reasonably short period of time. Today, 12 to 18 months is usually considered adequate to maintain the integrity of the original market studies and projections. Any program that

has a time frame longer than 18 months in today's highly competitive market increases the risk that the product will be obsolete by the time it arrives in the marketplace.

There is a second element here, which relates to the type of technology used. In the initial stages of the program, after the investors have formed the partnership and the contract for R&D has been given, some kind of technology is used to develop the product. Is that technology "advanced" or "intermediate"? Advanced or high technology is usually at the leading edge of the industry. Because it often depends on a breakthrough for success, it is an outright gamble. The investors are gambling that during the R&D program, they will be able to apply a new technology that did not exist when the contract was given. Maybe they will, but maybe they won't.

Intermediate technology typically employs state-of-the-art methods. It is technology that is proven but still relatively new. It should be obvious that programs which rely on advanced technology tend to be riskier than those that rely on intermediate technology. In the advanced technology, if a hoped-for breakthrough is not achieved, the program may fail or be delayed until further research is completed. This delay can result in the obsolescence of the product. If the delay costs a year or two, even though the final product is developed, the market may no longer exist.

A wise investor will look specifically for offerings that include the risk-minimizing features listed above. You might still be wondering, however, just how risky R&D projects are in general. Perhaps the best answer can be given by a comparison of R&D with oil and gas. The Corporations Commission of one state has made the following comparison which may prove helpful.

An R&D program which is a *single-product* program, which uses *high technology*, which has a *long lead time*, which must achieve a *high market share*, which has *more than just final development left*, might be compared to investing in an exploratory well program.

On the other hand, an R&D offering which involves *multiple products*, uses *intermediate technology*, has a relatively *short lead time*, requires a *small market share*, and has *only final development* left, might be compared to a developmental well program.

Consider the Company

There is one last thing a potential investor can do to minimize risk: he can look closely at the technology company, which often is the general partner in the offering. How does the investor really know if the general partner is a good company? How does the investor recognize those companies that have the track record, the capital, and the support to carry out a successful R&D program?

Here is a detailed list of criteria which should be considered in determining if the general partner(s) has the capability to support a successful R&D program.

Technology Company
1. A going concern
2. Most recent fiscal-year gross revenues of at least $5 million
3. Demonstrated gross profits of at least 40 to 50 percent
4. Strong capital base and favorable ratio of assets and liabilities
5. Ready access to financial institutions for acquisition of working capital support (lending institutions, equity capital, etc.)
6. Research and development budget of at least 10 percent of gross revenues

Support Personnel
1. Good financial personnel including employees in accounting, budget control, and financial planning
2. Manufacturing personnel experienced in the technology of partnership products
3. A research and development team experienced in the technology to be used
4. A marketing organization familiar with the licensees, distributors, dealers, and users of the partnership products, as well as advertising organizations, trade shows, conferences, and so on
5. Management
   a. Officers and directors with substantial experience in new product development from concept to commercialization
   b. Management with prior experience in running a company of at least $10,000,000 in annual gross revenues
6. Outside experts available for consultation in the following areas:
   a. market analysis
   b. technology
   c. subcontracting fields
   d. vendors
   e. accounting
   f. securities and corporation counsel
   g. patent counsel

136

h. investment and commercial banking
i. insurance

Since R&D partnerships have a relatively short history, it is often hard to find companies with proven track records. In cases where there is no previous track record with R&D partnerships, you might want to consider the company's track record in bringing out successful products on its own. A highly successful company may simply not have used the partnership vehicle to raise capital before and should not, on these grounds alone, be eliminated from consideration.

It bears repeating that the strength of the organization behind the partnership is the key to success.

CHAPTER SEVENTEEN

LEASING FOR
TAX SHELTER

Leasing is a very popular investment vehicle which can provide either shelter or strong income, or sometimes both. In this chapter we'll consider primarily the tax-shelter benefits of leasing. In the next chapter we'll go into leasing as an income-producing vehicle.

Almost everyone knows what a lease is. If you've ever rented a home or a car or a piece of equipment, chances are you signed a lease. There were two parties involved. There was the owner or *lessor*, who rented the equipment to you. And there was you, the tenant, or *lessee*.

When we speak of investing in leasing, we are dealing with these same two parties: the lessor (owner) and the lessee (tenant). In this chapter, however, we will not be talking about real property (real estate), but about personal property. This can be almost anything from a truck to a barge to a computer. Additionally, we are not speaking of you as an individual. Most leasing is done by individual investors involved in limited partnerships.

How does a limited partnership in leasing work? Taking it one step at a time, let's assume that you or I put our money into a partnership that will do the investing for us. The partnership now goes out and buys a piece of equipment. It might be a truck from General Motors or a computer from IBM. The partnership either pays cash for the equipment or, as is more often the case, finances its purchase. Once the partnership owns the equipment, it leases it to a company that needs it. For example, the partnership might lease the truck to a delivery company and the computer to an accounting firm. The partnership is the lessor. The ultimate user of the equipment is the lessee. In a nutshell, that's how leasing works.

Of course, it really isn't that simple. Why would a delivery company or an accounting firm lease the equipment instead of buying it outright? How does the partnership make a profit? Why are you and I entitled to a tax shelter? Let's now turn to these questions.

BENEFITS OF LEASING TO THE LESSEE

There are many reasons that companies rent rather than buy the equipment they use. The principal reason has to do with capital. In order to buy a truck that costs, say, $50,000, a company must come up with either the entire amount or a substantial portion of it for a down payment. The company can lease the same truck with virtually no capital expenditure. And frequently its lease payments are no more than loan payments would be.

Further, a company that buys a piece of equipment outright must capitalize the cost of that equipment over its life-span (usually 3, 5 or 10 years), but when it leases a piece of equipment, it may expense all lease payments in the year they are incurred. All lease payments for equipment used in business are fully deductible. Finally, leasing provides companies with a great deal of flexibility. It is possible for the companies to structure the lease so that the term can be established in accordance with its needs.

In the final analysis, the advantages of preserving capital, getting a fully expensed tax item, and greater flexibility make leasing highly desirable for a vast number of companies. In fact, today businesses lease more equipment than they buy.

As I noted earlier, almost anything can be leased. But, here's a list of items that are leased with increasing frequency today:
railroad cars
trucks
barges
aircraft (both small private and jumbo jets)
computers (including word processors)
computer-related devices, including programs
restaurant equipment
printing equipment
technical equipment in almost any other field

BENEFITS OF LEASING TO THE LESSOR

There are also many benefits to the partnership that leases. Topping the list is tax deferral. Leasing can provide a large write-off over a period of years through depreciation of the lease equipment. In addition, there is the residual value of the equipment. Depending on the type of equipment purchased, there may be a significant residual value after the lease time has expired. This is particularly true during inflationary periods when the cost of replacing the equipment continues to rise. The partnership benefits from the residual value of the equipment by selling it or by re-leasing it. Of course, such revenues come to the partnership as ordinary income.

THE TAX ADVANTAGES OF A LEASING PROGRAM

As individual investors, you and I might be asked to put up as little as $5000 or as much as $100,000 to join a partnership. Since the investment can be sizable, we want to be sure we can handle it from the standpoint of income, assets, and emotional well-being.

The partnership now has our money. Typically, it will use it (along with the money gathered from other investors) as a down payment on the purchase of equipment. Let's say that our partnership purchases a fleet of trucks with a value of $500,000. The partnership might put a $100,000 down payment on the half million dollar purchase price. The balance would be financed.

$100,000   Down payment ($10,000 apiece from 10 investors)
+400,000   Financed

$500,000   Purchase price of trucks

The partnership now leases the trucks to a company on a long-term lease (typically three to seven years). The company, or the lessee, makes monthly payments to the partnership.

The partnership then uses the lease income to cover its expenses. In this case the principal expense is the monthly payment on the $400,000 loan.

There can be some small positive cash flow if the monthly rental income is greater than expenses, but usually the expenses equal the income. The partnership, however, is able to depreciate the equipment. And depreciation can create significant tax write-offs over a period of years.

How Depreciation Works

Leased equipment can be depreciated by the owner (the partnership) over a period of 3 to 25 years depending on the equipment. The most commonly used terms under the new tax law are 3, 5, and 10 years.

The 1981 Economic Recovery Tax Act largely eliminated the old ADR system of determining useful life for equipment. (The ADR [asset depreciation range] assigned all personal property a taxable life that reflected its actual useful life.) Under the new law, equipment, depending on its type, is given an arbitrary life that may or may not be related to its actual useful life. In addition, the term of depreciation is specifically set down. The most common depreciation term is five years. Most equipment fits into this category. (Autos and some other types of equipment are given three-year terms; other items, ten years.)

Under the five-year depreciation term, the write-off is structured as follows:

Year	Amount of Depreciation
1	15%
2	22
3	21
4	21
5	21
	100%

Let's look at the write-off structure of a piece of equipment that $500,000. Here's the depreciation breakdown over five years.

Year	Amount to be Deducted
1	$ 75,000
2	110,000
3	105,000
4	105,000
5	105,000
	$500,000

What this means is that the partnership gets a depreciation expense of $75,000 the first year, $110,000 the second year, and so forth. Of course, there's the income from the equipment rental. However, as we've already seen, the rental income tends to offset the loan expense.

This, then, is how leasing works from a tax standpoint. The partnership uses rental income to cover the expenses of financing. The tax benefits come from the write-offs for depreciation.

Once the equipment is fully paid off, the lease term has expired, and the partnership must decide whether to re-lease (if possible) or to sell the equipment for its residual value. If the equipment has been fully depreciated and then sold for its residual value, the gain from the sale must be fully recaptured by the partnership.

(There would be no capital gain.) Needless to say, the individual partners, because of the pass-through feature of limited partnerships, receive all the benefits along the way. These include tax write-offs as well as income from the sale or re-lease of the equipment.

INCOME DURING THE INITIAL LEASE PERIOD

In most leasing programs, the income from leasing provides a cash flow to the partnership. In leasing programs emphasizing tax shelter, however, this is not always the case. The following example will illustrate this.

You purchase a piece of equipment for $100,000 and finance 80 percent of the purchase price with a five-year loan.

$ 20,000	Capital
80,000	Financed
$100,000	Purchase price

Each month you (the partnership) must pay back a certain portion of the $80,000 loan plus interest. Let's say your monthly payback is $2000. Ideally, you would like to rent that equipment out for more than $2000 per month. If you could rent it for $2500, for example, you would clear $500 per month. This would come back to the partnership as income. Unfortunately, in today's highly competitive market, it simply isn't possible to get a long-term lease return for much more than the cost of your debt. If you have to pay $2000 a month on debt service, then chances are your income from leasing will be close to $2000 a month.

In a sense it is a wash. What you take in roughly equals what you pay out. Of course, from a tax standpoint, it is not entirely a wash because a portion of your $2000 monthly payment goes to repay principal and a portion goes to interest. The interest portion is, of course, deductible; the principal is not.

A Full Pay-Out Lease

The preceding example described a "full pay-out" lease. What this term means is that the rent on the equipment is sufficient to pay off the entire debt. The income from rent, however, may not be sufficient to pay off both the debt and return the money put up by the investors. Remember, that equity was sued as a down payment on the equipment. The investor's original capital, thus, must be retrieved from the residual value of the equipment. The investors get their money back when they sell the equipment.

Other definitions of "full pay-out" are used in the industry today. Sometimes, it means that the rent from the equipment is sufficient to recover not only the loan costs but also the equity invested by the partnership.

Leases on equipment are often renewed. In many cases the equipment is fully paid off at the end of the first lease or the beginning of the second. This is the point at which the partnership begins receiving positive cash flow.

OTHER ASPECTS OF FINANCING

It should be clear now that the tax advantages of the programs just described are a direct result of the way the equipment was financed. What may not be quite so clear is that the extent of the leveraging also helps to determine the after-tax return to the partnership. The greater the leveraging, the higher the return. Similarly, the lower the leveraging, the lower the return.

Let's look at it from two standpoints. In both cases we are buying a $100,000 piece of equipment. In both cases the first year's depreciation will be $15,000. But in one case the partnership is only 50 percent leveraged. (The partnership invested $50,000 worth of capital in the equipment and borrowed the remaining $50,000.) Assuming that the individual investors in the partnership all happen to be in the 50 percent tax bracket, what is the after-tax return on this investment?

$15,000	Depreciation
×50%	Tax bracket
$ 7,500	Tax savings

Now we apply the tax savings to the amount of capital invested.

$$\frac{\$\,7,500}{\$50,000} \quad \text{After-tax return on investment} = 15\%$$

That may not seem to be a bad return until we consider the second case, in which the partnership is 90 percent leveraged. (The partnership spent $10,000 worth of capital and borrowed the remaining $90,000.) Again, we assume that the individual investors are all in the 50 percent tax bracket and that the after-tax savings is $7500.

$$\frac{\$\,7,500}{10,000} \quad \text{After-tax return on investment} = 75\%$$

Of course, in the first case there might have been positive cash flow (because of the reduced debt) adding to income, whereas in the second case there might have been negative cash flow caused by the heavy leveraging. The point is that the heavier the leveraging, the greater the tax advantages. But, as I have always stressed, the investment must be economically sound first. A big write-off should not be the prime consideration. You may get hurt further down the road.

OTHER COSTS

Thus far, we've only considered debt costs and depreciation; there are, of course, other costs. Typically, these are maintenance of the equipment, insurance, and personal property taxes.

In most tax-shelter leases arranged today, the lessee is responsible for both maintaining the equipment and paying the personal property taxes on it. They are, in effect, "net, net" leases.

A tax-shelter lease program is created by doing basically two things: Highly leveraging the cost of the equipment (typically, 4:1 or 5:1) and extending the period of the lease over the full depreciable life of the equipment. This permits a full pay back of money borrowed and a residual sale or re-lease.

As a result of the above structuring, the investor gets a strong write-off during the term of the lease and then recovers his investment at the end (with some profit). For an investor in a high tax bracket, the advantage comes primarily from the tax-savings features of this program.

There is another kind of lease program — the investment program that offers some shelter, but whose basic goal is income. We'll discuss investment leasing in the next chapter.

CHAPTER EIGHTEEN

LEASING FOR INVESTMENT

If your financial goal is tax shelter plus growth, you should consider investment leasing. An investment leasing program gives the investor not only some tax shelter (in the form of deferred income), but also strong cash flow income. Years after his initial investment has been recovered, the investor continues to receive monthly or quarterly income checks. For a retired person or an investor looking for growth, investment leasing can be a marvelous opportunity.

HOW INVESTMENT LEASING DIFFERS FROM TAX-SHELTER LEASING

In investment leasing, the basic approach is almost identical to tax-shelter leasing. There are, however, several important differences. The first has to do with financing.

Financing

As we saw in the last chapter, in a tax-shelter lease program the partnership borrows four or five dollars for every one it invests. This is not the case in investment leasing. Since the goal is income, investment leasing uses fewer borrowed dollars. Typically, the leveraging in a leasing program is 50 percent or less. In some programs, the investors put up the entire amount needed to purchase the equipment — no money is borrowed.

Low leveraging increases the positive cash flow. (In the last chapter, we saw how the monthly rental income from leasing was canceled by debt payments.) If there is no borrowing at all, all the rental income comes directly to the investors.

In the last chapter we used an example of a piece of equipment that brought in a monthly rental income of $2000. None of that, however, went to the investors because the equipment also had a

$2000 monthly loan payment. In investment leasing, with all or most of the loan payment eliminated, the $2000 comes back to the investors in the form of income.

Depreciation

Depreciation remains the same, whether the program is for tax shelter or for income and growth. In investment leasing, however, a substantial portion of the depreciation write-off must go toward offsetting income generated by rentals. Therefore, the amount of depreciation left for tax shelter is reduced considerably. In an investment lease, the tax shelter is probably no more than 30 to 40 percent in the first year. This figure drops to around 10 percent in the second year. Although you lose the write-off advantage, there is something else to be gained — income.

Consider the following hypothetical lease program.

Monthly expenses	$ 300
Depreciation	1,000
Total expense	$1,300
Income	$1,000
Loss	$ 300

Because the books show a loss, the investor has a tax write-off of $300. Now let's look at cash flow in this same program.

Income	$1,000
Expenses	300
Positive cash flow	$ 700

The program is yielding a positive cash flow of $700 at the same time that it is showing a loss on paper of $300. As a result, the $700 income is not immediately taxable. That income is tax deferred.

Income Shelter

Consider the advantage of tax-deferred income. The investors do not need to add their portion of the $700 to their other ordinary income and pay taxes on it. Because the lease is showing a loss, there's no immediate tax to pay on it; the investors can spend the money.

This example was exaggerated to make a point. In an actual investment leasing program, the depreciation would probably not be sufficient to eat up the income. In most cases, some portion of that cash income might be tax deferred and some might be taxed as ordinary income. The point, however, is a valid one. In an investment program cash goes directly to the investors. And a portion of that cash is not taxable in the year received.

INVESTMENT TAX CREDIT

Any new equipment purchased may qualify for a 10 percent investment tax credit. Tax credit is a bottom-line deduction. That is, it is subtracted directly from the investor's tax bill, not from his taxable income. A 10 percent investment tax credit can make a significant difference to an investor. For example, if the investor puts $10,000 into an investment leasing program that is fully capitalized (no borrowed money), he or she would get a 10 percent, or $1000, bottom-line credit in the first year of the investment. This credit reduces the amount of the original investment by 10 percent (or shelters $2000 of the investor's other income — depending on how you want to look at it).

What's important to understand is that the 10 percent investment tax credit is normally available in an investment leasing program, but not usually in a tax-shelter program. You will see why in a minute.

The government wants to make sure that people do not form partnerships just to get investment tax credits. For example, if a partnership bought a piece of equipment worth $100,000, it would be entitled to a $10,000 tax credit (10 percent). But, if a partnership had borrowed 90 percent to buy the equipment (or had taken out a $90,000 loan on it), and still received a $10,000 investment tax credit for the purchase, the piece of equipment would essentially be free — with the government picking up the entire tab.

Tax Credit Rules

To keep heavily financed partnerships from obtaining investment tax credit, the government says that in order to qualify for the credit, *the lease can run for no more than half of the useful life of the equipment*. This is fairly straightforward and easy to understand. The useful life of the equipment is supposed to be something close to its actual economic life-span — the period of time during which it can be successfully rented.

In the past the government had a directory in which it listed the life-span of all types of equipment. It was called the ADR tax life. Most equipment had a useful life of about six or seven years. This system was also used to determine the depreciation term for equipment. As we mentioned in the last chapter, the 1981 Economic Recovery Tax Act changed the definitions of useful life to 3, 5, or 10 years, depending on the type of equipment. The old ADR system has been abandoned, with one exception: it is still used to determine useful life for the purpose of determining eligibility for an investment tax credit.

149

To apply the no-more-than-half rule is quite simple. If a piece of equipment has an ADR life of six years, then the lease cannot run for more than three years if the investors are to qualify for the tax credit. If the lease runs more than three years, no credit is allowed. If it runs for less than three years, the credit can be claimed.

As we saw in the last chapter, most tax-shelter leases run for the full life of the equipment. This is the only way investors can recoup enough money to pay back the money borrowed to buy the equipment. Investment leasing partnerships normally do not have to pay off big loans. They can therefore offer leases for much shorter periods of time and thus qualify for the 10 percent investment tax credit.

ECONOMICS OF INVESTMENT LEASING

The investor considering an investment lease program might well ask, "How good is the lease going to be if it's only for half the useful life of the equipment?"

In the last chapter we mentioned that almost anything could be leased, from tank cars to restaurant equipment. This is true, but investment leasing generally deals with a special class of equipment: technology equipment.

Many large corporations use computer equipment. Often they buy the computer itself (the CPU). But they do not want to buy the peripheral equipment — the numerous terminals and storage devices associated with the computer. Why? There are two good reasons. First, they simply don't want to spend the capital. Most companies would rather use their capital for improving their product line. Second, companies don't want to buy equipment that will be obsolete in a short time. They know that the state-of-the-art computer of five years ago is an antique today. Companies prefer to rent these items on short-term leases. These short-term or "operating" leases are essentially the bread and butter of investment leasing.

But what about the leasing of computers and other high technology equipment from the investors' standpoint? What will the investors do with the obsolete equipment when it is returned in three years? Is owning obsolete equipment somehow less risky for the lessor than for the lessee?

There is an answer to this apparent paradox. Lease income tends to be significantly higher on short-term than on full pay-out leases. The income stream from an operating lease is higher than that from a tax-shelter lease. Lease revenue in investment leasing recovers the capital investment within three-and-a-half to four years on most leases. But, even if the investors recover their capital within a relatively short period of time (through income flow, tax credit, and write-off) how can they show a profit when they have nothing to sell but an obsolete piece of equipment?

The answer has to do with the word "obsolete." What is obsolete for one company may be state-of-the-art for another. Not every company wants to pay the price of having state-of-the-art equipment. Many are satisfied to pay a much lower lease rate and take their chances with older, so-called obsolete equipment. (Often the only difference between old and new computer equipment is memory size and speed. For some companies, this is not an important consideration.)

The investors can re-lease old equipment at a reduced rate. Since their capital has been returned, this income, though reduced, is pure profit. And it could easily continue through an additional three-year lease term.

Finally, as with tax-sheltered leases, there is the residual value. In the case of computer equipment, what is its residual value after the six-year useful life period is up? Isn't it just relegated to the junk heap? Not at all. Consider the IBM 360 computer. When this computer came out over 16 years ago it was state-of-the-art. Today, however, newer computers one-tenth its size can do far more work. The 360 is obviously obsolete, but is it also worthless? Hardly. An IBM 360 in good working condition has a value that even today is roughly 20 to 25 percent of its original cost. There are companies out there who will buy 360's and use them.

It should be obvious by now that investment leasing has the potential to generate substantial profit for the investor over a long period of time.

THE 15 PERCENT RULE

The difference between an individual investor and a partnership investor is analogous to the difference between an entrepreneur and a salaried worker. The person who can handle the challenge usually goes it alone. The person who doesn't have the time or the temperament to strike out on his own goes into the partnership. In most cases, the tax advantages are the same for both.

Not so in leasing. In general, a single investor cannot get the 10 percent investment tax credit. It is not that single investors are prohibited from obtaining this credit. It's just that as a practical matter they are prevented from getting it by the 15 percent rule.

The 15 percent rule states that to qualify for the 10 percent investment tax credit, the partnership must have operating expenses of at least 15 percent of its rental revenue. If the rental revenue is, say, $1000, the partnership has to show expenses of at least 15 percent, or $150, to claim an investment tax credit. It is not, as you might think at first, easy to qualify. Why? Because two important items — interest and taxes — do not qualify as expenses under the 15 percent rule. Those items that qualify are management, maintenance, and insurance.

The individual investor would find it difficult to come up with management expenses, simply because he or she is normally the manager. Insurance is usually paid for by the lessee. That leaves maintenance. Since maintenance usually only comes to 10 percent or so of the monthly revenue, it's not usually enough to qualify.

For a partnership, the story is quite different. The general partner normally charges a management fee to the limited partners. This might be in the area of 6 to 7 percent of the monthly revenue. This fee is completely deductible.

In addition, many partnerships are set up so that the lessee signs a maintenance contract with the owners. (This is the same kind of maintenance contract you may be asked to buy when you purchase a new car or washing machine.) Then, a portion of the lessee's rental payment is allocated for maintenance expenses (roughly 10 to 12%). This money is then paid out to a maintenance company that contracts to take care of the equipment. The 10 to 12 percent from the maintenance contract added to the 6 to 7 percent management fee charged by the general partner usually qualifies the partnership for the 15 percent rule and thus for the 10 percent investment tax credit.

RISKS OF LEASING

Finally, we come to the risks involved in investment leasing. In a short-term lease situation there is always a risk that after the initial lease is up, the investors might not be able to find someone else to buy or to re-lease the equipment. However, since the investors in a short-term lease probably have recovered their capital by the end of the three years, the worst that can happen is that they will not make a profit.

The real risk in leasing comes not so much from the lease as it does from the lessee. Both the investment and the tax-shelter lease are based on one important assumption, that the lessee will be able to continue making specified payments for the term of the lease. The financing and the capitalization are usually based on this assumption. But if the lessee gets into financial trouble and is unable to continue making payments, the investors could be in jeopardy.

If the lessee can't make the payment, the remedy, obviously, is to take the equipment back. But, will it be possible to re-lease what is now second-hand equipment at the same rate the original lessee was paying? Will it be possible to find another lessee who will want such equipment?

Therein lies the risk. (Note: suing the lessee for the unpaid rent on the equipment may not be a very good alternative, particularly if the reason the lessee is defaulting is because he is bankrupt.)

Minimizing Risk

The risk of lessee failure can be minimized in two ways. The first way is to check out the lessee thoroughly. The general partner should have complete knowledge of the lessee's financial background. Second, the lessee company should have been around for a number of years, have a good credit history, and have good future prospects. The worthiness of the lessee should be reflected in the terms of the lease. For example, if partnership had offered a lease to Chrysler Corporation when it was in the midst of its government bail-out and financing troubles, it probably would have offered a lease for no more than a single year. But that same partnership might have offered a three- or five-year lease to Toyota during the time it was setting import car sales records. If a company is not rejected out of hand because it is a bad risk, then the term of the lease should relate to the credit worthiness of the company.

Finally, there is the matter of the equipment itself. If the equipment is standard, such as a computer or a truck or a piece of restaurant equipment, the risk from the lessee defaulting is minimized simply because there will surely be other companies around willing to lease it. On the other hand, if the equipment is a specially designed lifting truck or a single-use processing table, then the risk might be more significant. If the lessee of special-use equipment defaults, it might be impossible to find another company to lease it to. Leasing multi-user equipment also tends to minimize risk.

Leasing can be a tax shelter, a revenue-producing investment, or both. It can also provide long-term growth. The choice is up to you.

CHAPTER NINETEEN

THE CATTLE INDUSTRY: BREEDING

Investments in cattle have a long and successful history as tax shelters. Depending on the investor's priorities, there are opportunities for shelter and growth or for shelter and quick profit. For investment purposes, the cattle industry can be broken down into three categories: breeding, feeding, and packing.

Cattle breeding, which will be discussed in this chapter, is exactly what you think it is: breeding stock is purchased and put out to pasture to increase and multiply. Several years later, when the size of the herd has increased (and the investor's taxable income has decreased because of the tax shelter provided) some or all of the cattle are sold for profit.

The second category, feeding cattle, involves fattening beef cattle for the market. It is a short-term venture, usually no more than six months in all. It offers the investor a potential for quick profit as well as the opportunity for tax write-offs as high as 400 percent. We'll go into feeder cattle investments in the next chapter.

Packing is the slaughtering and processing of meat for market. Investment opportunities in this area are limited to the purchase of securities in the various publicly owned companies engaged in this business, such as Armour, Cudahay, Wilson, and Iowa Beef. Cattle-packing investments are not tax shelters.

CATTLE BREEDING — YESTERDAY AND TODAY

The present cattle-breeding industry has its roots in the Old West. In the early days, land was cheap, cowboys worked for $5 a month, and the demand for beef far exceeded the supply. The first cattlemen bought a few head of cattle, took advantage of the cheap grazeland, and saw their herds multiply. But there were problems. A bad winter could kill off the cattle. Hoof-and-Mouth disease could wipe out a herd. But the biggest problem of all was transportation. How did the cattleman in Texas get his cattle to the market in Kansas City? The cattle drive, which has been romanticized in so many movies, was the answer.

Today, it's a different story. Feed is flown in to snowbound cattle, largely eliminating the problem of harsh winters. The miracles of modern medicine have cured virtually all livestock diseases. Today, the worst disease cattle are likely to get is a bad case of measles. And, with rail and truck transportation, getting the cattle to market is no longer a problem.

There are a variety of opportunities in cattle breeding. For example, there are breeders of purebred beef cattle. These breeders maintain high quality herds that supply breeding stock to the commercial producer who wants to upgrade the quality of his herd. Dealing in purebred cattle requires experience and skill and is not usually for the uninitiated. In addition, artificial insemination and embryo transplants (the latter is used largely in the dairy industry) offer investment opportunities. But the largest area of investment opportunity involves the breeding of commercial beef cattle. It is here that most investors, either through direct arrangements with cattlemen or through limited partnerships, participate in the cattle industry.

A TYPICAL CATTLE INVESTMENT

The investor buys cattle under an arrangement with a cattleman. The cattleman (who is more often than not a large cattle ranch) takes care of acquiring, breeding, and feeding the cattle. The investor pays for the cost of his cattle and feed and pays a management/maintenance fee to the cattleman.

The investor holds the cattle for a period of time. During that time the cattle breed. As a rule, a well-cared-for herd will produce annually an 80 percent calf crop, of which half will be male and half female. Generally, the males are sold when weaned or raised for slaughter. They provide income to the investor. The females are for breeding to increase the size and ultimately the value of the herd. Annual herd growth is normally somewhere between 35 and 40 percent.

It is generally assumed that for at least the first three years, the herd will not be self-sustaining from a financial standpoint. The income from the sale of the calves will not be sufficient to pay for feeding and maintaining the herd. If, however, beef prices are strong and the costs of feed and maintenance reasonable, the investor can expect to see profits beginning in the fourth year.

The length of time a herd is kept is frequently determined by tax considerations. It is not uncommon to see some herds liquidated in as few as five years and others kept for as long as 20 years.

TAX ADVANTAGES

There are several. The first and easiest to understand is the investment tax credit. Upon purchasing his cattle, the investor may take an immediate 10 percent investment tax credit. As with all credits, this is a bottom-line figure, deducted not from taxable income but from the tax itself.

Then there is depreciation. Under the new 1981 Economic Recovery Tax Act, the depreciation period for cattle was lowered from seven to five years. What this means, essentially, is that the cost of the cattle can be written off very quickly. And, when the investor sells his cattle, the income from the gain will be taxed as a capital gain providing that the herd has been held for a minimum of two years.

What exactly can be written off in a cattle operation? A typical write-off might include the following expenses:

Depreciation

Costs (feed and maintenance)

Interest (on leveraging)

Added to this, of course, would be the first-year investment tax credit of 10 percent.

BORROWING TO BUY CATTLE

It is almost always possible to get financing on cattle. The reason is that the collateral, the cattle themselves, is always growing. (Cattle are valued on a per pound basis.) It is possible, in fact, to get almost 100 percent financing. (It should be pointed out, however, that financing may not always be available through banks. It may be necessary to get it from the cattle ranchers themselves.)

The costs of feed (which vary according to climate and the amount of range available) may also be partly financed. However, feed bills are usually paid a year in advance. An estimate is made in January and the investor has to come up with the total payment all at once. Maintenance costs, which include water and other expenses, can also be prepaid (and written off 100%). Feed costs are written off in the year the feed is consumed. Therefore, the investor can finance both the cost of the cattle and a portion of the cost of the feed.

The important point to remember here is that an investor can only deduct leveraging for which he or she is directly liable, that is, only for "recourse" borrowing. Thus, the investor who borrows for cattle breeding, hoping to increase leveraging and the resulting tax shelter, must be very careful. High interest rates can turn an otherwise profitable venture into a losing one. Finally, since the investor is responsible for the payment of the financing regardless of how the venture comes out, it could turn out to be very expensive to borrow excessively.

To sum up, since the cattle can be completely financed and the cost of maintenance and feed is an expense item that can be written off in the year paid, and since depreciation is allowed, the investor can take a significant tax write-off (well over 100 percent) both in the year of purchase and in subsequent years.

TWO WAYS TO INVEST IN CATTLE BREEDING

Cattlemen throughout the West and Southwest offer breeding programs. These can be very small programs designed for a single investor or large offerings designed for a partnership. Typically they take two forms.

Investment Contract. In this program an investor can buy anywhere from 50 to 100 (or more) head of cattle. It is basically a range-cattle deal. There are two parties. One is a person in the cattle business; the other is the investor. The cattleman agrees to sell the investor so many head of cattle and to maintain and manage them for a set price. In this arrangement, the investor is not in partnership with any other investors. He owns his own cattle under a contract arrangement with the person in the cattle business.

Once a year the cattleman consults with the investor to make decisions about the disposal of the herd. The male calves can be kept or sold; the herd expanded or liquidated. In such cases the decision on what to do with the herd is usually made on the basis of the investor's tax needs.

It should be pointed out that the investor must trust the judgment and business integrity of the cattleman. Since the investor's role is basically passive, he will want to make sure that the cattleman he is doing business with will fulfill the active part of the contract. The investor should take a look at the size of the cattleman's operation, its efficiency, and most important, its track record.

Partnership Offering. It is also possible to get into cattle breeding by means of a partnership offering — either a large publicly registered partnership or, as is often the case, a smaller private offering. In a partnership investment, the cattle ranch or the cattleman becomes the general partner. The partnership as a whole buys an entire herd, with the general partner handling management and maintenance. Partnership offerings vary enormously in size, but generally the smallest cattle limited partnership is likely to be in the range of $5000 per investor. Generally speaking, the smallest practical herd size is 60 head.

Although the limited partner is strictly a passive investor, this does not mean that he never sees his cattle. Typically, before entering into a partnership agreement, potential investors are taken out to the ranch to see the operation and to take a look at the cattle that are going to be part of the herd. Although the investor does not exactly become "cowboy for a day," he does get a chance to see what he is buying.

THE RISKS OF CATTLE BREEDING INVESTMENTS

Assuming that the investor has found a responsible rancher to deal with, the risks in modern-day breeding comes down to basically one — price. If the price of cattle is high when the investor sells the male calves or liquidates the herd, the potential for profit can be very strong. On the other hand, if prices are soft, the investor might just break even or lose money.

The amount of the profit to be made, of course, depends on the costs that were incurred. Since feed is a major portion of the cost of the investment, feed prices affect the profit picture. If prices have been extraordinarily high, it is conceivable that an investor could sell his cattle even in a moderately strong market and still not make much money.

The investor should become acquainted with price trends in the cattle market. If the cattle market is likely to see weak prices (and the feed market, high prices) for several years, then investing in cattle might not make a great deal of economic sense. (As I've said before, all investments, even those that offer strong tax shelter, must make good economic sense. That is, they must have a potential for profit.)

CATTLE BREEDING — THE FUTURE

What is the cattle market likely to do in the next few years? Although it's impossible to predict with accuracy, certain trends are taking shape at the time of this writing. Throughout 1979 and 1980, cattle prices were high. Traditionally, during periods of high prices, cattle ranchers try to sell as many of their animals (steers and cows) as possible. A big selling period obviously greatly reduces the herd sizes of the future. Fewer cows mean that there will be fewer calves. In Russia, so many cattle were slaughtered during the feed shortage of a few years ago that there is no longer enough beef to meet the needs of the population.

In the United States, the long-term results are similar. Because of high prices in 1979 and 1980, herd sizes were down by 20 percent (about 21 million few heard) in 1981. The result should have been very high beef prices. However, this did not happen in 1981 primarily because consumer demand decreased almost as much as the supply of beef. Faced with inflation in general, and high beef prices in particular, consumers switched to pork and poultry. The result was somewhat lower beef prices.

In 1982, however, the prices for pork and poultry should be high enough to make beef prices again competitive. For the following three years, then, we should see a return to the normal demand for beef. Therefore, because the supply of beef wil still be limited (it takes time to increase herd size — a minimum of 18 months but usually three years or more), we are likely to see prices for beef firm and rising for three to five years.

Cattle breeding does offer many advantages to the investor. To summarize, there is the large tax write-off possible in the initial year because of depreciation, leveraging (if desired), and a 10 percent investment tax credit (ITC). In addition, depending on how the herd is managed, this tax write-off can continue for a number of years, often until the herd is sold. And, finally, when the herd is liquidated, the gain comes back to the investor not as ordinary income, but as capital gains.

CHAPTER   TWENTY

THE CATTLE INDUSTRY: FEEDING

If you ordered beef in a restaurant, and were served a piece cut from a steer right off the range, chances are you wouldn't like it very much. The meat would be tough, stringy, and essentially tasteless. Your grandparents might like it, however. The only beef they could buy in their youth came from range-fed cattle. (If you want to know what range beef tastes like, order a steak the next time you're in Australia. Virtually all Australian table beef comes from range cattle.)

Today's tastes are different. You are used to meat that has a strong flavor and that is marbled with fat (which makes it more tender). The particular flavor and texture we have learned to expect from table beef comes from the special intensive feeding cattle are given six weeks to six months before slaughter. (The time depends on the condition of the grazing land they came from.)

The cattle are brought together in giant feedlots. Essentially, these are simply large corrals in which the cattle are closely confined and then fed a very high protein grain diet. The special diet creates both an enormous weight gain and the kind of meat that the American consumer has come to expect.

The process of cattle feeding offers a special tax-shelter opportunity for the person who is looking for short-term income deferral.

FEEDER CATTLE SHELTERS

To understand how the shelter works, you must first understand the two basic elements of the operation:

1. The entire feedlot process takes a relatively short time: usually six months at the maximum, three months at the minimum.

2. The cost of the feed is high. A high protein diet is expensive.

The critical point here is timing. Typically, tax-shelter feedlot cattle are purchased in the summer or fall. They are fattened and then sold early the next year. The investor has two major expenses: the cattle (largely financed) and the feed (possibly financed). If properly structured, almost all expenses occur in the year the cattle are purchased. The cattle are sold in the following calendar year. All income, then, is produced, and taxed, in a subsequent year. The result is a one-year tax deferral.

It is important to understand here that the income received from the sale of the cattle is ordinary income. It is not capital gains.

THE ADVANTAGES OF A FEEDER CATTLE SHELTER

There is basically only one advantage to the investor of feedlot cattle — a one-year deferral of taxes on income. This is particularly beneficial for the investor who has an unusually large income one year and anticipates a smaller income the next. There are, however, many high-income investors who use cattle feedlots to defer taxes even though their income in the year of the write-off may not be particularly high. A wealthy investor, for example, could defer a great portion of his current income to the following year. But the next year he would have not only that year's income to pay taxes on, but also th eprofits from the cattle sales. Some investors then buy twice the number of cattle in the next year and roll the whole thing over into the third year. They continue this process of "doubling down" almost indefinitely.

RISKS OF A FEEDER CATTLE SHELTER

The risk in cattle feeding, as in cattle breeding, comes from price. When an investor buys feeder cattle, he anticipates selling them six months down the road at a price that will cover all the expenses incurred. There could be a problem, however, if beef prices tumble during that six-month period. The result could be a substantial loss. There is a way to protect against this loss. The method is a commodity futures contract. Let's see how it works.

The investor has just bought the cattle he plans to fatten and sell six months later. He, of course, knows what he paid for them and what the price of feed will be. Because he also knows approximately how much the cattle will weigh at sale time, he can determine their selling price at today's going price. He knows he will at least break even if prices hold. But what if they go down?

To protect himself against that eventuality, the investor purchases a contract to buy cattle on the futures market at today's prices. The investor has essentially *guaranteed* the ultimate sale price of his cattle, even though the date of sale is still six months in the future.

The operation of the commodities futures market is beyond the scope of this discussion. It is important to understand, however, that with futures, the investor can often hedge his or her investment to a very large degree, thereby significantly reducing the risk of loss.

SPECIAL CONDITIONS OF A CATTLE FEEDER SHELTER

Certain special conditions must be met to qualify for the one-year tax deferral.

1. Only the feed actually consumed by the cattle during the calendar year can be deducted for that year. In other words, even if you prepay your feed bill for the whole six-month period, you can only deduct the amount consumed in the calendar year. It is wise, therefore, to try to arrange to have your cattle delivered to the feedlot in time to consume nearly all the feed bought in the year. (Remember, feed is the major expense item.) The investor should try to sell the cattle as close as possible to January 1 of the next year so that as little feed as possible is consumed in the year of sale. (The price of feed consumed in the year of sale is deducted in the year of sale.) This eliminates a lot of December investments in feedlots (although this may still be sometimes possible, in a properly structured limited partnership).

2. No interest prepayment is allowed. This is not a new rule, but it bears repeating. Typically in feeder programs, 75 percent of the cost of the cattle can be financed. However, only that interest actually paid in the tax year can be deducted. If cattle are purchased, say, in November 1983 and not sold until late February 1984, half the hoped-for tax advantage (of 1983) would be lost.

Many limited partnerships handle feeder cattle. These partnerships can be purchased from financial planners and security brokers. Typically, the minimum offering is $5000.

HOW MUCH IS THE WRITE-OFF?

The write-off is virtually unlimited for the following reasons.

In a feedlot program, the investor may invest as little as 25 percent of the total cost of the program. Seventy-five percent may be financed by either the feedlot owner or the bank. An investor who comes in with $10,000 could write off $40,000 in the year of the investment. And that's why these programs have been so popular, particularly among wealthier investors.

A person in the 50 percent tax bracket could not only have the government finance his or her entire investment (a 200 percent write-off), but could get significant shelter as well (a 300 percent write-off).

It must be remembered, however, that what is lost one year must be found the next. The deferral is for one year only. And that, of course, is the reason that once into these plans, many investors find themselves returning year after year.

Feedlot programs are not for everyone; but, for the person who needs a short-term income deferral, they can be a godsend. Properly used in a well-planned program of tax shelters and investment, cattle feeding can bring great advantages and benefits to the right investor.

CHAPTER TWENTY ONE

INVESTING IN AGRICULTURE

The gentleman farmer of old farmed for pleasure rather than profit. He sat on his veranda, sipping a cold drink, watching his prize bulls or thoroughbred horses. Today, there is a new breed of gentleman framer, the taxpayer who goes into an agricultural investment, not for pleasure but for tax shelter and profit. And, like the gentleman farmer, he rarely lifts a finger to do the work.

Because of new provisions in the 1981 Economic Recovery Tax Act, today's investors are looking closely at vineyards and orchards, as investment possibilities. Almonds, apricots, avocados, figs, citrus fruits, peaches, plums, grapes, and walnuts are popular prospects. Agricultural investments have provided significant tax shelters and strong profits for investors for years, and they are worth a few moments of serious consideration.

WHERE THE PROFIT IS

There's an old saying, "A farmer lives poor, but dies rich." It's true that farmers (unless they own thousands of acres) rarely make fortunes from farming. Often they are able to do little more than feed, clothe, and shelter themselves and their families. Farmers die rich because the old homestead has turned into a choice piece of residential property. What the farmer paid a few dollars an acre for years ago is now worth $50,000 or more an acre. The farmer never made much off the land. But by holding it, he died a very rich man.

The same thing may happen to investors in agricultural property. At first, there's not going to be very much profit. In fact, there will be only losses, including negative cash flow, for at least the first five years. In a new orchard, chances are the break-even point won't be reached for six years. But, if you chose wisely when you bought your land, there can be an enormous gain when you sell it.

Let's look at that potential gain on sale more closely. How does it occur? It occurs through a change in usage. Land is valued principally for what it can be used for. Orchards and vineyards are valued for the crops they can produce. That value can be translated into dollars and cents by capitalizing the income you receive from the land. For example, if the net income from your orchard is $5000 a year, you can determine the value of your land by capitalizing the income at a rate of 10 percent ($5000 divided by 10 percent yields a value of $50,000). That is one way to determine how much your land is worth *for agricultural use.*

But, let's say that during the five or ten years you've owned your ten acre orchard, the city has crept closer and closer. Your farm is now in the suburbs. If your trees were cut down and your land developed for residential use, your orchard could be worth $30,000 an acre. The ten acres now have a total value of $300,000. It's important to understand that the agricultural value of your land hasn't gone up. For agricultural use, it is still worth only $50,000. But for residential use, it is worth $300,000. It's the change of use that could produce a big gain.

Agricultural land that is sold to investors today usually has as its ultimate goal, a change of usage to residential, commercial, or industrial land. Now that we've seen where the profit is, let's go back and take a closer look at how an agricultural investment works.

HOW TO CHOOSE AN AGRICULTURAL INVESTMENT

Agricultural investments can be made either by individuals acting alone or by limited partnerships representing a pool of investors. (Some agricultural entrepreneurs encourage individual investments by offering small parcels of land for sale.) Whether you plan to invest as an individual or as a limited partner, the procedure for finding a good investment is essentially the same.

With the aid of an expert (say, an agronomist), the investor scouts out a good prospect — either an already established farm operation or undeveloped land that can be converted to agricultural use. (The tax-shelter benefits often determine which will be purchased, as we'll see in the next chapter.) Let's assume that you, the investor, decide to buy an avocado grove in Southern California. The land is bare, ready for trees to be planted. You buy the grove, contract with a management firm to farm it, have the trees planted and an irrigation system put in, and then wait. The trees must mature, usually a minimum of three to four years, before they will start producing fruit.

For the first three years, you will have only a negative cash flow. You must pay your mortgage and all expenses for maintenance, management, water, pesticides, fertilizer, and so forth. By the fourth year the return from your crop should be enough to cover perhaps half the cost of managing your orchard. By the fifth year, it should pay for all the grove costs. By the sixth year, the crop can pay for grove care, taxes, and the mortgage payment. And, depending on how much you borrowed, by the seventh year there should be enough coming in to pay all your costs and provide a small income. This situation should continue until you can sell your land for a different use. The profit you make on the sale would be taxed at capital gains rates. Now that you have had a bird's eye view of how an agricultural investment works, let's come back to earth and take it one step at a time.

Finding The Land

Location is a critical factor in all real estate. If you're buying a home, you want it to be in a good neighborhood, near good schools and recreational facilities. Location is also critical for agricultural land. But, because the investor ultimately hopes to make a profit by selling the land for a different use, there are two factors involved: location for agricultural potential and location for conversion potential. (We will deal with conversion potential later in the chapter.)

You begin to look for land the same way you begin to look for a house. You drive around until you find an area of well-kept, attractive homes. Of course, you don't drive around aimlessly, looking for good land. You consult realtors and real estate development firms first. There are, after all, only certain areas of the country suited for the type of agricultural development we're speaking of here.

Once you've found what you believe is a suitable avocado grove, you must now investigate its production potential.

Evaluating Production Potential

The key to value in agricultural land is production — how many boxes, bushels, or sacks of crop can be taken from the land per year. For a producing grove or orchard, this is a fairly easy figure to come by. The owners will have production charts available. If these figures seem out of line, you can check with the packing house that handled the crop.

For a new grove or orchard, you will have to determine production figures by inference. Check with the owners of surrounding orchards of similar size for comparison figures.

Testing the Soil

After production, your next concern should be soil. You get a soil analysis from an agronomist. This helps you determine if the soil is suitable for avocados. (Chances are that land surrounded by avocado groves is suitable for avocados, but it's always a good idea to check.)

Checking for Disease

You will also want to check carefully into any local disease problems. Disease is perhaps one of the biggest risks in agriculture. And in avocado groves, the biggest disease is root rot. It is a disease that is caused in part by poor soil drainage. (Soil heavy in decomposed granite is best for avocados because it allows for adequate drainage.) If we were to compare tree diseases to human diseases, avocado root rot could be likened to cancer, whereas brown rot (a common citrus disease) is closer to a bad cold. Brown rot can be cured; root rot (which travels through the ground) cannot.

Does that mean that an avocado grove with root rot should be avoided like the plague? Not necessarily. In some cases, root rot can be slowed down to the point that diseased trees will produce fruit for years, even decades. And if you plan to sell the orchard as, say, commercial property one day, it might be worth taking a chance on.

The Rest of the Story

After you've considered soil and disease, you'll want to look at drainage, frost, and wind — all of which will contribute to the success or failure of your crop. Just because other groves or orchards are successfully producing nearby, don't assume that your grove will have no drainage, wind, and frost problems. These conditions can vary significantly for plots of land only a few hundred feet apart.

You have checked with experts in all the areas just mentioned and gotten the go-ahead signal. You purchase the land and then, under contract with a management firm, have the ground prepared, an irrigation system installed, and the trees planted.

The final ingredient is time. It takes time for trees to grow and crops to be harvested. You wait for these things to happen. Your costs are basically water, insecticide, and other disease controls. Eventually, your trees mature and begin to produce avocados. The land begins to pay for itself.

That is the basic scenario for agricultural land. The steps are essentially the same for all land, although the time frame varies with the crop. With row crops such as wheat or barley, the crop is sewn one season and harvested the next.

RISKS

The major risk, disease, has already been discussed. It can usually be minimized by careful management (and by choosing the right soil and location to begin with). The other serious risk is not to your produce, but your pocket. It is one that occurs in any commodity investment — fluctuating prices. There is no risk, of course, if the price of the agricultural product stays high enough to pay for the farming of it. This has not always proved to be the case in the past.

One area of highly successful product pricing is vineyards. The demand for wine has soared in recent years, far outstripping the ability of vineyards to produce it. Wine-grape prices, therefore, have also been high. Investors who bought into vineyards have reaped significant profits just through the agricultural use of their land.

Investors in avocados, row crops, and citrus have not done as well. Overplanting, caused in part by investors coming in for tax-shelter purposes, has caused prices to drop or to remain low for a period of years. As a result, investors in some areas have not been able to make agricultural usage pay off. Typically, they get enough back to take care of maintenance, management, and irrigation costs, but not (in the case of those who borrowed money at high interest rates) to cover their debt costs.

Some protection against loss due to low prices can be obtained by hedging in the commodities futures market. This, however, is no guarantee of safety, and it may not even be possible if there is no commodities market for the crop you are raising.

The biggest risk to agricultural investment, therefore, comes from low crop prices. In today's market, the investor who goes in looking for much more than a break-even situation is not likely to be pleased with his agricultural investment.

HOW TO CHOOSE GOOD CONVERSION PROPERTY

Thus far we've been considering the value of an investment in land restricted to agricultural use. We noted, however, that the potential profit in such an investment comes from a change of usage — from agricultural to residential or commercial. To be successful here, the investor has to use a whole different set of selection criteria.

When I was talking about buying for agricultural usage, I said that a good location was an area where the crops would grow well, where they would be reasonably protected against frost, disease, and wind. These criteria remain important, of course, but with a mind to long-term profit, the investor must add a new one — "Where is the path of development?"

Finding the Path of Development

Some of the best agricultural land is often out in the middle of nowhere. To reach it, you drive down country roads, passing picturesque barns, stands of weeping willows, and babbling brooks. Although the pastoral scene is charming, it is (or should be) irrelevant to the investor who is looking for potential higher-usage land. In fact, chances are that if the agricultural land is miles from the city, buying it for higher-use development is very risky. Yes, it might develop in the sense that all land might develop. But how soon? Can you afford to wait 20 or 30 years?

The wise investor usually looks for land that is close to a city. In many areas of the country, even in the heavily populated areas of the East Coast, farmland stretches to the edges of the city. This land may not be quite so attractive from an agricultural view-point. But, if the city is growing, and the land happens to be in the path of growth, its conversion possibilities probably far outweigh its agricultural liabilites.

Determining which way the city will grow, therefore, is critical. There are a variety of ways to do this, but probably the safest way is to join forces with an agricultural syndicate that specializes in just such development. These partnerships look for land that may now be marginally agricultural, but which has great conversion potential. They have real estate experts who do nothing but evaluate potential conversion properties.

It should be noted that in such cases land prices are frequently determined by the land's potential for higher use. Land that is worth only $10,000 an acre for agricultural use might go for as much as $50,000 an acre. A citrus grove that is right on the edge of an attractive new housing development would also have a very high price because of the high probability of imminent conver-sion. On the other hand, an avocado grove ten miles out of town, with no residences or industrial activity nearby, would very likely have a very low price in comparison, even if it was right in the path of development, simply because that development is still years away.

Back in the mid-1970's, many investors went into agricultural land with the anticipation of huge profits. With certain exceptions, such as vineyards, that dream did not come true. Today's agricultural investor has his eye on conversion possibilities, usually through a partnership that specializes in such areas. While waiting for the profits from the sale of his land, the investor enjoys certain tax advantages, which have been greatly increased since the passage of the 1981 Economic Tax Recovery Act, as we'll see in the next chapter.

CHAPTER TWENTY TWO

AGRICULTURAL TAX SHELTERS

Agricultural tax shelters work the same way that most others do. Basically, they defer ordinary income to some time in the future when, presumably, it will reappear in the form of capital gains. An agricultural shelter is created by depreciation, tax credits, and leveraging. Let's see how a typical program works before considering each item individually.

Typically, when an investor buys agricultural land, he or she borrows to finance part of the purchase. The amount borrowed is often between 50 and 70 percent of the value of the property. If a producing grove is purchased, the investor allocates a certain portion of the total purchase price to the various elements of the investment. These elements are the actual land cost, which is typically 15 to 25 percent of the purchase price, the trees, about 60 percent of the price, the irrigation system, and any buildings that happen to be on the property. Once the property has been allocated, it can be depreciated. As we've seen, no depreciation is allowed for the land. But the other elements are usually all depreciable.

If you buy nothing but bare land, then obviously there is nothing to depreciate until the land is agriculturally developed. Then, the irrigation system and the trees may be fully depreciated.

In addition to depreciation, there is an investment tax credit on any equipment purchased. (In orchards, this generally means the irrigation system.) If a new irrigation system is installed, the 10 percent investment tax credit can be taken the year it is installed. Finally, all expenses are deductible the year they are incurred. These include pesticides, fertilizer, water, and management. One dollar is written off for each dollar spent.

These are the elements of an agricultural tax shelter. Now, let's look at each more closely.

FINANCING

It is wise to get the highest leveraging possible, for two reasons. Depreciation is taken on the cost of the total investment (minus land), no matter how the investment is financed. Therefore, the write-off in relation to actual capital invested is going to be much larger for the investor who borrows 70 percent than for the investor who borrows 10 percent. Let's look at a situation in which the cost of the depreciable property is $100 and the depreciation allowance for the first year is 15 percent.

$100	Total investment
×15%	Depreciation
$ 15	Write-off

If the investor puts up the entire $100, the write-off is 15 percent of his capital investment. If the investor, however, only puts up 10 percent, or $10, the write-off is 150 percent.

$15	Write-off
$10	Investment

The difficulty with financing agricultural land is that institutional lenders such as banks are hesitant to make large loans. To get financing, therefore, the investor usually borrows from a combination of sources. Typically, the person who owns the property already has a mortgage on it, either from an institutional lender or the previous owner. (If it was an institutional lender, chances are it was for far less than 50 percent of the property value.)

The new investor might assume the old mortgage. Then, he might go to a bank and try to get a second mortgage on the property. (Lending institutions, surprisingly, are often more willing to issue short-term second mortgages than they would be interested in long-term first mortgages. Of course, short-term second mortgages carry a higher interest rate.) Finally, the seller may take back "paper" in the form of a third mortgage.

The result is that the buyer finances about 70 to 75 percent of the cost of the property. But, in order to do so, he has to have a combination of mortgages that carry high interest rates. It should be remembered, of course, that the interest on these mortgages is an expense item that can be used to offset income from crops. However, if no income from crops is generated, and the interest paid is sufficiently high, it could become a tax preference item.

In today's high interest rate market, many agricultural investments are short run investments. As we saw in the last chapter, investors hope to buy conversion property and sell it after a few years for a substantial profit. Today's interest rates make high leveraging in a long-term agricultural investment almost prohibitive. The interest payments would absorb all the income the crops could produce and more. Generally speaking, the people who go into agriculture today for the long term either pay cash up front or have enough money to take care of the high interest rates.

DEPRECIATION

In the past, orchards and other farm operations were depreciated on their actual useful life. Fruit trees, for example, could only be depreciated in terms of how long they would actually survive. Lemons, for example, were typically given a useful life of 40 years, figs 55 years, and some vineyards 33 years. It's easy to see that depreciation was not a significant factor in agriculture in the past. This all changed with the 1981 Economic Recovery Tax Act, which instituted a new Accelerated Cost Recovery System (ACRS). (It should be noted that under the old law, the ADR system was used to estimate the useful life of a variety of items including trees and vines. However, because of its complexity, the ADR system was rarely used in agriculture. Rather, legal precedent and guidelines drawn up by the IRS were used to determine useful life.)

Under the new ACRS system an arbitrary life-span is assigned to many agricultural commodites. The new ACRS system is the ultimate in simplicity: All crops can be fully depreciated over five years (with no allowance required for residual value).

To understand the dramatic impact that the ACRS system has made on agriculture, look at the following table, keeping in mind that every item listed now can be depreciated in five years.

Crop	Old Depreciation Term (in years)
Almonds	40
Apricots	25
Avocados	25–40
Figs	25–55
Lemons	35–40
Nectarines	15
Olives	50
Oranges	33 to 40
Peaches	15
Plums	20 to 33
Vineyards	7–33
Walnuts	33–40

The beauty of the new system is that the taxpayer does not have to go through an elaborate procedure for determining useful life. The write-off rate, as we've already seen, is also specified by the 1981 Economic Recovery Tax Act. For the aid of this discussion, however, it is repeated here.

Write-Off Percentages for Years 1981 to 1985

Year	Depreciation
1	15%
2	22
3	21
4	21
5	21

To see the effects of the new write-off schedule and to see how it works with leveraging, let's consider an investor who buys an orange grove. We'll say that the total cost is $150,000, of which $100,000 is the value of the trees. Only the $100,000, therefore, may be depreciated.

We'll further assume that the investor arranged for 70 percent financing. Thirty percent of $150,000 is $45,000, the total capital invested. Now let's consider the depreciation. Under the old method, the grove was depreciated over 40 years. Let's say that the grove was already 20 years old when the investor bought it, which means it has a remaining useful life of 20 years. Let's further assume that it was depreciated using a 150 percent declining balance accelerated method. What is the first year's depreciation?

Old Method

$100,000	Value of trees
÷20 years	Term of depreciation
$ 5,000	First year's depreciation (straight-line)
×150%	Accelerated rate
$ 7,500	Total depreciation, first year

Under the old method, the most that could be depreciated was $7500. And this is assuming that the property was purchased on January first and thus qualified for a full year's depreciation. Should the property have been purchased later in the year, only that percentage of the year it was owned could be deducted.

Now, let's consider the new rule. The calculations are extremely simple. The first year 15 percent may be depreciated. Fifteen percent of $100,000 is $15,000. You have twice as much depreciation as under the old method.

Under the old rule, an investor who purchased the property on December 1 would have been entitled to only one-twelfth of the year's depreciation. Under the new rule, an investor who purchases the property even as late as December 31 is automatically entitled to a half year's worth of depreciation.

The advantages of the new rule are even more dramatic the second year. While under the old rule the amount deducted would have been somewhat less than $7500, under the new rule the amount deductible is 22 percent, or $22,000. Now, let's see how this works out in relation to capital investment. (We're assuming for the moment that the income from the oranges offsets other costs including mortgage debt, water, and management.)

Year	Write-off in relation to capital investment	
1	$\dfrac{15,000}{45,000}$	or 33%
2	$\dfrac{22,000}{45,000}$	or 49%
3	$\dfrac{21,000}{45,000}$	or 47%

Of course, as we've noted, income may not be sufficient to pay for mortgage debt, management and actual expenses involved in growing. This would produce a negative cash flow that affects the write-off. (If income were higher, it would produce a positive cash flow also affecting the write-off.)

INVESTMENT TAX CREDIT

The investment tax credit is applied to the purchase of new equipment, including irrigation systems. If a farmer, for example, puts in an irrigation system that costs $1000 per acre and he has 20 acres ($20,000), under irrigation, he is eligible for a $2000 investment tax credit.

Leveraging can work here as well to increase the actual effect of the credit. For example, if 80 percent of the money to install the irrigation system was borrowed, that means that the farmer put up only $4000 in capital. The $2000 investment tax credit represents 50 percent of the total investment.

The investment tax credit covers a period of five years. If the owner disposes of the property sooner, a portion of the credit must be recovered, at the rate of 20% a year.

TAX ROLLOVER

There is another form of agricultural tax shelter that is not widely used these days, for reasons that will soon become apparent. It is the rollover shelter.

The rollover is generally available to investors in row crops — barley, beets, alfalfa, and the like. Unlike fruit-bearing trees, row crops live through only one life cycle — they are planted and harvested over a single season. The rollover shelter works like this. The crop is planted in one calendar year, and all costs incurred in the planting (the cost of the plants themselves, the fertilizer, the cost of planting, ground preparation, management and so forth) are written off that year. When the crop is harvested in the next calendar year, it is sold and, if prices are adequate, returns to the investor the costs involved in planting.

Because, however, the costs were written off the previous year, the profit received in the year of harvesting is recorded as ordinary income.

The rollover basically defers ordinary income from one year to the next. The basic drawback to the rollover is that it is a dollar for dollar transfer. Each dollar that is actually spent in the first calendar year can be deferred to the next, but no additional dollars. The only method of increasing the write-off is to use leveraging. The farmer would have to borrow money to purchase the plants, the fertilizer, and so forth.

If, for example, the cost of the crop was $50,000 and the farmer borrowed $25,000 to finance it, the effect would be a $25,000 write-off in the year the crop was planted. While this would, of course, come back as ordinary income the next year, it would effectively reduce income by the amount of the write-off during the first year.

The investor could, of course, continue deferring to following years and, doubling up each year, continue the write-off. If, however, in any one year if the cycle were to be broken, a large amount of ordinary income would suddenly be incurred with its accompanying tax liability.

This rollover in agriculture is similar to the rollover in cattle feeding described in the chapter on cattle investments and tax shelters. It is not recommended for the ordinary investor.

Agricultural tax shelters are not as popular today as they were five years ago — probably for obvious economic reasons. When only working farmers were involved in crops, they usually planted only as much as the market would bear. The result was that market prices tended to be strong, and the farmers frequently showed profits. When investors became involved in agriculture, however, their motives for planting were often quite different.

The result was an overabundance of agricultural commodities in virtually all areas that were popular as agricultural tax shelters. The resulting large crops drove down prices and made it extremely difficult for anyone to break even, let alone make a profit. And, as I have noted often, if an investment does not make good economic sense before tax considerations, it should be looked at very carefully.

The one bright area in agricultural investment is the partnerships that involve land development. Here investors go in with the specific goal of changing the use of the land and thereby realize their profits.

If you're thinking of agriculture as an investment or a tax shelter, be sure to examine all the angles carefully.

CHAPTER TWENTY THREE

CABLE TV TAX SHELTERS

In the mid-1970's, the "earth stations" of cable television began picking up programs bounced off satellites parked in geostationary orbit 22,300 miles above the equator. Now, just about everything you can transmit on land is being transmitted via satellite — voices, data, printed matter, and, of course, video. And, not only can a cable television subscriber receive this kind of data, but it is just a matter of time before he can "talk" back to his television set. This opens up a myriad of possibilities including home banking, home shopping, home security, and business information.

These exciting developments have attracted many newspapers, broadcasting companies, and other major corporations — as well as individuals — to investment opportunities in cable television. In the last few years, major corporations have moved into cable, with the result that many of the largest multiple systems operators (MSO's) are owned by companies like Time, Westinghouse, Warner Communications, American Express, Cox Communications, and Storer Broadcasting.

But there are some 4300 cable systems throughout the nation, and many are still owned by their founders, whose vision of cable television was simply good quality television reception for people who lived too far outside major metropolitan areas to pick up clear broadcast signals with rooftop antennas.

Many of these small- and medium-size cable system operators were willing to turn their initial, small investments into retirement profits by selling their systems. The first limited partnerships that invested in these then little-known systems provided both appealing capital appreciation possibilities and tax shelters. These early limited partnerships have been overlooked by many potential investors both because they were privately offered and because they typically required sizable minimum investments of

$20,000 to $150,000. (In order to qualify as a private placement, the number of contacts must be limited. Therefore, early investors were usually people who were closely associated with the industry or who specifically searched out investment oportunities in cable television.)

But now cable is beginning to attract individual investors through publicly offered limited partnerships promoted by general partners (usually cable companies), financial services, or securities firms specializing in cable television. These publicly offered partnerships offer large and small investors alike an opportunity to take part in the expanding cable-television industry.

The riskiest cable ventures are those that finance the starting-up of new cable-television systems or the securing of franchise permits. But many partnerships buy one or more existing systems and invest their capital in upgrading the quality and reach of the system (for example, to give subscribers access to such pay-TV offerings as HBO, Showtime, Cinemax, Escapade, and Bravo). These "premium services," which the subscriber pays for in additional monthly charges, are growing in popularity at a faster rate than basic cable service, which is typically the retransmission of the big network broadcast stations, distant independent stations, cable networks specializing in sports, news, religion, and ethnic programming, and public access channels.

In a hypothetical case, "Golden Cablevision" has been servicing a community of 8000 households and maybe 4000 existing subscribers for a number of years. Because of lack of capital, inadequate management, and aging facilities, it has provided adequate but not exemplary service. There were frequent breakdowns in service, picture quality was below par, and subscriber dissatisfaction was high. Professional marketing and community affairs efforts were minimal.

Golden Cablevision may be a suitable candidate for acquisition by a limited partnership.

DETERMINING A PRICE

Operating income in the cable industry is defined as net income, plus all noncash charges such as depreciation and amortization and prior to any form of debt service (including interest and principal charges), before taxes. Typically, the approximate sales price of a cable system is determined by multiplying operating income for the most recent year by a "multiplier." This produces a rule of thumb that can help establish value.

The multiplier is arrived at by comparing other companies sales price to operating income ratio and by factoring in several other critically important elements such as the growth rate of the community served by the system, the system's penetration (how many subscribers it has compared to how many it could have), and the age of the equipment.

Once the multiplier is determined, the approximate purchase price of the system can be calculated and evaluated against other acquisition opportunities. In our Golden Cablevision example, let's say that operating income is $300,000 annually and the multiplier is 10. This gives the system a value of $3 million. If the limited partnership buys Golden Cablevision at that price, it might put up one million in cash, pooled by the individual investors and general partner, and then borrow the remaining $2 million.

IMPROVING SERVICE

Now the partnership owns Golden and it immediately — again using investors' capital and borrowing potential — begins making improvements by modernizing the equipment, offering more pay-TV services, instituting professional marketing, sales, and community affairs programs.

As a result of the improved operations, the company gains more subscribers, improves its market penetration, and may even find new sources of revenue, say, from local advertising. Because the system's operation has vastly improved, the management may have valid reason to request a rate increase from the authority, usually the city council, that regulates basic service prices. Pay-TV services are usually not regulated.

Let's say that Golden has done so well that its annual operating income increases from $300,000 to $400,000. It is immediately obvious (if you remember the multiplier of 10), that the system's sales price has increased to $4 million. Since it was purchased for $3 million, the value of the asset increased by $1 million. And because the limited partnership was leveraged two to one, the return on equity is 100 percent.

REWARDS

Of course, what I've described is an investment that has the great advantage of being purely hypothetical. I simply didn't bother to take into account costs that got in the way of our figures, such as working capital and the costs of improving the system, and I did not consider all the things that can get in the way of success. Nevertheless, the example does demonstrate how limited partnerships can provide capital appreciation.

Typically, a limited partnership buys with leveraging that is close to two to one, and uses multiples in the range of eight to twelve. It hopes to hold the system anywhere from three to seven years and then sell it for a substantial profit.

What is the potential return? Of course, it varies from offering to offering. The return may be in the four to one range, but it will probably take at least five to seven years to attain this return.

Tax Shelter

In addition there is the tax shelter. The advantage offered through limited partnership investing in cable is essentially of the deferred-income variety.

A cable television system has two basic assets: one is its hardware (the system facilities, wire, earth stations, and the like) and the other is its franchise (the right to operate a cable system in a certain community).

In the Golden Cablevision example, the hardware might represent two-thirds of the price, and the franchise the remaining one-third. Typically, both the franchise and the hardware are written off (depreciated). Most of the hardware is written off in five years. Because the hardware is used equipment, it is frequently depreciated by the 150 percent declining balance method. The value of the franchise is normally depreciated over its remaining life. Finally, there are investment tax credits, which may or may not be available to the investor. It's impossible to provide a rule of thumb. Investigation on a case-by-case basis is critical.

The noncash deductions on depreciation and amortization usually result in substantial losses, for tax purposes, during the early years, and most partnerships allocate most of these losses to the investors who can benefit most from deducting them from their other income. Also, investors may get some tax benefits if a system is sold within five years. Because there is recapture on the equipment depreciated for five years, a portion of the investor's return will be ordinary income. But a portion will also be capital gains subject to the lower capital gains tax. In a typical sale, 40 to 50 percent of the gain will be taxed as ordinary income, and 50 to 60 percent as capital gains.

It should be apparent at this point that in a well-run limited partnership, it is possible to get both significant shelter and good growth potential. But, as in all investments, it is unwise to only consider the upside. There is always a downside risk as well.

RISKS

The risks in cable television are far fewer than in many other types of investments. I have listed them below.

Bad Management

If the management of the limited partnership does not have the expertise or ability to make sound decisions on acquisitions, there will probably be trouble down the road.

The limited partners, obviously, are better off when the deals are structured so the general partner has lots of incentive to make the venture succeed. Here as elsewhere, it is probably the track record of the general partner that will be critical. Has the general partner ventured into cable before? Does he (or it) understand the industry and the territory where the possible acquisitions are located?

Technological Change

In some major urban markets, STV (subscription television) and MDS (multi-point distribution) systems compete with cable television. These two technologies deliver through scrambling mechanisms a pay product very similar to HBO, The Movie Channel, and Showtime. However, they are limited to a single channel delivery method (as opposed to the 54 channels currently being delivered by cable) and thus have a limited competitive life. Several firms have opposed direct broadcasting facilities from the originating transmitter via satellite to the home. This technology is designed to serve remote rural areas, where it is not economically feasible to construct a cable system. Like STV and MDS, channel capacity is very limited.

Government Regulation

The ultimate extent of government regulation of cable television is not known at the present time. Changes are occuring at all levels of government. Frequently, local government exercises control over rates and conditions of service. The FCC exercises jurisdiction over cable at a federal level. Changes in this regulatory climate could adversely affect cable TV in general and certain systems in particular.

Economic Collapse

Since many of the cable systems targeted for acquisition by limited partnerships are located in communities outside of major metropolitan areas and serve only a few thousand subscribers, any changes in the economic base for that community could have a profound impact on the economic well-being of the cable system. For example, if Golden Cablevision was located in a Wyoming town highly dependent upon local mines, what would happen if the mines closed? Ghost towns don't need cable television systems.

Cable television is a new and exciting investment medium for many small and large individual investors. When a person invests in a cable television system, he or she is investing in an appreciating asset much like real estate. Both the facility itself and its location are the elements that give it value. If the building is kept in good repair — or improved — and the location becomes more attractive to residents, the value of the real estate goes up.

For those whose primary long-term objective is growth and whose short-term objective is tax shelter, investing in cable television may be an important investment opportunity.

More information on publicly offered limited partnerships in cable, can be obtained from one of the many offices of Integrated Resources, Inc.

CHAPTER TWENTY FOUR

OFFSHORE TRUSTS

For most people, the idea of an international trust seems remote at best. Many of us simply do not really know what a trust is. Others who have considered trusts wonder why they should bother with an "offshore" or foreign version. And finally there are those few who have looked into offshore trusts and have seen what appear to be insurmountable problems — finding a competent attorney in the foreign jurisdiction, knowing foreign exchange controls, learning foreign law, and so on.

Yet, if you have assets of at least $50,000 and income of at least $25,000, an offshore trust can provide tax and other benefits to you. In addition, today setting up an offshore trust can be a relatively simple and clean operation. Offshore trusts are no longer the domain of only the very rich.

INTERNATIONAL TAX PLANNING

One of the major reasons for considering an offshore trust comes from looking at our tax picture not just from a national basis, but from an international perspective. It is possible to conduct tax planning that includes multinational factors thereby extending the national tax scheme to include a foreign influence.

The advantages of linking two tax systems are that we increase the possibilities of minimizing and/or deferring taxes. The disadvantages are that if we're not careful we would end up with double taxation and problems in dealing with foreign legal and administrative systems. The simple fact of the matter is that when we deal with international tax planning we increase the tax and non-tax factors to be considered whether good or bad.

Do the advantages outweigh the disadvantages?

In many cases they do. It is possible today to secure the aid of an expert in foreign trusts who can prepare all the documentation, set up the trust and provide advice for its operation. This expert must, of course, thoroughly understand both domestic and foreign tax matters. He or she must have a thorough knowledge of your tax situation. And the expert must have a strong track record.

WHAT IS A TRUST?

A trust is essentially the right of one party to hold property for the purpose of benefiting another party and is a most common entity. Parents sometimes set up trusts to provide income for their children.

Trusts generally involve two or three parties: the grantor (the person who sets up the trust), the trustee (the party who directly handles the property placed into the trust) and the beneficiary (the person who is going to benefit from the trust, often the grantor). The grantor could, for example, put real estate, cash, or stocks or any other property, real or personal, into a trust. The trustee would then administer that property as directed by the grantor. The instructions on how the property is to be administered are contained in a document called the "declaration of trust."

USES OF A TRUST

Trusts are legally treated as independent entities, just like corporations, whether they are international or domestic. Because of this fact, the trust can own property, sign contracts and even go into court in its own name. When the grantor, trustee and beneficiaries all reside in the same country, the trust is subject to the laws of that land. When this is the case, the trust comes under intense scrutiny from taxing authorities to determine if the trust is independent of, or merely the alter ego of, the beneficiaries.

However, when trusts are located in countries other than those in which the beneficiaries reside, they are beyond the legal jurisdiction of the home countries. This is not to say that anyone should use trusts for illegal purposes, only that the discretion of international trusts is far wider than domestic trusts.

A person with an international trust can deliver to that trust a certain amount of money. Instructions on that money can then be given. The trustee can buy and sell foreign currencies, blue-chip stocks, precious metals, domestic or foreign properties. It can conduct whatever business the grantor instructs it to conduct. But, because it is a *foreign* entity, it is not subject to the same tax laws that you and I are as domestic residents. It will be subject to the laws in the country in which it exists.

Your international trust can serve as a passive repository of your wealth, if you so choose. Or it can be a dynamic conduit for speculative investment and active trading. You can gain the benefits of real estate speculation, commodity trading and securities transactions potentially without onerous income or capital gains taxation. In using your international trust for investments, you may either let your trustee trade on your behalf and sit back and relax, or you may give detailed instructions as to when and what you want traded.

The important thing to remember is that your international trust is a separate legal entity. When it acts, it acts as a foreign citizen and *not* as you. It is, of course, subject to the regulation and taxation of the country it is located in. But, if that country is well chosen, these can be minimal.

You, of course, are subject to the regulations and taxation of your country, the United States. But these should come into play, normally, only when you receive a distribution from your trust. And you can decide how that is to be handled.

There are other uses for trusts, besides investment and the protection of gains from immediate taxation. These include protection against having your possessions seized.

If you are faced with a frivolous lawsuit, an unmeritorious domestic claim including a tax deficiency, you stand to lose your property — unless you don't own much property.

If you have sufficient cause to fear such seizure you can reorganize your financial planning to include a discreet international trust. The trust would be the owner of the property. And because it was an international (foreign) trust, it would not be subject to the laws of this country — including seizure.

The final use of the trust is in the transfer of property. In the case of most trusts, the beneficiary interest can be assigned to someone else. This can be to another individual such as a spouse or a child, or to virtually anyone you choose. This can be done simply utilizing "bearer certificates" which entitle the bearer to become the owner of the trust. Or it can be done as part of the trust documents. The new beneficiary does not directly receive any property. Rather, the beneficiary receives the right to control the trust and to do as he or she wishes with whatever property happens to be in it.

SETTING UP AN INTERNATIONAL TRUST

We'll go into the actual documentation and how a trust is set up in a few moments. But first, let's consider how a grantor might transfer property to a trust.

Land, securities, or businesses may require nominal sales by you to the trustee (or its nominee). Of course, there could be taxes due on the gain from such sales; however, these can be minimized by carefully structuring the sales price and terms.

Transferring cash to the trust can be somewhat more difficult because of the restrictions that many countries have in allowing the transfer of more than very small amounts of cash across their borders. To stay within the law you should not exceed your country's daily transfer limit.

LOCATING A TRUST

It is important that both the grantor and the trustee be located outside the jurisdiction of the beneficiary's country of residence. This is so that they are beyond the subpoena or regulatory powers of the beneficiary's country. This maximizes security. In essence, a properly structured international trust should be in a country with which the beneficiary has no other contact.

Trusts, however, are not universally recognized by law; basically they exist only under English common law. This means that foreign trusts must usually be established in English speaking countries. These might include the following:

Switzerland

Hong Kong

Bahrain

Bahamas

Caribbean islands including Anguilla, St. Vincent and the Cayman islands.

Finally, the choice of where to set up a trust must be made with an eye to the types of controls and taxation in the foreign country. Ideally the location would have virtually no taxes or taxes levied exclusively on affairs only within the country. (No tax on international transactions.) In addition, some areas grant privileges to certain businesses which come to their areas, and there can be benefits here.

HOW A TRUST IS SET UP

There are some people who, because they desire secrecy in their foreign trust, set it up themselves. There is at least one organization charging relatively large sums of money which will teach you how to set up your own trust. Yet, virtually all the information required to do it yourself, should you choose, is available at your local library in the law section.

Since doing it yourself is not recommended, another method is to have an attorney draw up the required documents for you. To be sure of competence on the attorney's part, it wil probably be necessary to have an attorney in the foreign country handle the documents. (A domestic attorney might simply not know how to handle foreign law.)

Yet another method is to have a bank trust department handle the trust for you. This will require the use of a foreign bank. Domestic banks and trust companies are only interested in managing trusts locally. They determine the site (almost always local) of the trust.

Finally, there are organizations in the U.S. that operate as "trust arrangers." They act as a go-between for you. They arrange for a trustee in the foreign country, assemble all the documents and give counseling and advice. Unfortunately, their fees are often very high, typically in excess of $10,000.

What many individuals who are interested in a foreign trust are doing is avoiding all of the alternatives just suggested. They are opting instead for a "pre-granted" trust. This is simply a trust already in existence at the time it is acquired. The trustee has been named, the management fee established and all the necessary foreign arrangements made. No records concerning to whom the trust is sold exist in any place other than in the documents held by the purchaser-beneficiary and the trustee.

The trustee in these pre-granted trusts is usually a foreign bank in an appropriate country. The pre-granted trust, besides offering simplicity and thrift, also offers the very highest degree of financial privacy.

Once we've established our trust, have a trustee with whom we feel secure (a foreign bank) and put our money or other property into it, the question arises as to how we get out property out.

DISTRIBUTION FROM A FOREIGN TRUST

We may wish to have funds from our trust given to us for a wide variety of reasons. We may have a general use for cash, as, for example, money to live on a day-to-day basis. Or we may need cash from the trust for emergencies. (Remember, we probably wouldn't need money from the trust for investment purposes. That sort of money would be invested directly by the trust.) How do we "expatriate" our money from our trust?

Money from the trust can be wired to us directly. Or it can be sent through the mails in the form of a check from the foreign bank. Of course, should it be desired, these methods of receiving funds can be done discreetly. Nevertheless, funds received from a foreign trust would be subject to the laws and taxation of the United States. Should there be gain involved, appropriate taxation may be levied.

Indeed, if it were established that the foreign trust were not truly a real entity, but the grantor's alter ego, all of the activities of the trust could be subject to U.S. law and all gain potentially taxable. Of course, the fact that the trust is outside U.S. territory and not subject to U.S. law might make application of law and even seizure somewhat difficult if not impossible. But the beneficiary, in any event, would not want to leave him or herself open to any sort of tax evasion charge. Under current U.S. tax law a grantor may be taxed on the income derived from property transferred to the trust simply by virtue of being a grantor or transferror. *The rules are complex and this discussion should not be viewed as exhaustive or as legal advice to be relied upon in a particular transaction.*

One common method used of transferring funds from the trust outright is to get a loan. Your trustee bank can lend you whatever funds you may require using the trust property as collateral. The money, since it is borrowed, is not normally taxable. And the interest you pay on the money is deductible. Of course, there is the necessity of repaying the loan, but this could be handled almost indefinitely by rolling over and increasing the debt with further loans.

In addition, with a foreign trust, there are endless possibilities if you don't want to bring your money home. Want to spend a vacation abroad? Simply use the money from the trust wired to your vacation site. Want to lease or even buy a villa on the Riviera, use the trust. Want to buy a fur coat, jewelry or gifts for personal use on a trip? Use the trust. (Of course, bringing such items back would make them subject to U.S. import duties.)

Finally, if your offshore trust conducts business in your home country or owns a business there, it can give its valued officers, employees or agents such perks as a company car, corporate retreat, adult education benefits, generous expense accounts and business-related travel vouchers. In the case of income property owned by an offshore company, this could mean a free manager's office or apartment. This list is certainly not exhaustive and the creative corporate officer, employee or agent can extend it almost without limit. Such expenditures are deductible business expenses as well as tangible benefits to the recipient frequently without a direct tax consequence to the recipient.

In summary, international trusts offer a form of security available in no other way in today's modern world. If we place money in a bank, everyone has access to knowledge of the fact. If we buy real estate, our name is recorded on the county records. If we buy stocks, the brokerage company maintains records of our transactions. Yet, if we do all these things through a foreign trust, we can do them in complete secrecy — secret from everyone.

We can use a trust to preserve our wealth and to ultimately pass it on. We can use a trust to invest and trade either actively or passively. And we can use a foreign trust to protect us from seizure of assets and exchange control regulations.

Finally, lest there be suspicions among readers, it should be noted that the creation and operation of a foreign trust is not illegal under the laws of the United States. As citizens we have the right to establish such trusts as we desire.

It is illegal, however, to avoid paying taxes on any gain that we personally may have. We normally, however, do not have to pay taxes on a gain that someone else has, even including a trust. Domestic trusts (see the chapter on estate planning) are being set up constantly as a legal means of having an income grow without taxation or having that taxation deferred to later years or handed down to our children.

The difference between the foreign and the domestic trust is simply one of latitude. In a foreign trust, because it is set up under the laws of a foreign country, the activities of that trust can be far broader than in a domestic trust. And, if it is set up in an appropriate country, the gains on the investments of the foreign trust can be tax free. (Domestic trusts are taxed as domestic entities.)

It is the utilization of differences of multi-national laws and taxation that allow for the benefits of an international trust.

It must be understood, however, that international trusts are not for everyone. The individual with little money and few assets could probably not benefit financially. In addition, the person who is financially unsophisticated might find the entire concept difficult to grasp.

Sound legal advice and counseling is essential to setting up an effective and legally structured international trust. To help in this matter the following two books which provide additional information on foreign trusts should be considered: *Anyone Can Profit With a Secret Foreign Trust* and *How to Profit From Offshore Banking*. Both are published by the Gold Depository and Loan Company, Inc. — Publishing Division, 2124 Union Street, San Francisco, California 94123.

Should you get a foreign trust?

That question is best answered with the aid of your attorney and financial planner.

CHAPTER TWENTY FIVE

DIAMOND INVESTMENTS

There is no other investment quite like diamonds. If you chart the history of these beautiful, rare stones over the past 70 years, you will see only continuous strong appreciation in value. Those who bought diamonds in that period, and held them for the minimum waiting period of at least three years, have made profits — often substantial profits. But why a three-year waiting period? Let's find out.

DEBEERS AND THE DIAMOND MARKET

The giant DeBeers organization essentially controls the world diamond market. This control obviously influences prices, but perhaps not in the way you would expect. DeBeers rarely acts to move prices upward; the benevolent giant more frequently acts to force prices down.

The truth of the matter is that the vast majority of diamonds sold end up as jewelry in wedding bands, bracelets, earrings, and so forth. If investors were allowed to push the price of diamonds too high, then jewelry manufacturers would be forced out of the market, making a major crash inevitable. (That is something which has occasionally happened in collectibles and in gold and silver bullion.) During periods of high investor speculation in diamonds, DeBeers introduces more rough stones into the market, thereby holding prices down. When there is a slack period, such as the recession of 1981, DeBeers restricts the flow of rough diamonds, thereby stabilizing prices.

These benevolent actions of DeBeers (which are really only self-interest, since DeBeers stands to make even greater profits from a healthy diamond industry) are what make a minimum three-year holding period necessary. It works like this. Over a period of time, DeBeers may allow prices to accelerate. Then, if prices accelerate too rapidly, DeBeers will increase the flow of diamonds into the market to stabilize prices. Prices might remain stable for a fairly long period of time. Traditionally, this time period has been about three years.

Then DeBeers might allow prices to rise again. The investor has to be prepared to wait for this eventuality because he cannot know at what point in the cycle his purchase was made. If it happens to be just before a big price rise, then the waiting period could be only a month or two. But if it's early in the cycle, then it could be quite a bit longer.

But many people still talk of diamond prices falling. If DeBeers has the kind of influence just described, how can diamond prices fall? The answer is that DeBeers acts only on the "rough" market. Rough stones are stones taken from the ground; they are still uncut and unpolished. The result is that the hand of DeBeers, though it moves throughout the industry, does not move smoothly or equally. When news of a price increase is heard, diamond merchants immediately raise their selling prices in anticipation, even though the initial price increase occurred at the farthest end of the pipeline. By the time the new rough has been cut and polished and found its way to the dealers, the diamond merchants often discover that the prices they had arbitrarily raised are not sustainable. And then prices fall back. What's important to see here is that when DeBeers acts it's like a boy throwing a stone into a quiet pond. He knows his action will make circular waves, but he doesn't know how big they will be when they reach the shores of the pond.

Over the years the price of diamonds has increased and stablized, increased and stabilized over and over again. No other investment in the world, including stocks and bonds, real estate, bullion, or even collectibles, can equal a record of such sustained growth.

Although the fact is not widely known in the United States, diamonds are regarded as currency in many parts of the world. In Switzerland, for example, bank accounts may be opened in currency, gold, or diamonds, the queen of monies. Diamond accounts are the most cherished. And in times of crisis, diamonds provide easily transportable wealth. Gold and silver are too heavy. Currency would probably be worthless. But a fortune in diamonds could be carried in just one pocket. And there would be no problem at national border crossings. Although the movement of gold and currency is restricted, it is perfectly legal to bring in a king's ransom in diamonds.

PRICING DIAMONDS

Unlike gold and silver, diamonds do not have a "price." What many people do not realize is that each diamond, like each snowflake, is unique. (There are processes, including photoprinting by laser beam, which can fingerprint diamonds so that each stone can be identified and differentiated from every other diamond in the world.) Therefore, when someone asks the price of diamonds, the only appropriate response is another question, "To which particular diamond are you referring?"

Carat

Of course, there are ways to classify diamonds. One has to do with the stone's weight, which is measured in carats, exactly one-fifth of a gram. Each carat is divided into 100 points. A quarter-carat stone, therefore, is 25 points.

Stones under 20 points are referred to as "melee." (At one time melee weighed between 20 and 50 points, but demand for this size stone lowered the weight requirements.) Melee are used primarily to set off larger stones. They are purchased primarily for the jewelry trade and used in rings, bracelets, and so forth.

Another market exists for stones between 20 points and half-carat. These are used for engagement rings. Four out of five first-time brides in the United States receive a diamond engagement ring. (In Japan the ratio is even higher!) Another market exists for one-carat stones. These are bought primarily by more mature buyers as gifts for anniversaries and other occasions. Finally, there is the market for stones above one carat, which is primarily a collector's market.

The market demand for diamonds of different weight categories varies. The half-carat market may be moving while the melee and one-carat are quiet. Or the one-carat may be moving while the half-carat, melee, and larger stone markets are quiet.

Cut

The standard American round "brilliant" has exactly 58 facets. It is cut to produce the greatest possible brilliancy, or return of light. When a brilliant (or any other traditional cut) meets the industry's standards, it is called an ideal cut. In the diamond-cutting process, however, more material is lost in making ideal cuts. Since for most people weight remains the big determiner of value, cutters are generally unwilling to create ideal cuts. (Often the shape of the rough diamond will preclude an ideal cut.) A stone that has an ideal cut is in one category of demand. That which has a less than ideal cut (by certain margins) is in another.

There are other types of cuts. There's the 17 facet cut (used frequently on melee), a European cut with a deeper pavilion, an earlier modern cut developed by Marcel Tolkowsky in 1914, a heart-shaped cut, and on and on. These other cuts, although in less demand, have their own markets.

Clarity

Many people think that diamonds are naturally clear stones. Almost none are. Most have minor flaws. Perhaps it's the formation of a tiny second diamond within the first, or a cleavage in the stone. (A big misconception about diamonds is that because they are hard they won't break. Hardness has nothing to do with brittleness. Hit a diamond with a hammer and you'll shatter it into a thousand pieces.) The Gemological Institute of America (GIA) has established grading standards for diamond clarity. The scale looks like this:

FL	Flawless
IF	Internally Flawless (a European standard)
VVS1	Very, very slightly included
VVS2	Very, very slightly included
VS1	Very slightly included
VS2	Very slightly included
SI1	Slightly included
SI2	Slightly included
I1	Imperfect
I2	Imperfect
I3	Imperfect

Obviously the most perfect stones are at the top of the list. What is fascinating about this scale is that in general only those stones graded imperfect have flaws visible to the naked eye. In grade above I, the flaw can usually only be seen with a 10-power magnifying glass — the standard magnification used for grading.

Grading has created two distinct market categories for diamonds. Stones in the imperfect category are almost always found in rings and other jewelry. Investor stones are in the top six categories. (The S1 category is a sort of twilight zone, which in recent years has become of increasing interest to investors as the quality of stones taken from the earth continues to go down.)

Color

Some diamonds are colorless — the so-called white diamonds. Others, however, have a distinct color, usually yellowish. The GIA also has a grading scale for color ranging from D which is colorless, all the way down the alphabet to X. (The scale does not start with A, to avoid confusion with older scales.) Grades from D through I generally appear colorless to the untrained eye. Grades D through H are generally considered investment stones.

Color has always been important in grading diamonds. However, it became particularly important in 1978 when diamond investors suddenly demanded the most colorless stones. Those with the higher grades of color saw their value increase enormously.

The four Cs of diamonds, therefore, are *carat, cut, clarity,* and *color.* It's easy to see that there are ultimately thousands of different diamond classifications possible. And that is why it's so difficult to talk about price. If we were to narrow the discussion down to a specific category, and even more precisely to a specific stone, we could get a much clearer answer.

INVESTING IN DIAMONDS

More and more people are beginning to "bank in diamonds" as a hedge against inflation. Single investors are the largest category of diamond investors. But recently, pension funds have begun to invest a small percentage of their portfolios in diamonds.

There is a problem, however. The world's supply of diamonds is dwindling. The great diamond mines of Africa are running dry. A mine, in any case, has only a relatively short life-span, perhaps a few decades. In most of the major mines, the best diamonds have already been removed, and today miners are reworking old tailings and digging into less productive host rock. In 1960 about 50 million carats were produced; in 1979 only 39 million came out of the ground. Although it is hoped that new mines in Russia, China, and Australia will raise production, it is unlikely that it will ever exceed or even equal earlier figures.

Today's investor faced with a dwindling diamond supply (perhaps only 1 or 2 percent of all diamonds mined are suitable for investment), a controlled market, and appreciating prices may find diamonds very tempting.

But investors should remember that diamonds do have drawbacks. There is the waiting period of at least three years before any appreciation is likely to be seen. There is also a fairly wide spread between wholesale and retail diamond prices (because of the enormous risks the cutting entails). And, of course, diamonds are not as liquid as other investments; if you have to sell before the minimum waiting time is up, you could lose money.

If you're considering diamonds, look for the most reputable dealer you can find. Look for a good track record and look for price. Above all, know what you are getting. Diamonds are usually sold with a "certificate" attesting to their quality. Be sure that the certificate is from a reputable laboratory.

CHAPTER TWENTY SIX

GOLD AND SILVER INVESTMENTS

Gold and, to a lesser extent, silver have through the ages been universally accepted as a medium of exchange and a store of wealth. In ancient Egypt, gold was used as an item of barter, although at that time, silver was considered even more valuable because of its greater scarcity. In 400 B.C., King Croesus minted what were perhaps the first gold coins. Silver coins were minted in Lydia as far back as 800 B.C.

The point I want to make is that gold and silver are money. Even though today they are not considered "official" currency by most governments, they have become a kind of universally accepted "super currency." There is no country in the world that will not accept gold or silver in payment for virtually any purchase.

The acceptability of gold and silver as mediums of exchange is most clearly demonstrated in times of crisis. Should there be a flare-up in the Middle East or unrest in Czechoslovakia, individuals, corporations, and governments in neighboring countries, fearing an escalation of hostilities, trade their own endangered currencies for a currency that is not — gold and, to a lesser extent, silver. These "currencies" do not depend upon the survival of any particular country for value. They are international and independent of border lines.

GOLD — A BRIEF BACKGROUND

At various times between the Civil War and the Great Depression, the U.S. paper dollar was backed by gold. (Remember the "gold certificates"?) In 1933, however, President Franklin Roosevelt, as part of his economic recovery plan, made owning gold currency and bullion illegal. There were still gold certificates around, but these were restricted to use in international trade. For most of the time from the Great Depression until President Richard Nixon closed the gold window in 1971, foreign countries could exchange their gold certificate dollars for gold at the rate of $35 dollars per ounce.

Prior to the closing of the gold window, the U.S. dollar had been devalued several times. Nevertheless, since all foreign currencies in the Western world were defined in terms of their value in dollars, they were also defined in terms of gold.

Today the value of currencies, including the U.S. dollar, are expressed not in relationship to gold, but in relationship to each other. The German mark, for example, rises and falls in relationship to the dollar according to how individuals, corporations, and governments view their relative strength. For example, if Germany has a lower inflation rate than the United States, chances are that the Deutschmark will be stronger. On the other hand, if the United States offers higher interest rates, foreign investment money would flow to the United States and (all other factors being equal), the dollar would grow stronger.

Since the time Nixon took the United States and in essence the world off the gold standard, the total world monetary reserves (not including gold) have increased over sevenfold. This increase can be appreciated even more when we compare it to the 29 percent increase that occurred between 1950 and 1959. Although there has been a currency explosion in the world, there has not been a gold explosion. Quite the contrary, the amount of gold has actually declined. Today, there is much more paper currency available in relation to gold than there ever has been in the past. What does this tell us?

We have seen that gold is the currency that people rely on whenever there is a crisis. Even during relatively stable times, people tend to hold some gold, just in case. Yet, the number of dollars, Deutschmarks, francs and so on, has increased enormously in relation to gold. The result has been a rapid increase in the value of gold. In a sense the inflation of currencies has driven the price of gold up.

The prospect for continued inflation of all world currencies remains strong. In the United States, for example, the government constantly increases the number of dollars it produces. The efforts of recent administrations to control the money supply have not been in the direction of keeping it constant or even reducing it, but rather merely slowing down the rate of increase. Because the same situation exists in other countries, the value of gold in the future is likely to continue to increase relative to the value of international currencies (including the U.S. dollar).

202

SILVER — A BRIEF BACKGROUND

Although gold and silver are frequently linked in the minds of investors, they are in reality two separate metals and as mediums of exchange behave according to different principles. The basic element affecting silver is supply and demand. As we all know, the price of anything rises if either the supply decreases or the demand increases. Either factor by itself can cause the price to go up. But with the two factors combined, a substantial price in-increase can be anticipated. That is the case with silver.

Since 1955, the gap between supply and demand has steadily widened. To see why, let's first consider supply.

Silver Supplies

Silver ore is found primarily within the top 200 feet of the earth's crust. Although some veins do run down to great depths, the highest grade ore is generally on top. As a result, virtually all major deposits of silver have already been discovered and mined.

During the mid-1800's, silver was taken in great quantities from the famous Comstock lode in California and Nevada. By the late 1800's, however, the cost of recovering it had become so high that the owners closed down the mines. The silver that remained was so expensive to recover that producing it was not justified by the world price of the metal.

In the United States today, there are very few, if any, mines dedicated solely to producing silver. Generally, silver is produced (in this country and in many others) only as a by-product. (Copper, lead, and zinc deposits usually contain some silver as well.) There are, of course, other countries, such as Mexico and Bolivia, which do in fact mine silver directly. But even there, the margin between the world price of silver and the cost of production is very close. Generally speaking, with world prices at or near the $10 level, even low-labor-cost areas cannot afford to produce much silver. In fact, 70 percent of the silver produced in the world today is the by-product of some other mining venture; only 30 percent is either mined directly or comes from other sources.

The largest other source is silver scrap and salvage. There are two kinds of silver scrap. *Old scrap* consists of silverware, plates, jewelry, coins, and anything else made of silver that is turned in and melted down. *New scrap* is the material lost in the production of any silver object. For example, when a silver spoon is crafted, a certain amount of scrap material is either shaved or stamped away in the process.

Finally, there is *silver salvage*. As must be apparent, silver, like gold, is relatively immutable. It can be used and used again. For example, when film is sent to laboratories for developing (roughly half of all silver used goes to make photographic film), much of the silver (in the form of silver halides) is recaptured. This salvaged silver amounts to about 30 percent of all silver that was originally used to make the film. Once salvaged it can then be used again. The amount of silver salvaged has been constant for some time. Quantity of new scrap has also been constant, but the amount of old scrap has varied considerably.

When the price of silver soared to $50 an ounce in 1980, the amount of old scrap increased enormously. At one point close to four million ounces a month were turned in. Once the price of silver dropped back down below the $10 mark, the old scrap market almost disappeared, dropping below half a million ounces per month.

Part of the problem is that there simply aren't that many old silver coins left. Most have already been melted down. Another problem is that people are often reluctant to part with their silverware or silver jewelry unless the price gets extremely high. At $50 an ounce many were willing; at $10, few were.

At the present time, the supply of silver from scrap and salvage is low — far below the demand. (Back in 1955, the supply of new silver roughly equaled demand. By 1980, however, there was a 170 million ounce discrepancy between new supplies and demand. This was, of course, met by scrap and salvage.) Today the supply of silver would most likely be inadequate if it weren't for the U.S. government. In October of 1981, the government began selling roughly one million ounces a month on the open market. Current plans call for the sale of 46.5 million ounces in the fiscal year 1982-83, 44 million in the fiscal year 1983-84, and 15 million in the fiscal year 1984-85. In response to this move, silver prices have become both depressed and stable.

The U.S. government has sold silver before. Its original stockpile was about 2000 million ounces, but during the 1960's, most of this was sold in order to keep silver prices down, thereby discouraging citizens from withdrawing silver coins from circulation and melting them down for their silver content. Until recently, the government had roughly 139 million ounces remaining in its strategic stockpile. In 1981, Congress granted the government permission to sell about 100 million ounces, but only to purchase other strategic metals.

When this last silver sale is completed, the government will be out of the silver business, probably for good. There will no longer be that overhang of silver left to depress and control prices. At that point, we can expect to see a significant increase in the price of silver.

SILVER DEMAND

The demand for silver has increased rapidly since 1955. The largest user is the photo industry, consuming about half of all silver production. Other large users include electronics, jewelry, silverware, bronzing, soldering, and dentistry. All these industries, and in particular electronics, have substantially increased their use of silver in recent years.

While overall production of new silver has remained fairly constant over the years, the increase in usage has nearly doubled in the last 25 years. Indications are that this increase is likely to continue in the future. When the government sells off its silver, we can expect to see prices rise.

The price of silver might still be held in check if the private reserves of silver held by investors were to come onto the market. It is most unlikely that these investors would alow substantial portions of silver to be sold unless they felt that inflation had been halted. These investors hold silver for two reasons: to act as an emergency currency in time of crisis and to serve as a hedge against inflation. Since inflation is not likely to recede in the foreseeable future, a large amount of silver from private reserves is not likely to enter the market. Silver, therefore, remains a strong contender to rise in price over the years.

HOW TO INVEST IN GOLD AND SILVER

There are basically five ways. We'll cover each separately:

1. *Bullion*. Bullion is essentially metal in bar form. Gold is generally stored in either 100 or 400 ounce bars of .999 fineness. Silver is kept in ingots that come in a variety of sizes. Commodity silver (that which is used for the futures market) is generally in either 1000 or 4000 ounce bars. Ingots produced by Handy and Harmon, and other silver refiners come in sizes all the way down to a one-ounce piece.

2. *Coins*. In gold the most popular coins are the Krugerrand, the Maple Leaf, the Austrian Korona, and the Mexican 50 peso. A potential investor should know that the fineness, or purity, of gold

varies by type of coin. The Maple Leaf, for example, is .999 fine, whereas the Krugerrand is only .916 fine. Both coins, however, contain exactly one ounce of pure gold.

For silver, most investments are in "junk" silver or in coins minted before 1964 that have no numismatic, or collector, value. These coins which are 90 percent silver, are sold in bags. The price of the bag is determined not by the face value of the coins (usually $1000), but by their silver content. Most bags contain roughly 714 ounces of silver, and their value, therefore, is 714 times the price of silver per ounce. Bags often have a premium — as much as 30 percent over the price of silver. It is also possible to buy silver dollars. (The bags contain only dimes, quarters, and halves.) Silver dollars are also sold at a premium above the price of silver.

3. Both gold and silver can be purchased in the form of jewelry, nuggets and specimen material. When buying gold jewelry, it is important to know the carat value, or purity, of the gold. Twenty-four carat is solid, or 100 percent, gold. Fourteen carat is 14/24, or roughly 58 percent, pure, the remainder being base material. Most investment grade jewelry is 18 carat or higher in purity.

4. *Options.* Stock options on gold and silver mining companies are readily available from any stockbroker. Options on physical gold are available from several sources including Mocatta Metals in New York.

5. *Stocks* in gold or silver mining companies. There are numerous mining companies listed on the New York Stock Exchange and on foreign exchanges. The price of these stocks fluctuates with the price of gold.

Tax Considerations

There are basically four tax considerations. The first applies to all gold and silver investments. The rest apply only to mining ventures.

1. *Capital Gains.* If you hold your investment in bullion, coins, jewelry, or mining stocks for more than one year, your profit on resale will be taxed as a capital gain rather than as ordinary income. Gold and silver, therefore, make sense as an investment from a tax standpoint. In addition, these metals provide excellent liquidity and may increase in value relative to paper currency at a rate either commensurate with or better than the rate available on short-term interest rates.

2. *Investing in a Mine* as a tax shelter. It is possible to invest in an operating gold or silver mine. You could get into a mine development program directly, either by ownership or by lease, or join a limited partnership specifically set up to develop gold and silver mining properties. There are two advantages here: (1) the ability to offset expenses with the excess deductions obtained from the mining venture and use it to shelter other income, and (2) should the project be successful, it may be possible to sell your share in the partnership and obtain a capital gain treatment on the income received.

3. *Depletion Allowance.* There is normally a 15 percent depletion allowance available for minerals. Although the rules are quite complex (a qualified tax expert should be consulted), it may be possible to obtain a 15 percent depletion allowance in a properly structred ventured.

4. *Gold Profit.* There is no profit in a mining venture until the product is converted. In the case of gold, it must be converted into money, or, as the tax authorities define it, U.S. dollars or federal reserve notes. Consequently, if you were to keep all of your production from the mine in gold concentrate, gold bars, or some other form, you would not show a profit for tax purposes until after you actually sold your gold. You might want to keep it in gold form for quite some time.

Expert advice should always be sought in any mining venture. The investor should also be aware that the existence of high-grade ore alone does not guarantee a successful investment. The mine must be so located that the ore can be extracted cheaply enough to make the end product profitable. Finally, honest management is indispensible.

Gold and silver are shining investment mediums. They can provide both tax benefits and profits. I think that perhaps the most important thing to remember about them is that 100 years from now, when our paper money has turned to dust, people will still be buying and selling gold and silver.

CHAPTER TWENTY SEVEN

RARE COIN AND
CURRENCY INVESTMENTS

Coin collecting has been a popular pastime for 2000 years, and there is every reason to believe that it will continue to be popular long after present forms of money have been replaced by plastic cards and computer banking.

Coins have traditionally been collected for a variety of reasons — historical value, aesthetic value, rarity, and collectibility, and even as a convenient way to transfer large sums of money in times of emergency.

Coin collecting, as most Americans think of it today, got its start in the early 1930's. Whitman Publishing in Racine, Wisconsin, a manufacturer of children's games, introduced a new "toy" — a simple slotted piece of cardboard designed to hold a set of Lincoln pennies taken from circulation. Once the set was completed, it could be redeemed through a local dealer for a little more than its face value. From this humble beginning, millions of Americans learned about collecting coins.

Nevertheless, the serious coin collector continued to dominate the field until the 1960's when, with gold and silver values rising steadily, the government was forced to remove silver from coins. This called great public attention to value of bullion silver. What before only collectors had known, that there was money to be made in coins, was suddenly known by almost everyone in America. The day of *investing* in (as opposed to collecting) coins had dawned.

The transition from collecting to investing has been an involved process. There is now a clear delineation between the two, although it is sometimes difficult to see because there will always be an overlapping of interests and motives. The blending, however, has broadened the field considerably. Whereas at one time collecting and investing were limited almost exclusively to coins, today paper money, tokens, and, in fact, almost any kind of an item that might be considered numismatic is saved. Of course, the key factors of *supply*, *demand*, and *condition* still determine value.

Since the 1960's, and the advent of serious investing in coins, there have been three major boom periods: 1963-64, 1973-74, and 1978-80. Each boom period significantly altered the investment potential of coins, with the most recent period having the strongest positive effects. This period, 1978-80, owes its long-lasting effects to the following factors:

1. The incredible rise in bullion prices and subsequent input of profits from bullion dealers in the rare coin market.

2. Concurrent media coverage of the bullion and rare coin market.

3. The advent of sustained double-digit inflation, which caused investors to examine alternative investments.

4. The U.S. government approved the inclusion of rare coins in retirement plans, including IRS's and KEOGH's. (This latter privilege, which applied to self-directed plans, was taken away by the 1981 Economic Recovery Tax Act, but strong efforts are underway as of this writing to have it restored.)

5. The money managers who in the past had viewed coins as a fringe investment became aware of their value as a hedge against inflation.

During the 1978-80 boom period, top quality coins were heavily promoted. Because these gold, silver, and copper coins were truly rare, the market sustained high prices for a long period of time. By late 1979, tremendous increases in the price of bullion and the resultant influx of bullion-related money into the rare coin market caused prices to shoot up dramatically. In addition, high ticket rarities and proof gold coins shot up in value quickly as speculators clamored to buy any coin in top quality condition regardless of price. In just a few months, we saw proof $20 gold pieces increase in price from $25,000 to $85,000. Panama-Pacific sets rose in value from $45,000 to $225,000. Naturally the market could not sustain these prices (particularly since the collector had been left on the sidelines several months earlier). In April of 1980 and for several months thereafter, the market went through a readjustment period once again.

What makes this recent boom period particularly significant, however, is its long-lasting effects. The movement of so-called smart investment money into coins is now an established fact. Coins are no longer viewed as an exotic investment. In fact, it is not uncommon today to hear the most conservative of money managers advise their investors that as much as 5 percent of their assets should be placed into hard assets, in particular into rare coins.

ADVANTAGES OF RARE COINS AS AN INVESTMENT

1. *There is a limited supply and an increasing demand.* As more and more investors enter the field, they must draw from a supply that is both fixed and limited. Today we know that the government is no longer issuing coins of any significant intrinsic value (they're all base metal), and today no one owns a hoard of this type of material which could be dumped upon the market to change the supply/demand equation.

2. *Pricing is established daily on the basis of supply and demand.* Few outside the field realize that dealers are tied into coast-to-coast wire networks and that bid and ask prices on virtually every type of rare coin are broadcast constantly. Weekly industry publications provide similar data. The *Coin Dealer's Newsletter* gives weekly and monthly summaries of the U.S. coin market. *The Currency Market Review* presents monthly and quarterly bid-ask levels for U.S. currency. In addition, there are two national newspapers (one, *Coin World,* is often as thick as the New York Times) and two international magazines devoted exclusively to numismatics. The largest, *COINage*, runs full color photographs and is well over 100 pages each issue.

3. *Investors have learned to search for top quality.* The demand for top grade, scarce material is ever increasing.

4. *The rare-coin and currency market is undervalued compared with other areas of investment* — art, gems, and so on.

5. *The rare-coin and currency market is not subject to the whims of other markets.* If the price of gold declines, this does not mean that the price of rare coins (even those containing gold) will necessarily decline. Current events do not affect the price of coins and currency as they do the stock and bond market.

6. *Liquidity is assured by an international dealer network and numerous auctions.* A purchase agreement is no stronger than the dealer in question, but some have been in business for 40 years or more — far longer than many comparably reputable firms in other sectors of business and industry. Rare coin auctions occur almost every day, and millions of dollars worth of material is sold in unrestricted and unreserved sales.

7. *There is a standardized grading system to establish values.* The grading standards are outlined in the American Numismatic Association's book *Grading Standards for U.S. Coins.*

Of course, there are certain disadvantages in rare-coin and currency collecting. While these by no means preclude the field from consideration as an investment, they must be taken into account.

DRAWBACKS OF RARE COINS AS AN INVESTMENT

1. *As with all hard assets, rare coins and currency produce no income until sold.* A stock gives a dividend, a bond interest, real estate rent, but a rare coin gives only beauty, until it's sold. For an individual who is seeking a continual source of income from an investment, rare coins are not the answer.

2. *Rare coins require storage and insurance.* Unlike real estate, rare coins are easily transferable. The owner, therefore, must protect them. A bank safety deposit box is usually the safest repository for rare coins. There is, of course, the minimal cost of the box plus any insurance the investor might want to carry.

3. *Rare coins and currency require expert evaluation.* As with stamps and diamonds, the average person probably will not know a rare and valuable coin from a common piece. Therefore, in order to invest with assurance, the individual must establish a relationship with a reputable coin and currency dealer or with a financial planner with a similar relationship developed through thorough "due diligence." Then the investor must rely on the dealer's or adviser's judgment of the quality of materials purchased. Many dealers are very proud of their reputations. These reputable dealers will often guarantee the items they sell. Should there, say, be an error in grading, they will make up any loss the purchaser has suffered.

4. *Investing in rare coins and currency usually involves spending some time learning about the field.* Although many investors have made large amounts of money simply relying on the expertise of their dealer, most find that they need or want to learn more about rare coins and currency. The more knowledgeable the investor, the greater the chance that he or she will be able to buy wisely.

5. *Rare coins and currency investing is a long-term investment.* If you happen to buy at the beginning of a boom period, you might see your investment skyrocket in value. But, if you purchase during a slow period, it could take years before a substantial price increase occurs. During this time, as mentioned earlier, the investment will not produce any income. The investor, therefore, should only invest in rare coins and currency with money that he or she has available for the long term.

Investing in coins is a time-honored way to accumulate wealth. In the past it was limited to those few knowledgeable collectors who realized the potential. Today it is open to everyone.

$25,000 INVESTMENT PACKAGE

This investment package consists of

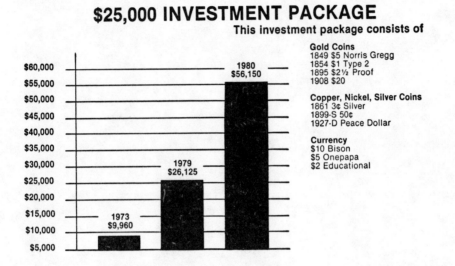

Gold Coins
1849 $5 Norris Gregg
1854 $1 Type 2
1895 $2½ Proof
1908 $20

Copper, Nickel, Silver Coins
1861 3¢ Silver
1899-S 50¢
1927-D Peace Dollar

Currency
$10 Bison
$5 Onepapa
$2 Educational

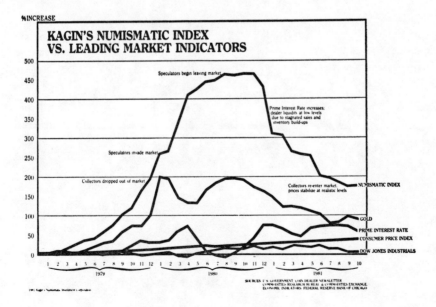

CHAPTER TWENTY EIGHT

STAMP INVESTMENTS

Chances are every time you mail a letter, you lick a stamp and without a second thought, stick it on an envelope and drop the envelope into the nearest mailbox. Stamps, which are common-place items to most of us, are also a highly successful investment medium. During the 1970's, stamps (along with other collectibles) were looked at with new interest by investors who saw in this popular hobby a potential for rapid growth, a hedge against inflation, and a tax shelter for the high-income taxpayer.

When you buy a first-class stamp, you are paying for the privilege of having the postal service deliver your mail. This pay-for-mail process dates back a long, long time. And while today's common stamp probably won't be worth very much (unless it is extremely unique), those stamps which were issued long ago may have become very valuable. For example, a one-cent British Guiana stamp issued over a hundred years ago was sold in 1980 for a stupendous price of $935,000.

That's for a one-cent stamp! Who would pay so much for a tiny, fragile piece of paper? The answer is the key to the whole price appreciation of stamps — the collector. Collectors are people who have been bitten by the stamp bug. For them, acquiring a particular stamp or a series of stamps is a hobby. How many collectors are there? No one knows for sure. But most guess that there are more collectors of stamps than collectors of anything else. There are, for example, about a million elementary school students who are members of the Benjamin Franklin stamp clubs organized by the U.S. Postal Service. It is probably safe to say that there are millions upon millions of stamp collectors in the world. And when the figures get that high, what does it matter what the actual number is?

Stamp collectors look for a variety of things in their stamp purchases. Some are collecting for the stamp's design. They may collect only those stamps with planes or those with buildings. Other collectors may want only stamps issued in the United States or in Germany, or only during certain periods of history.

With so many government postal services issuing stamps daily, collectors of modern-day issues have little trouble expanding their collections. But eventually nearly all serious collectors want to expand their horizons as well. They may want to collect stamps that were issued 10, 20, or even 100 years ago. There's the rub. The supply of stamps issued a hundred years ago is very small. In some cases, it may only be a handful. The large number of collectors competing for the very few old stamps is the basis of upward stamp prices. Scarcity, or, as it is more commonly called, rarity, is what makes a stamp expensive.

Now enter the investor. The investor may or may not be a collector; chances are he isn't. For the investor, stamps are seen as an avenue for making a profit, not as a hobby. The investor looks to the eventual resale value of the stamps, while the true collector usually does not even consider selling. While the collector is the foundation on which stamp investing is built, it is the investor who builds on this foundation by adding to the competition for rare stamps. The combination of investor and collector competing in the marketplace drives the price of stamps constantly upward.

It is important to note that the base of collectors is ever expanding. At the same time, the number of investors entering into the field is also growing. The net result is that the prices of stamps are higher than ever. If we look at the performance table for the period between 1925 and 1980 — 55 years — we can compare the performance record of stamps with that of London gold prices or the Dow Jones average. Even a casual glance at this chart indicates that selected stamps have outperformed inflation, gold, and the Dow Jones by tens of thousands of percent. Equally remarkable, stamps show an incredible performance even for the short term.

PERFORMANCE TABLE: 1925-1980
Selected U.S. Stamp Issues vs. Dow Jones Industrial Average
London Gold Price & Cost of Living Index (CPI)

Scott Cat. No.	U.S. Stamp Issue	1925	1980	Approximate Percent Increase
1-2	1847 First Issues (set)	$ 180.00	$ 18,000.00	10.000%
230-45	1893 Columbian Expo (set)	45.33	11,169.00	24.000
285-93	1898 Trans-Miss. (set)	23.83	4,827.00	20.000
C 3a	1918 24¢ Biplane (invert)	750.00	115,000.00	15.2000
	TOTAL	$1,001.29	$149,438.00	14.800%
	Comparative Indices			
	Gold Price (London)	$ 20.67	$ 512.00	2.300%
	DJIA	159.40	838.74	425
	Cost of Living (CPI)	52.50	230.00	338

WHICH STAMPS SHOULD I BUY?

Unless you're a collector, choosing stamps to buy should be done with the assistance of a professional. There's a lot to know about stamps besides price and rarity. You need to know the condition of the specimen, and you need to be able to identify stamps that have been counterfeited or doctored.

While most stamp investors usually build their portfolio with the aid of an expert, other alternatives for the beginning investor do exist. Limited partnerships in stamp purchases are available; the general partner or stamp professional provides the guidance necessary to choose the successful investment. In any case, there are several guidelines that even a newcomer can understand and practice.

Purchase Stamps That Have a Proven History

The wise investor will purchase stamps that have histories that are easy to trace. Stamps often have pedigrees. In many instances it is possible to find out where a stamp was issued and who the collectors have been that owned it. Through research, it is sometimes possible to trace ownership back many decades. With a proven history, a stamp's true price appreciation can be determined.

Buy Stamps That Are Truly Finite in Number

As noted earlier, the rarity of a stamp is critical to its monetary value. Therefore, the serious stamp investor will not waste time and money buying modern-day issues. Instead, serious consideration should be given to stamps issued before the 1900's.

217

Since U.S. stamp issues are never reprinted, it is possible to determine the age of any American stamp. If we know the quantity of the issue, we can make an educated guess about how many have been used and how few remain for collecting and selling.

Choose Popular Material

A stamp can be very rare, but if it is not in demand the price may not be high. In addition to rarity, which is the supply side of the equation, there has to be popularity, the demand side of the equation, for a stamp to be highly valued. Particularly popular stamps have included the Columbian's, the Trans Misses, the Washington-Franklin series, Scott's numbers 1 and 2 (Scott makes a stamp guide that lists stamps by number), and the Graf Zepplin series.

The smart stamp investor will rely on a trusted professional to know what's popular and what isn't. Because of the professional's constant contact with the market, he knows what's selling and what isn't.

Although stamps do offer a potentially substantial return, there are some less than perfect aspects associated with stamp collecting that should be considered before making an investment in this area.

WHAT ARE THE DRAWBACKS?

Stamps Do Not Produce Income

Stamps should only be purchased as part of a diversified financial portfolio. Stamps are an investment that should be made after other needs are satisfied. Do you have enough cash in the bank to handle any emergencies that might arise? Do you have substantial life and health insurance? Do you already own a portfolio of stocks and bonds that offer liquidity in case you should need additional cash? If you can answer yes to all of these questions, then you can consider a stamp investment portfolio.

When you buy stamps, you will not receive monthly, quarterly, or annual income. You buy the stamps and then hold them. They do nothing for you financially until you sell them. This means, therefore, that only disposable income should be used for purchasing stamps. No more than 10 percent of your investment portfolio should be in stamps if you want a balanced investment package.

Be Prepared To Wait

Unless you happen to make a stamp purchase just before an unexpected move in the market, you must be prepared to wait for a return on your stamps. The minimum waiting period is three to five years. It's important to understand that stamps are quite different from investments such as stocks or bonds. For example, the stock investor can watch his stocks, and if he is quick, he can buy low and sell high on a very short-term basis. This is more difficult with stamps. In the recent past, quality material has seen some very strong price advances. But as a general rule, this flurry of action does not last. To receive a profit, the investor has to have the patience to wait several years.

Stamps Are Only Paper

It is important to understand that stamps are fragile. They are subject to damage from water, humidity, and fire. Stamps should be stored in a bank vault and insured. (Most people think that their banks carry insurance for the vault. While many do, not all offer enough insurance in case of damage or fire.)

LIQUIDITY

We've already seen that stamps are not liquid. Buy they are not illiquid either. While you cannot and should not try to sell your stamps as quickly as you might sell your stocks, that does not mean that they cannot be sold. If you do need to cash in your stamps, there are auction houses and dealers who will handle the sales for you.

DIVERSIFY FOR PROFIT AND SAFETY

If you have $10,000, should you buy a single stamp or many? With $10,000, you should be able to buy 10 to 50 investment quality stamps. Each stamp should have both collector popularity and a history of strong demand. Diversification increases the probability that a particular stamp in your collection might shoot up in value. In any case, you are not stuck with just one stamp that may not go up in price at all.

Overall, stamps are not that expensive. If you have ever tried to buy antiques, rare coins, or paintings, you can appreciate the fact that with only $10,000 you can buy a good number of stamps.

BARGAINS

There simply are no bargains in stamps. If you find someone offering you a bargain, watch out! Valuable stamps conform to the age-old adage, "You get what you pay for."

CONDITION AND QUALITY

Be on the lookout for stamps with detracting features that may influence the selling price. Many features, including glue or gum on the back, the vibrance of the color, and whether the stamp has been hinged, contribute to the value of stamps. If you are not an expert, find one that you can rely on to tell you the quality of the stamp. What may look perfectly good to you may be seriously flawed when viewed by the discriminating expert.

STAMPS AS A TAX SHELTER

As you've seen, stamps can be immensely profitable. By diversifying, using a deposit box with insurance, relying on an expert, and being aware of the stamp market, your chances for earning profits are greatly increased and your risks substantially minimized.

What we haven't discussed yet is the tax advantage in stamp investing. There is no tax credit on stamp purchases, and there is no depreciation or depletion allowance. Rather, the tax advantage to be obtained from stamps comes entirely from leveraging. And leveraging is only for the investor who is in the 50 percent tax bracket.

The investor borrows money using the stamps (or some other item) as collateral. If the investor has $50,000 in cash and borrows an additional $50,000, the total $100,000 can be used to purchase stamps, which are then held for three years. During the three years, the investor pays interest on the $50,000 borrowed. With an interest rate of 20 percent, the investor pays $10,000 a year in interest on the loan ($30,000 over the three years).

This $30,000 amounts to a write-off for the investor. At the end of three years, the investor sells the stamps. If they sold for $150,000 (not unreasonable in light of past performance), the investor has the original $50,000 back, enough money to pay off the loan ($50,000), and $50,000 profit.

But look what happened from a tax viewpoint. The interest the investor was deducting each year ($30,000 total) helped reduce his ordinary income. The $50,000 the investor gets back now is in the form of a capital gain since the stamps were held for more than one year.

220

Along the way, the investor converted the $30,000 he paid in interest, into $30,000 in capital gain — a substantial savings. In addition, there has been a $20,000 profit made on the original investment.

$50,000		Capital invested
$50,000		Capital borrowed
$100,000		Value of stamps purchased
	$150,000	Sales price
	$100,000	Less purchase price
	$50,000	Profit
	$30,000	Less interest paid on capital
	$20,000	Return on original capital

Stamps are classified as a high-risk tax shelter because they depend on appreciation for the investor to come out on top. Nevertheless, should appreciation be good over the period of time involved, both a substantial profit and a healthy shelter (deferring ordinary income to capital gains) can be achieved.

CHAPTER TWENTY NINE

THE EXOTICS: MOVIES, ART, RECORDS

There was a time a few years ago that investors poured millions of dollars into the so-called exotic investments. Limited partnerships were started every day to sponsor a record or a movie or even a piece of art. This is no longer the case. Today there is relatively little actual investment in these fields, yet investors still ask me about the exotics. This chapter answers many of the questions I am asked.

NON-RECOURSE PAPER

Before the 1976 Tax Reform Act it was possible to invest in exotics (among other things) using non-recourse paper. These were loans that the borrowers did not have to sign personally and, in the event of loss, did not have to repay.

Non-recourse paper was obviously a great advantage in creating tax shelters. Investors could participate in limited partnerships and leverage their positions 8 or 9 to 1, thereby increasing the write-offs enormously. Write-offs of 400 percent in the first year were not uncommon in the exotics.

Because the money borrowed was not the personal responsibility of the investor, if things went bad the investor simply walked away and let the lender worry about the loss. The investor had the write-off, which at 400 percent in a 50 percent tax bracket meant a dollar in profit for each dollar invested, just on the basis of the shelter!

In 1976 the government disallowed non-recourse loans (except in real estate), and that was the end of most of the exotics as viable investments. Since that time the volume of investment in exotics has plummeted to perhaps only 1 percent of 1976 levels. The reason for the decline in exotic investments is high risk. There is, of course, the possibility of high rewards—but the risk scares most investors away.

MOVIE PRODUCTION SERVICE

We have all heard of movies that made millions of dolars. *Star War, Raiders of the Lost Ark, Superman I* and *II*, were all blockbusters in terms of profit.

But in talking with industry specialists it became abundantly clear that for each *Star Wars* or *Superman*, there are perhaps a hundred other movies that are box-office losses. Those are the movies that never return the initial investment. In some cases, they barely make back the costs of distribution, which can mean that the investors who initially financed the production showed a total loss. The odds do not favor success here. Yet each year there is a spate of new movies.

The movie studios and the distributors do take substantial losses. But the profits from a success like *Star Wars* or *Raiders* can support them through a hundred losses. Since they are the actual originators of the films, they are in a position to average out the good with the bad and, overall, make a profit. (Sometimes they don't; we have seen many studios fold over the years.)

The individual investor is not usually in this position. For the American investor in an American movie, it's hard times. Going into a limited partnership to create a movie means bucking the tide. It was one thing when potential loss could be overlooked because most of the money had been borrowed via non-recourse paper. But today when an investor borrows it may all be recourse paper. That means if there's a loss, the investor is still liable for repayment of the loan.

As indicated in previous chapters, most investors want low-risk investments with high return. Usually these two demands do not go together. Most investors are happy to preserve their capital and obtain some tax benefits. In other words, they want their money back and want to make a few dollars too. Generally in a low-risk investment, your return will be modest—you are not going to make a fortune. Let's examine one interesting type of investment that purports to answer these needs.

MOVIE DISTRIBUTION

Major movie studios are mostly in the distribution business. But in order to provide enough product (films) for distribution, they were forced to go into the production business. Production can be very risky. Production costs vary, and much of what can go wrong often does!

When the film is completed, the studio is anxious to recoup its production investment. It can take on the risk of distribution, hoping to pay back costs and start producing at a profit. Or the studio can sell the distribution rights (or part of the rights) to an outside party to recoup the investment, and take a percentage of distribution as its profit.

THE "IDEAL" MOVIE INVESTMENT

Let's examine a so-called low-risk, modest return, good tax shelter movie investment. This investment will acquire the rights and distribution, title, and every interest unto, of a completed film product. This would include worldwide distribution, TV rights, in-flight planes, cable, network, pay TV, satellite, video cassettes and discs, publishing, merchandising (dolls, T-shirts, etc.), sound trade and other so-called non-theatrical rights. According to industry claims, income from the above all-media sources could equal 70 to 120 percent of the money invested. The investor could make back the investment from these rights alone, even if the movie were never shown in a theatre.

Think of this movie product as a house (or any other real estate you may acquire). It belongs to you or your partnership and you may make use of this property any way you wish.

One of the tax advantages of the movie over real estate is its depreciation schedule. The IRS allows a 5-year depreciation write-off as the projected life of the movie property. This compares to the current 15-year depreciation schedule for real estate. Therefore, in comparison to real estate, the investor receives three times the depreciation tax benefits. In addition, a full 10 percent Investment Tax Credit (ITC) is allowed as a deduction, assuming 80 percent of the movie was produced in the United States.

OTHER TAX BENEFITS

As shown above, tax benefits come from depreciation write-offs and investment tax credits. In addition, during the first year advertising and promotional costs are expensed and the investor will incur interest expense on notes. Taken together, these deductions can equal up to five times the initial cash investment and provide the investor a high tax deduction to apply against other income.

Recently I was contacted by a syndicator offering a year-end film distribution investment. The partnership he represented had acquired the distribution rights to two extremely popular films.

The total amount necessary to release these films was over $20 million. A look at how such a syndication would work out will illustrate movie investments in general.

Cash	$ 25,000
Letter of credit (2)	125,000
Recourse note	525,000
At risk	$675,000

First Year Write-Off:
Investment Tax Credit (ITC)
Depreciation $125,000
Expenses

or a total first-year write-off of 5 to 1 of cash invested.

There is an additional $100,000 write-off in the second year due to depreciation, costs, and interest on amounts borrowed using letters of credit as collateral. The total write-off over four years should be over $350,000. However, should the movie be an immediate success, the cash flow starts earlier, less borrowing is needed and write-off will be reduced.

The investor, of course, is liable on both the letters of credit and the huge recourse notes. Because it is expected that the films would be successful, the assumption is that the revenue from distribution will pay for these costs. Initially the investors will receive 30 percent of the gross profits from the film distribution and less after they've gotten back all their money for an average of 14 percent of gross distributions. You can't go running to the bank with these profits, however, since these revenues will be used to pay off the notes.

While the tax incentives are high, it is important to consider the partnership from an economic viewpoint. One optimistic projection is a profit of $10,000 to $15,000 over a five-year period, not considering tax benefits. This converts to a rate of return somewhere between 7.2 and 10 percent on an annual basis. Considering that these are blockbuster films, that's not much of a return!

Additionally, the profit is based on *gross* returns. That means that the minute the first person walks into the theatre the partnership begins receiving money. Most movie partnerships are based on *net* return. That means that there is no profit until all costs have been paid. On net distributions usually your great grandchildren will die before any payment is received!

ADVERTISING PARTNERSHIPS

The third type of investment involving the movie industry is called an advertising partnership. All monies are used to promote a film. The production of an average film costs approximately $8 million. Advertising and promotion should not exceed 50 percent of the cost of production. Usually 15 to 20 percent of the gross receipts are earned by the partnership until all investment is returned. After full cash recovery, this percentage drops to between 10 and 12 percent. There are no recourse notes to sign. There is no film property to depreciate. Therefore, without high leverage and without depreciation, this tax shelter offers write-off to a maximum of 1 to 1. Your liability and your tax write-off is limited to the amount of your investment.

OTHER EXOTICS

There is one additional reason that most investors have stayed out of the exotics: "shams," or false deals.

Let's consider records. In the past investors have been offered the rights to a particular recording in exchange for putting up the money for production and distribution. Once the record sold, they would be entitled to a share of the profit.

But what is the value of the rights to a record? If we're dealing with real estate, we can get an independent appraisal. If we're dealing with leasing, we can find the retail value of a truck or a computer. If we're in cattle, we know what beef is selling for on the hoof per pound. But how do we know what the rights to a record may be worth? It's an unproven commodity and the rights are valued basically by guesswork.

There are informed people in the industry who can estimate fairly accurately the value of a recording artists's name and sound on a recording. The trouble is that these informed people were not the ones offering syndications. Someone else, either knowingly or through ignorance, was offering limited partnerships. A recording worth $5000 might have been offered to the public for $100,000. Who knows the difference? Generally investors had little or no idea of the true value and the syndicator only a vague idea. It is very, very hard to know the true value of the rights until *after* distribution and marketing, when the buying public has had a chance to make its feelings known.

While the profit potential could be enormous—a record purchased for $100,000 might make millions—too often they make nothing.

ART

In the past, syndications have been granted to promote the art of famous painters. Perhaps the painter would do a serigraph or a limited-edition lithograph and the partnership would underwrite the costs.

Here, with a well-known painter, the risk was considerably lessened. The name of the artist was sure to sell at least a minimal number of prints. The investors could roughly calculate the minimum that could be sold and arrive at some sort of break-even. If things went well they would sell thousands, but even if they didn't go well they would probably break even.

The problem is that there aren't many living painters whose names are known well enough to guarantee sales. Consequently, syndications have been put together featuring painters of lesser renown. The paintings had to carry the entire burden of sales just like movies or records. If they were well-distributed and if the public liked them, sales and profits could be high. Usually this did not happen and the investors lost a sizeable portion of cash invested.

If you are an expert in a particular field—movies, art or records—then you will know enough to invest on your own. But if you are a person on the outside looking for a good tax shelter and a good profit potential, my feeling is that the risks here are too high to justify an investment.

ESTATE PLANNING

Estate planning is essentially a very simple concept. It involves protecting (and possibly increasing) the assets you hold today for the people who will inherit them tomorrow. If estate planning were to be broken down into stages, then, it would be broken down according to the two activities implicit in the above definition. One involves planning for the disposition of your estate upon death. The other involves the protection of your estate while you're alive.

ESTATE PLANNING FOR DEATH

Most people think of estate planning as involving the disposal of assets upon death. They are concerned with reducing or legally avoiding the federal estate taxes which may be triggered at that time. It is important here to discriminate between two terms — *estate tax* and *inheritance tax*.

The federal government taxes the estate of a deceased person. Many individual states, however, place an additional tax on the inheritors. This is an inheritance tax. Inheritance tax and estate tax are different.

In California, a person who dies will have his or her entire estate taxed by the federal government (after certain exclusions). However, the person who inherits through a bequest will have only a portion of the inheritance taxed.

The amount of inheritance tax that must be paid in California is in direct proportion to the relationship the deceased bore to the inheritor. For example, a minor child will have a very large portion of his inheritance exempted. An adult child will have less exempted. A mother, father, brother, or sister will have even less. And a friend will only a few hundred dollars exempted.

Our purpose is not to examine the inheritance laws of the various states. For that, you will need to consult a local attorney. Rather, I'm going to give an overview of estate planning with regard to federal taxation.

DO YOU NEED TO WORRY ABOUT ESTATE TAXATION?

It all depends on the size of your estate. Exemptions are given to estates. If your estate happens to be below the exemption, then you don't have to worry about estate taxation.

In the past the equivalent exemption was $175,625. The 1981 Economic Recovery Tax Act increased the exemption equivalent which will reach $600,000 by 1987. Here's the new exemption schedule.

Year	Amount of Credit	Exemption Equivalent
1981	$ 47,000	$175,625
1982	62,800	225,000
1983	79,300	275,000
1984	96,300	325,000
1985	121,800	400,000
1986	155,800	500,000
1987 and later	192,800	600,000

As can be seen, with the exemption going up significantly, your estate may not be taxed at all. If you think, however, that your estate will be large enough to be taxed, you should consult an attorney or some other expert in the field. (Each individual's situation is unique). The material we're going to look at in this chapter is, by its very essence, general in nature. It is designed to give only an overview of estate planning, not specific guidelines.

There are essentially two ways to transfer assets to our inheritors that will reduce estate tax.

GIFTS

The first method is outright gifts. These are made during the taxpayer's life. Today, the exclusion on these gifts is $10,000. (With gift splitting by spouses, it is increased to $20,000.) The word "exclusion" here means the amount that may be given without having to pay gift tax. In addition to the $10,000 just mentioned, a taxpayer may now also give gifts for medical expenses or for school tuition without gift tax consequences.

TRUSTS

The second method is the trust. A trust is simply an arrangement whereby the title to real or personal property is transferred from the taxpayer to a trustee who holds it to benefit a third party, called the beneficiary. (In certain trusts the taxpayer/creator might also be the beneficiary.) A trust can be set up upon death (a testamentary trust) or while the grantor is still living. There are many advantges in the latter case, which we'll discuss shortly.

In the past, one of the most common trusts was the "split estate." In it the spouse who died first had his or her funds put into a trust for the ultimate benefit of the children. However, the income from the trust went to the surviving spouse. The advantages of the split estate trust was that there was only one estate tax to pay, upon the death of the first spouse. Without the trust, the estate would have been taxed twice — once upon the death of the first spouse and again upon the death of the survivor.

The 1981 Economic Recovery Tax Act changed all this. The ERTA established an *unlimited marital estate tax deduction*. The transfer of the decedent's portion of the couple's community property to the surviving spouse qualifies for this deduction. Therefore, the earlier trusts set up to avoid double taxation are largely unnecessary today. There is still, however, the need for estate planning when it comes to "stepped-up basis" for community property versus joint tenancy.

Community Property

I have seen many books suggest that the way to avoid probate and to handle estate planning is to hold everything in joint tenancy, which means that the surviving joint tenant automatically inherits upon the death of the other. Although you should consult an attorney about your own situation, I can see cases in which joint tenancy can be a disadvantage, particularly in community property states (Arizona, California, Idaho, Louisiana, Nevada, New Mexico, Texas, and Washington).

The reasoning is as follows. Let's say you own a home that you bought for $50,000 years ago and is today worth $250,000. Your basis in the home is $50,000; your potential gain is $200,000. Now, let's say that you want to sell. On what part of the sales are you going to have to pay taxes? If you answered on the $200,000 gain, you are correct. The entire $200,000 will be taxable.

Now, let's say that a couple owns this house as joint tenants. Upon death, the deceased's interests automatically go to the surviving spouse. At this point, the survivor is automatically assigned a "stepped-up basis" for that half of the property. That means that the basis is no longer tied to the property's original purchase price, but to its current value. What does that mean when the surviving joint tenant goes to sell the house?

Remember the current market value of the house is $250,000. Half of $250,000 is $125,000. This survivor now owns two halves of the same house: the deceased's half with a basis of $125,000 and his or her own half with the old basis of $25,000 (half of the original purchase price). The total basis is $150,000. If the house were now to be sold, the survivor would have to pay taxes on the difference between the basis and sale price.

$250,000	Sale price
150,000	New basis
$100,000	Taxable gain

But, now let's say that the couple owned the property not as joint tenants but as "community property." On the death of either spouse, the property transfers to the remaining spouse and the entire property gets a stepped-up basis.

$250,000	Market value
250,000	New basis
—0—	Taxable gain

In community property, either spouse owns the entire house. Therefore, when either spouse dies, the entire house qualifies for the stepped-up basis.

It's easy to see why holding property as community property instead of as joint tenants works better for some individuals in community property states.

ESTATE PLANNING FOR LIFE

Estate planning for life essentially means setting up a variety of trusts to hold your property (or gifting it). Usually it means naming your children as beneficiaries. The advantage is that once the property is in the trust, it no longer is yours, and it is no longer taxed at your ordinary income rate.

Short-Term Trust

The short-term or Clifford trust must be funded for at least 10 years and a day. The advantage of this trust is that when it ends, the property reverts back to the grantor, the person who set it up initially. A further advantage is that the income produced by the assets in the trust is not taxed at your own presumably higher rate. If minor children, for example, are named as beneficiaries, the income is taxed at the children's rate. These short-term trusts are very helpful in transferring assets out of a high tax bracket into a lower one. There are some disadvantages. The principal one is that once started, the 10-year clock does not stop. If additional funds or property are added to the trust, it starts the 10-year clock all over again. The trust ends 10 years from the time the last property was added.

Charitable Remainder Trust

In this trust, the income from property placed within it can go back to either the creator of the trust or to designated beneficiaries. When the beneficiary dies, however, the property in the trust is turned over to a charity, which is usually already named. This trust allows the creator to get both an income and a charity deduction. Additionally, the estate that is left after the beneficiary dies gets an additional charitable deduction.

Totten Trust

This is the kind of trust account that people use all the time at their bank or savings and loan. Typically a parent opens an account and names a child as the beneficiary with the parent as trustee. The trustee can make deposits or withdrawals at will. Since the trustee has such broad powers, the account is considered the property of the trustee for income tax purposes. Therefore, it has no particular tax benefits.

Spendthrift Trust

This is a trust designed for an individual who for one reason or another may not be capable of handling his own money. It is usually set up so that the beneficiary receives income from the trust, but cannot touch its assets. The beneficiary, therefore, can't waste the money or use the assets as collateral. Under a spendthrift trust, the creditors of the beneficiaries have no claim on the assets until they are actually passed on to the beneficiary.

Sprinkling Trust

Here the trustee is granted total discretion. The trustee can decide how to distribute the assets and income to the beneficiaries — how much and over what period of time.

Revocable Versus Irrevocable

Trusts can be either revocable, meaning they can be taken back by the grantor, or they can be irrevocable, in which case they can't be taken back.

The revocable trust has no particular tax savings to it. The irrevocable trust has strong tax consequences. If you set one up, with someone else as the trustee, you do not have to pay taxes on it. (It's no longer, in fact, your money.) The money is taxed separately.

These, then, are some of the more common trusts that people set up to preserve their estates. As I noted at the beginning, the establishment of a trust is only one part of estate planning, which in itself is one part of overall financial planning. It does not make sense to run out and establish a trust for yourself until you have established and studied your long-term financial goals. Further, you should not attempt to do your own estate planning unless you are a professional. There are many in's and out's that must be taken into account, and a great deal of fine print that must be read. A good attorney is your best bet in estate planning.

CHAPTER THIRTY ONE

CONCLUSION:
FINDING YOUR INVESTMENT

Americans enjoy an unparalleled freedom to select their own investments, but almost every investment sold in this country today requires some degree of suitability. Brokers who sell stocks or bonds are required to follow a "know your customer" rule, which prevents them from selling an aggressive go-go stock to a little old lady who wants only to preserve her capital. Before a reputable insurance agent recommends a $100,000 policy, he must first be certain that the buyer needs and can afford that amount of coverage. Banks and finance companies require information on income and credit before making consumer loans. Real estate brokers once sold dreams to newlyweds. Now, in an era when few newlyweds can afford homes, brokers must consider the home-seeker's ability to obtain and pay off a mortgage.

Financial planners who work with many types of investments see a common thread of suitability tying together most financial services. Yet, in terms of delicate matchmaking between people and investments, tax shelters are in a class by themselves.

It is not just a matter of projecting budgets, tax liabilities, and rates of return. Good accountants can do that. Recommending a tax-sheltered investment requires more than an intimate knowledge of tax laws and regulations. Not all tax lawyers who can quote verbatim from the tax code have the makings of a shelter adviser.

In addition to knowledge of numbers and the current tax law, tax-shelter advisers need interviewing skills, intuition, and the imagination to determine how investors will function under duress or loss. They must be able to dig below the surface of sales talk and automatic responses to discern the real character and motives of both clients and promoters. They must have the business skills to survive in a volatile industry, in which one mistake

235

can wipe out the results of a dozen successes. Finally, they must have a clear perception of the direction to which the economy and the tax law will move in the next decade because many shelters are essentially frozen for that long or longer.

It is not a coincidence that many of the most active tax-shelter advisers are also full-service financial planners. If you know enough about clients to keep recommending shelters successfully year after year, you should also be able to fill needs for insurance, equities, and income-producing investments.

A financial planner is also familiar with the offering circular or prospectus of the investment. Every prospectus for a publicly resistered shelter contains a section on suitability, often titled "Who Should Invest." (For the sake of accuracy, it should be titled "Who Should Not Invest".) Usually, but not always, this section is located on the first few pages of the prospectus. "Who Should Invest" determines who should bother reading the rest of the prospectus.

To invest in a public real estate program, the law requires the investor to have a net worth of $20,000 and annual gross income of at least $20,000, or a net worth of at least $75,000. For oil and gas drilling programs, the requirement is a net worth of $225,000, or a net worth of $60,000 combined with a taxable income of $60,000. (Net worth, for these purposes, excludes personal possessions such as home, car and furniture.) I can tell you from long experience in tax shelters that there is little correlation between these requirements and successful shelter investing.

With the help of experience and other financial planners, I have developed my own tests for suitability, which fall into two groups — financial and human. Of the two, the latter is the more important to me, because the true test of compatibility between investors and shelters is the investor's expectations. Rarely are those expectations purely financial.

Your success on the rest of your journey into the realm of shelters will depend upon your answers to the following questions. While it is hard to quantify something as complex as an individual's investment temperament, count your yes answers to the questions. Any yes should cause you to think twice about certain types of shelters, principally those with high risks, high write-offs, or long-term commitments. Three or more yes answers, and you might want to ask yourself if shelters are right for you.

First, let's look at the kinds of human questions I ask my clients.

1. *Do you lie awake nights thinking about your investments?* I call this the sleep test. "If an investment interferes with your

sleep," I tell clients, "don't get into bed with it." Tax shelters cause more sleepless nights than any other investment. If you toss and turn with commodities or options, you can at least call your broker in the morning and sell your investment. Not so with most shelters.

I have learned that it does not help my business to recommend shelters for worryworts. I tell them, "If the investment is going to drive you crazy, then you will probably drive me crazy." We have plenty of other investment choices for these people.

2. *Is your marriage about to go bust?* Illiquid investments do not mix well in domestic dissolutions. In California, we have experienced our share of divorces among clients. The fact that ours is a community property state does not help in the division of assets.

3. *Does the thought of a tax audit give you the cold chills?* Some people have an irrational fear of being audited, and it's a fact that tax shelters increase the possibility of being selected in the IRS's annual "audit lottery." Tax shelters do give taxpayers a higher profile. For example, some shelter programs do not distribute their K-1 forms, the declaration of tax information, until near or after the April 15 filing deadline. It is a simple matter for the taxpayer to file for an extension in these cases, but an extension request can sometimes increase the probability of audit.

4. *Does your attitude toward investments vary greatly over a short period of time?* I call this the Dr. Jeckyl and Mr. Hyde syndrome. One month a person can't wait to get into a shelter. The next month he can't wait to get out. I once had a salesman who came to me seeking a shelter. He had earned a lot money, more than $100,000 that year, and didn't realize the tax impact until December. He had never made an investment in his life other than his own home, and he insisted that I help him cut his taxes with a shelter.

Because of his nervous nature, I advised him to wait until January, at which time we would calmly begin planning his taxes for the following year. When we came to that point, his attitude changed totally. He read the prospectus and was shocked that the president of the company sponsoring the shelter earned $250,000 a year. Nobody should earn that much, he believed, and he refused to invest in the shelter. Had I helped him with a shelter in December, I would have had trouble on my hands in January.

5. *Might your income or tax bracket change dramatically in the next few years?* A tax shelter is rarely a one-time commitment. It is not unheard of for shelters to solicit additional contributions from limited partners after the first year. Oil and gas partnerships have

what is called "rights of presentation" and conversion offers, which are ways to increase participation or swap partnership units for other interests. These can result in additional contributions or revised tax benefits.

Not long ago, a cattle-breeding program in which our clients invested ran into a cash shortage. Our investors were given a choice of accepting a loss or buying the cattle individually (with the cattleman continuing to feed and manage the herd). The second choice was clearly the best, but some of our investors who had just retired were not in a position to select the best option.

6. *Are you so surrounded by protective accountants, attorneys, or relatives that you will not be able to implement the shelter program recommended by your advisor/broker?* This can be a difficult question to answer, because the line between a helpful second opinion and interference is a fine one. Like most good financial planners, I will not make tax-shelter recommendations unless I am in a position to implement them and monitor the investments.

7. *Are you bothered by paperwork and reports about your investments?* Owning tax shelters is not as easy as clipping coupons on bonds. Reports, tax information, income distributions, and other paperwork does demand some attention and discipline. I have one woman client who owns nearly 20 tax shelters and was so bombarded with paperwork that she no longer knew what she owned. I helped her set up a color-coded series of file envelopes and told her not to even open the reports when they arrived. At the end of the year, we sort out the important material, and throw the rest away. The paperwork burden is not really much greater than with other investments, but the investor may feel that it is.

The following suitability questions pertain to finances and taxes.

8. *Will your tax-shelter investment put a squeeze on your budget for living expenses?* Even if the tax savings are substantial, people who dip.into liquid cash reserves to finance shelters are asking for trouble. If, for some reason, your tax deductions are not allowed by the IRS, will you have enough cash to pay extra taxes? What if an unexpected need for cash arises? I always try to convince my clients to establish a comfortable cushion of reserves, in money market funds or liquid securities, before investing in tax shelters.

9. *In the year that you are sheltering, do you have either a long-term capital gain of more than $100,000 or abnormally large itemized deductions?* These two factors can trigger the Alternative

Minimum Tax, which became part of the tax code in 1978. If you are forced to calculate your taxes using this method, much of the write-off value of shelters could be lost.

10. *If you have a large estate, do you have sufficient liquidity in the estate to meet potential estate taxes?* Illiquid shelters can be a problem for estates that need to raise cash instantly. In some cases, before recommending shelters for wealthy people, we have had to do estate planning and recommend additional life insurance coverage or more liquid investments.

These questions should have given you more insight not only into shelters, but also into yourself as an investor. If you answered yes to several questions, it may not mean you should never invest in shelters. It may simply mean that you should tend to other investment priorities first.

If all of your answers were no, on the other hand, it may mean that you are ready to plunge ahead into a tax-sheltered investment. But which one? We've covered nearly a dozen in this book. Some may be suitable for you, others may not. How do you decide which is the right investment for your particular needs? To help you decide I include another group of questions. These will go a long way toward helping you determine which investment is correct for you.

CHOOSING THE RIGHT INVESTMENT

1. *Have you clearly identified your financial objectives?* In the first chapter of this book, I talked about financial objectives. A list of possible objectives was given along with suggestions on how to determine your own personal objectives. Now you must make the decision. Is your goal education for your children, more income right now, retirement, greater tax advantages, or some other? You can't begin to invest until you have a clear idea of your financial objective.

2. *Does the investment you're currently looking at meet your financial objectives?* While this may seem obvious, it's truly remarkable how many times we all slip up. Suddenly we see an investment that seems to have all kinds of potential. Yet, the potential is in a direction we don't want to go. Should we take it? Perhaps not. For example, let's say that you're retired. You have a fixed income and are in a relatively low tax bracket. Your financial objective may be "income now." But you find that you can get into a great "deferred tax shelter." Should you go for it? If there's

no income now, it probably would be a mismatch for you. Sometimes it's far better to let those so-called great deals pass by than to get involved in something that you really don't want or need.

3. *Have you thoroughly analyzed the potential return on the investment you're considering?* If you think about it for a moment, there are really only three ways to get a return from an investment.

Income. This comes from interest, rents, royalties, dividends, and so forth. It can be of two varieties. One variety is *tax free* or *tax deferred*. Tax-deferred income might come, for example, from real estate, where the property is actually producing a positive cash flow while showing a loss on paper. The advantage of this type of income is that you do not have to add it to your current taxable income.

The second variety is *taxable income.* It must be added to your current income.

The difference between the two is great. In the 50 percent tax bracket, for example, one dollar of the "tax-free" income is worth two dollars of the taxable income.

Tax Write-off. This return is in the form of a tax deduction. For example, you invest $10,000 in an oil and gas partnership; 80 percent of that amount is deductible in the first year. Your taxable income is then reduced by $8000 or 80 percent of your investment. If you are in the 50 percent tax bracket, you would save $4000 in taxes!

Growth, or Capital Appreciation. Finally there is the matter of growth. Will your investment be worth more 10 years from now (factoring in inflation) than it is today? You certainly hope to sell your investment for more than you paid for it and hopefully a sizeable portion of the gain will come back at the lower capital gains rate.

As investors you need to look carefully at each and every investment you are considering in light of these three kinds of potential return. If there isn't sufficient return in at least one of these avenues to make the investment worthwhile, why are you considering it?

4. *Is the return realistic?* You only need to apply common sense to answer this question. For example, if you're buying into agriculture, does the return that is anticipated assume that every year there is going to be a good crop and high prices? If it does, then the projected return is unrealistic because for any crop there will be some years when growth is low and prices are down.

This holds true for all investments. If only perfection is assumed, then the investment is unrealistic. I always look to see if "Murphy's Law" has been factored into every investment I consider for my clients. I assume that if something can go wrong, it will. There should be a sufficient margin for safety in every investment so that when what can go wrong does, the investment won't be lost.

5. *Have you checked the track record?* This is perhaps the single most important consideration. You want to know who's doing the management; how long they have been in the business; what their reputation is; and how much the success of the investment depends directly on their expertise. (Sometimes, a particular type of investment might not have a good track record, yet you might still consider it because the managers have a long history of success in the field.)

6. *Does the risk/reward ratio make sense?* This is a personal judgment. Some of us are risk-takers, others are not. Similarly, some investments have a great deal of inherent risk, while other ones are fairly safe. The riskier ones certainly have the greater potential for large profits. You need to examine the investment closely. Then step back and see if the risk/reward ratio makes sense to you. Never mind if it makes sense to someone else. Does it feel right to you?

7. *Are you overcommiting yourself?* This goes back to being able to sleep at night. When you look at a particular investment, you have to determine how much of your resources you are able and willing to commit to it. It may be the case that the investment is simply too big a bite for you to chew. By the same token, it could also be the case that the investment itself is too narrow in scope. If you read the material on research and development, you learned that you increase your chance for success through diversification. How diversified is the investment you're considering?

8. *Can you live with it?* Remember, an investment is something you take home with you at night. It's something that drifts back into your mind when you're not thinking about much else. Is the investment you're considering something you can live with?

The freedom that we have to select our investments can also be a terrible burden. We are not only free to choose, but we are also free to act wisely or to make mistakes.

It is my hope that this book has not only informed you about the many tax-shelter options available, but has also given you the

tools to make wise decisions. And when you make those decisions, I hope they bring you rich rewards by day and peaceful
dreams at night.

A P P E N D I X

AN ANALYSIS OF THE ECONOMIC RECOVERY TAX ACT OF 1981*

The art of taxation consists of so plucking the goose
as to obtain the largest amount of feathers
with the least possible amount of hissing.

*– J.B. Colbert (1619-1683), Controller
General of Finance to Louis XIV*

Monsieur Colbert would have been pleased with the art of taxation as practiced by U.S. tax collectors. Americans (after the Boston Tea Party) have historically yielded a great quantity of feathers with a minimum amount of hissing. Recently, however, taxpayers have been quite vocal in their dissatisfaction with the ever-increasing tax burden and with the way their government has elected to spend the revenues. Taxpayer concern came from many directions.

- A broad cross-section of individual taxpayers became fully aware of the effects of inflation and "bracket creep" on their spendable incomes.
- Savers saw their principal eroded as after-tax interest yields failed to match inflation.
- Corporate giants blamed declining productivity on antiquated and ineffectual depreciation systems.
- Small businesses complained of tax measures which prohibited effective competition.
- Closely held companies decried severe estate tax burdens which prohibit a family business from passing to succeeding generations.

The Economic Recovery Tax Act of 1981 addresses these major concerns as well as a variety of more specialized problems.

*Material used by permission of Alexander Grant & Company, certified public accountants.

243

Changes Affecting Individuals

RATES, DEDUCTIONS AND CREDITS

Ordinary Rate Reductions

The centerpiece of the Economic Recovery Tax Act of 1981 is a substantial across-the-board cut in the rate of individual income tax in all brackets, coupled with a reduction of the maximum tax rate from 70% to 50%.

Across-the-board rate reduction. The Act reduces the marginal tax rate applied to the taxable income of individuals by 25% across-the-board. This reduction is accomplished in three steps: a 5% rate reduction on October 1, 1981; a 10% rate reduction on July 1, 1982; and another 20% rate reduction on July 1, 1983.

A special transition rule applied for 1981. The October 1, 1981, 5% tax rate reduction is effected by providing a tax credit of 1¼% against regular tax liability before other tax credits. The tax rate schedules for 1982 and 1983 reflect the additional rate reductions. The first full year in which the full 25% rate reduction will be in place is 1984.

The following table compares the marginal tax rates for a married couple filing a joint return under prior law with the new phased-in rates, at selected income levels. Note that the range of rates of 14% to 70% under prior law is ultimately reduced to a range of 11% to 50%.

Taxable Income Bracket	Old Rates	1982 Rates	1983 Rates	1984 (and after) Rates
$ 3,400 to $ 5,500	14%	12%	11%	11%
$ 20,200 to $ 24,600	28%	25%	23%	22%
$ 29,900 to $ 35,200	37%	33%	30%	28%
$ 45,800 to $ 60,000	49%	44%	40%	38%
$ 60,000 to $ 85,600	54%	49%	44%	42%
$ 85,600 to $109,400	59%	50%	48%	45%
$109,400 to $162,400	64%	50%	50%	49%
$162,400 to $215,400	68%	50%	50%	50%
$215,400 and over	70%	50%	50%	50%

The impact of these basic rate changes on tax planning and financial and investment strategies is discussed later.

50% maximum rate on all income. Prior law made an important distinction between personal service income — wages, salaries, self-employment earnings, and deferred compensation payments — and unearned or investment income, such as dividends, interest or royalties.

That portion of taxable income attributable to personal service income was subject to a maximum tax rate of 50%. All other income was subject to rates up to 70%. Now, all income — whether earned or unearned — will be subject to a maximum tax rate of 50%. This change is effective January 1, 1982.

The rationale for the prior difference in treatment between earned and unearned income purportedly was that it is more equitable to tax those who work for their income at a rate lower than those who sit back and collect investment income. This equitable justification has now been subordinated to the economic argument that the nation's economy could be revitalized by providing incentives for individuals to put money in traditional income producing investments. Thus, all income, whether earned by labor or earned by investment, will be subject to a maximum tax rate of 50%.

Capital Gains Rate Reductions

As a result of reducing the maximum tax rate to 50%, the maximum rate of tax imposed on net long-term capital gains is reduced to 20 % from 28%. While the portion of a capital gain includable in income remains 40%, by applying a maximum tax rate of 50% to this includable portion of the gain, the maximum rate on a capital gain becomes 20%.

While the reduction of the top marginal rate for all income to 50% from 70% does not become effective until January 1, 1982, the change in the top capital gains rate to 20% from 28% is effective for gains resulting from sales or exchanges occurring after June 9, 1981.

This reduction in the tax on capital gains has significant and wide-ranging implications in terms of tax-planning strategies and investment planning and tactics. Many of these are discussed in the next section.

In order to make the alternative minimum tax (AMT) conform to the change in maximum tax rates, the new law reduces the top alternative minimum tax rate to 20%, from 25%, effective with respect to capital gains occurring after June 9, 1981.

Implications for Tax and Investment Planning

The conceptual simplicity of reducing the maximum tax rate from 70% to 50% belies the far-reaching implications of the change for individual tax and investment planning. Tax and investment planning will be affected in several basic ways. While the full array of consequences to the individual may not be immediately apparent, some conclusions can be stated at this point.

Tax shelters. The across-the-board rate reduction, coupled with the reduction in the top rate of tax, will not eliminate investor interest in tax-oriented investments. (Some cynics have observed that if tax rates were reduced to 2%, there would still be a mad scramble to avoid paying taxes.) However, the tax law changes may alter the way individuals assess and compare investments.

Investors who select particular investments primarily because of hoped-for tax advantages may now be less inclined to do so. Investors who made risky investments, with the knowledge that tax benefits could mitigate economic losses, may now review the need to take such risks and reevaluate the extent to which tax benefits can help recoup potential losses. The result may be that many individuals formerly in the 50%-plus bracket will now look for less risky investments having long-term appreciation potential — rather than for riskier investments that offer tax advantages. A 70% tax-bracket individual under prior law will see a 20% reduction in benefit from any tax loss resulting from a tax-advantaged investment. This may substantially alter that individual's assessments of the risks inherent in the investment.

Minimum tax on tax preferences. In one respect, analysis of the tax aspects of a shelter program becomes easier under the new law. A major concern of tax advisers counseling clients on tax shelters was the possibility of "maximum tax poisoning." This term describes the rule which required that personal service income subject to the 50% maximum tax rate be reduced by the dollar amount tax preferences — certain items receiving preferential tax treatment. Thus, there would be a dollar-for-dollar reclassification of income subject to a 50% tax to income subject to rates up to 70%.

By providing a 50% maximum tax rate for all income, this aspect of tax-shelter analysis is eliminated. Under the new law, investors no longer need be concerned that tax preference items will dilute or eliminate the benefit of tax shelters because of maximum tax poisoning.

Investors should, however, be aware that the possiblity of imposition of the minimum tax is slightly increased under the new law. This should be considered when studying shelter investments or when doing tax projections.

In general, the minimum tax (also referred to as the "add-on" minimum tax) imposes a tax at the rate of 15% on items that receive preferential tax treatment, reduced by the greater of $10,000 or one-half of the regular income tax liability for the year. For example, if the dollar amount of regular tax liability is $25,000 and the tax preference items total $15,000, the minimum tax is $375. ($15,000 — $12,500 × 15%.

As the regular tax liability is reduced due to rate reductions, the exclusion from minimum tax liability could be reduced by as much as 20%. (The difference between the 70% bracket and the 50% bracket.) As a general matter, the dollar impact of this reduction should be small. Given the elimination of maximum tax poisoning, the overall result is that the minimum tax on tax preference items becomes much less significant to tax shelters than under prior law.

Tax-exempt bond income. The economic value of an investment in tax-free municipal bonds needs to be reevaluated in light of tax rate reductions. The after-tax return of other investments may be more attractive now, when all of the economic factors are taken into account.

Depreciation recapture. The negative impact of depreciation recapture may be minimized to some degree by the rate reductions. This may spur individuals to consider disposition of depreciable business property.

In essence, depreciation recapture means that all or a portion of the gain realized from the sale or disposition of depreciable business property is taxed as ordinary income rather than as a capital gain.

For tangible personal property (referred to in tax jargon as Section 1245 property), all of the depreciation claimed on the property is recaptured as ordinary income, rather than as a capital gain, upon the sale of the property. In no case, however, can the amount of depreciation recaptured exceed the gain realized.

In the case of depreciable real property (known as Section 1250 property), generally all depreciation claimed in excess of the amount that would be allowable under the straight-line method is subject to recapture.

With the reduction in maximum ordinary rates to 50% and the reduction in the top capital gains rate to 20%, the spread between the two rates becomes 30 percentage points, down from the prior point spread of 42. This smaller "cost" of recapture may serve to remove previously existing obstacles to the sale or disposition of business property for individuals. This may become particularly significant in the case of businesses conducted as partnerships, where the tax consequences flow through the individual partners.

Conclusions. The simple act of reducing individual tax rates has widespread implications in planning transactions — especially for individuals formerly in over 50% tax brackets. Virtually every personal financial or investment transaction must now be carefully reviewed and analyzed in light of this rate change for possible opportunity as well as for possible pitfall.

Indexing Rates for Inflation

Beginning in 1985, the individual tax rate brackets, the personal exemption, and the zero bracket amount (formerly known as the standard deduction) will all be indexed for inflation.

This provision of the Act is designed to combat the phenomenon known as "bracket creep": the push upward into higher tax brackets attributable to inflation — resulting in an overall decline in taxpayers' real spending power.

From a tax and investment planning viewpoint, it may be too early to make judgments since the provision does not become effective until 1985. However, it appears that the indexing of rates for inflation will afford a degree of stability and certainty to individuals in their long-range financial and investment planning. Principally, the indexing rules will provide an incentive to avoid economically risky, tax-motivated investments.

Mechanically, the indexing provisions function to adjust tax brackets, personal exemptions, and zero bracket amounts to reflect cost-of-living increases as measured by increases in the consumer price index.

Relief for Two-Income Married Couples

With the sharp increases in the number of two-income married couples which occurred in the past decade, the so-called marriage penalty tax became more noticeable and more burdensome to many families.

A natural consequence of the tax structure is that a two-income married couple, with each spouse earning approximately the same amount (and filing a joint return), pays more tax than two income earning single individuals, each filing separate returns. While a married couple can elect to file separate returns, the tax law is structured so that filing separate returns will almost always result in a higher tax than a joint return.

Beginning in 1982, the new law provides a deduction intended to alleviate the marriage penalty tax problems.

Two-earner married couples who file a joint return will be allowed a deduction equal to 10% (5% for 1982) of the earned income (up to $30,000) of the spouse with the smaller earned income. Thus, the maximum deduction will be $1,500 for 1982 and $3,000 for 1983 and subsequent years. For example, if in 1983 a husband earns $40,000 and his wife earns $35,000, they may claim a $3,000 deduction.

The deduction is allowed from gross income in arriving at adjusted gross income. Thus, taxpayers may claim the deduction even if they do not itemize their personal deductions.

In general, earned income against which the 10% deduction (or 5% in 1982) is applied is defined as salary or wages and excludes pensions, annuities, IRA distributions and deferred compensation payments. Also, the earned amount must be reduced by trade or business and employee business expenses as well as by contributions to a Keogh plan or IRA. For example, if a wife earns $35,000 and her husband earns $30,000 but deducts a $2,000 IRA contribution, the marriage penalty deduction for 1983 is $2,800 ($30,000 − $2,000 × 10%).

Depreciation and Investment Tax Credit

The new law makes extensive changes regarding depreciation and investment tax credits for business property. Principally, these provisions affect business. However, it is important to note that those changes also apply to individuals who may have depreciable business property — such as the proprietor of a small business or the owner of a rental building. Also, these changes will affect the personal tax situation of individuals who are partners in partnerships using depreciable business property. The tax consequences of the partnership flow through to the individual tax returns of the partners. Thus, partnership depreciation and investment tax credits translate to deductions and credits for the individual partners.

Gain on Sale of Residence

The rules that afford many individuals selling their homes an important tax break have been expanded.

Under old rules, if an individual sells his or her home and, within a period beginning 18 months before the sale and extending 18 months after the sale, buys a new home at a purchase price equal to or greater than the sale price of the old home, gain on the sale of the old home may be deferred.

The new law expands the replacement period from 18 months to 24 months. Also, the $100,000 once-in-a-lifetime exclusion of gain on the sale of a home for individuals aged 55 and over is expanded to $125,000. Both changes are effective for the sales or exchanges of principal residences after July 20, 1981. The extension of the replacement period is also effective with respect to 18-month periods still open on July 20, 1981.

Charitable Deductions for Non-itemizers

Most Americans, regardless of income level, make at least some charitable contributions during the year. Yet, many individual taxpayers in the past were precluded from claiming a tax deduction for charitable contributions because their total deductions were insufficient to allow them to itemize.

The Act provides that beginning in 1982, deductions may be claimed for charitable contributions even if the individual does not itemize personal deductions. The deduction allowable is 25% of as much as a $100 contribution for 1982 and 1983, 25% of as much as a $300 contribution in 1984, 50% of any contributions for 1985, and 100% for 1986 contributions. After 1986 the provision expires.

Child Care Credit Expansion

The credit for child or dependent care expenses of working individuals is expanded under the new law.

Starting in 1982, the credit will be 30% of employment-related child care expenses for taxpayers with incomes of $10,000 or less. The credit reduces by 1% for each $2,000 of income over $10,000. Thus, for taxpayers with income of $20,000 the credit is 25%. Taxpayers with income over $28,000 are entitled to a 20% credit. Also, the maximum child care expenditure amounts for which credit is allowed are increased to $2,400 per dependent for each of the first two dependents.

SAVINGS AND RETIREMENT

Tax-Exempt Savings Certificate

In response to concerns voiced by the savings and loan and banking industries and by the housing industry, Congress established a tax-exempt savings certificate.

The tax-exempt savings certificate provisions of the new law are designed to encourage savers to place funds in traditional savings institutions (i.e., banks and S&Ls) as opposed to high yield sources such as money market funds. Also, the provision attempts to help the housing industry (and home buyers) by making more funds available for mortgages, thereby perhaps lowering mortgage rates.

The essence of the tax-exempt savings certificate rules is that interest earned by certificates meeting certain requirements is tax-free to the saver. A lifetime maximum of $1,000 (or $2,000 in the case of joint returns) is imposed on the amount of interest that may be earned without tax.

The specific rules governing the tax-exempt saving certificates are:

- The certificates must be one-year certificates issued after September 30, 1981 and before January 1, 1983.
- The yield on the certificates must be 70% of the current yield on one-year Treasury bills.
- The certificates must be issued by a bank, savings and loan association, mutual savings bank, or credit union.

The Act requires financial institutions issuing the tax-exempt certificates to use at least 75% of the proceeds from the certificates for housing or agricultural loans.

Partial Interest Exclusion

Since by its terms the tax-exempt savings certificates discussed in the preceding section are only temporary (they cannot be issued after December 31, 1982), Congress also enacted what it hopes will be an adequate permanent savings incentive — an exclusion from income of savings interest of as much as $450 per year on individual returns and $900 per year on joint returns. This new exclusion does not become effective until January 1, 1985.

Specifically, the Act provides that effective for taxable years beginning after December 31, 1984, an individual taxpayer may exclude from income an amount not to exceed 15% of the lesser of:

- $3,000 of savings interest (or $6,000 in the case of a joint return), or
- The excess of savings interest income over deductible interest expense, exclusive of mortgage or business interest expense.

Not all interest earned will qualify for the partial interest exclusion. In general, only savings interest such as that from bank or savings and loan accounts or certificates qualifies. Also, corporate bond, U.S. obligation, and certain commercial paper interest qualifies for the exclusion.

251

Interest and Dividend Exclusion Repeal

The Windfall Profit Tax Act of 1980 introduced a $200 dividend and interest exclusion ($400 in the case of joint returns) for 1981 and 1982. This dividend and interest exclusion replaced, for 1981 and 1982, the previously existing $100 dividend exclusion ($100 for husband and $100 for wife on joint returns).

Concluding that the dividend and interest exclusion is inadequate as an incentive for individual savings and unnecessary in light of the savings provisions discussed in the two preceding sections, Congress repealed it, effective for years beginning after December 31, 1981. Thus, starting with 1982, the old $100/$200 dividend exclusion returns.

Expanded IRA Contributions and Coverage

The deductible amount which an individual may contribute to an Individual Retirement Account (IRA) is increased, beginning in 1982, to the lesser of $2,000 (or $2,250 for a spousal IRA) or 100% of compensation. Spousal IRAs are for married couples with only one wage earner.

Besides expanding the deduction limitation for IRAs, the new law extends the coverage of IRAs to those previously precluded from establishing such retirement savings accounts. This change is very significant and will allow additional tax benefit to many individuals. Starting in 1982, employees who are active participants in their employer's qualified retirement plan may contribute and deduct $2,000 (or $2,250 for a spousal IRA), but not more than 100% of compensation, for contributions to an IRA. In this way it is possible for individuals to supplement — out of pre-tax dollars — whatever retirement savings may be provided by an employer.

The Act eliminates the old requirements that contributions to a spousal IRA be equally divided between the two spouses — i.e., $875 for the husband's account and $875 for the wife's account. Beginning in 1982, the $2,250 deductible amount may be divided unequally between the two accounts, provided not more than $2,000 is contributed to one account.

Expanded Keogh and SEP Contributions

The maximum amount which a self-employed individual may contribute to his or her self-employed retirement plan (known as a Keogh or H.R. 10 plan) will increase in 1982 to $15,000 from $7,500.

This increased contribution level may make Keogh plans more attractive to certain groups of self-employed individuals. For example, in recent years many physicians and attorney's practicing as sole practitioners or in partnerships formed professional corporations. In most cases, the principal reson for incorporation was that corporate retirement plans (pension or profit-sharing) afforded these high income individuals greater opportunity to set money aside for retirement than was possible with a Keogh plan. While as a general matter the corporate plans may still allow larger deductible contributions than the newly expanded Keogh plans, in some instances the gap between the two may be small enough to require more careful examination of the question of incorporation for professionals.

These changes in both IRA and Keogh rules may cause reevaluation of retirement plan options by employees, employers, and special groups such as owners of closely held corporations or professional people. For example, the individual covered by an employer's plan may now question whether he or she should establish an IRA or contribute to the employer plan. The employer may question the value of maintaiing certain plans, and certain groups of employers may assess Keogh or SEPs differently than before.

INVESTMENTS

Commodity Transaction Rules

The commodity straddle is a technique that had been successfully employed to defer tax liability. By this device a taxpayer who had realized gains during the year would defer the payment of tax on these gains by simultaneously buying long and selling short commodity futures contracts, and by closing prior to the end of the year that contract upon which a loss had been sustained. If the commodity price moved upward, the taxpayer would purchase a new contract at the higher price and cover his short sale, thus incurring a loss. If prices moved in a downward direction, the long contract would be sold, thereby producing a loss. In the next year, the converse trading activity would take place, thereby restoring the taxpayer to his original gain position, but allowing him to rollover his gain from one year to the next.

Congress believed that such transactions were tax-motivated and not reflective of true economic substance. Accordingly, in a radical departure from existing law, the new Act taxes unrealized gains and losses from straddle transactions by providing that a taxpayer must value all of his outstanding commodity futures contracts at the end of the year (market-to-market) and to pay tax on the unrealized net gains on commodity futures contracts. The taxpayer will treat 60% of the net unrealized gains and losses as long-term gains or losses and 40% as short-term gains or losses, the effect being a maximum 32% tax rate on net unrealized gains. Net losses under this concept may be carried back three years against market-to-market gains. Tax due on gains rolled forward from prior years into 1981 may be paid in five annual installments beginning in 1981. These rules apply to contracts acquired and positions established after June 23, 1981.

Present law allows a current deduction for interest and carrying charges for purchasing or carrying commodity investments. The new law requires that such charges be added to the basis of the commodity if it is part of a straddle.

In essence, the new law tends to discourage tax motivated commodity straddles.

INCOME EARNED ABROAD

Partial Exclusion

U.S. citizens working abroad for extended periods are, under the Act, entitled to exclude from income a portion of their "foreign earned income." The term generally refers to income attributable to services performed in a foreign country.

Income may be excluded as follows:

Taxable Years	Maximum Annual Exclusion
1982	$75,000
1983	80,000
1984	85,000
1985	90,000
1986 and after	95,000

The rules that apply to determine whether an individual is eligible for the foreign income exclusion are broadened. The exclusion now applies not only to U.S. citizens who are bona fide residents of a foreign country for the entire taxyear, as under prior law, but also to U.S. citizens or residents who during any period of 12 consecutive months are present in a foreign country at least 330 full days.

Qualifying individuals may also exclude from income foreign housing costs in excess of a base amount, where housing costs are provided by the employer. (A deduction for excess housing costs is available where the employer does not provide amounts for housing.)

Estate and Gift Tax Changes

Although not a significant producer of revenue for the Treasury, estate and gift taxes can wreak havoc on an individual estate. The Tax Reform Act of 1976 recognized that three decades of inflation had subjected many estates to unintended estate tax. At that time, the value of property permitted to pass tax-free at death was increased from $60,000 to $175,625. The 1981 Act more than triples this amount and provides relief from succession taxes in several other ways. The most distressing aspect of estate and gift taxation has been the impact on closely held or family businesses. Large estate tax liabilities resulting in severe cash deficiencies have made it difficult for a closely held business to pass to succeeding generations. Although the new rules will not eliminate this problem, they will certainly give estate planners more to work with in dealing with it.

ESTATE TAX

Unified Credit

The unified estate tax credit is an amount subtracted directly from the estate tax. The credit determines the minimum size estate which will pay estate tax. This amount is generally known as the credit equivalent. For example, under present law, the unified credit is $47,000 which is the estate tax computed on $175,625. When the unified credit is subtracted, the estate tax is reduced to zero. Therefore, the credit equivalent is $175,625 — meaning that a taxable estate of up to that amount can be passed to heirs free of estate tax.

The Act increases the unified estate tax credit over a six-year period. By 1987 it will be $192,800. The credit equivalent will then be $600,000. This means that a taxable estate of as much as $600,000 can be left to heirs without any estate tax being imposed. The table below shows the amount of credit and credit equivalent as the new provision is phased in.

Year of Death	Credit	Credit Equivalent
1982	$ 62,800	$225,000
1983	79,300	275,000
1984	96,300	325,000
1985	121,800	400,000
1986	155,800	500,000
1987 and after	192,800	600,000

Corresponding changes have been made in the estate tax return filing requirements to accommodate the many thousands of estates which will no longer be subject to tax.

Although the new unified credit will exempt many estates from tax, we continue to caution clients not to underestimate the size of their estates. Many persons will be surprised to find their estates exceeding $600,000 when the value of a residence, group life insurance, a closely held business and other property is considered. On the other hand, effective estate planning can keep your estate within the tax-free exemption.

Estate Tax Rates

The new law also makes an absolute reduction in the highest estate tax rates. The top rate on transfers of property will drop from 70% to 50%. This change will also be phased in over a four-year period. The table below shows this phase-in, together with the size of estate where the top bracket takes effect:

Year of Death	Highest Rate	On Estate Over
1982	65%	$4,000,000
1983	60%	3,500,000
1984	55%	3,000,000
1985 and after	50%	2,500,000

Unlimited Marital Deduction

When computing the amount of an estate subject to estate tax, a deduction is allowed for property passing to a surviving spouse. This deduction has always been limited to an amount equal to one-half of the adjusted gross estate (total value of property less liabilities). A 1976 provision also permitted a minimum marital deduction of $250,000.

The new law does away with these limitations. A marital deduction will be permitted for the entire value of property passing to a surviving spouse. This feature will often be very helpful in providing for the needs of a surviving spouse. However, it will not be desirable for many estates to claim the maximum marital deduction. Planning in this area will be more demanding in the future, calling for careful projection of estate values as well as a certain amount of clairvoyance. Consider the following examples. (In each case, it is assumed that the new rates and unified credit have been fully phased in. The facts are greatly simplified for better illustration.)

Example 1: H has an estate of $1,200,000. W has no estate. If H leaves the entire estate to W in a transfer qualifying for the 100% marital deduction, the following estate taxes will result. (Assume that H predeceases W.)

	H Estate	W Estate
Total estate	$1,200,000	$1,200,000
Marital deduction	1,200,000	—0—
Taxable estate	$ —0—	$1,200,000
Tentative tax	$ —0—	$ 427,800
Unified credit	192,800	192,800
Estate tax	$ —0—	$ 235,000

Although the entire estate of H passed to W free of tax, a substantial tax amounting to $235,000 was imposed upon the death of W. This tax could have been completely eliminated while still providing for W through the use of the traditional, non-marital trust technique. Under this approach, H would leave one-half the estate to W outright or in a trust *qualifying* for the marital deduction. The second half would be left in a trust giving income to W for life. As a terminable interest, the trust value would *not qualify* for the marital deduction and (assuming proper drafting) would not be included in W's estate upon her death. The results of this arrangement are shown below:

	H Estate	W Estate
Total estate	$1,200,000	$ 600,000
Marital deduction	600,000	—0—
Taxable estate	$ 600,000	$ 600,000
Tentative tax	$ 192,800	$ 192,800
Unified credit	192,800	192,800
Estate tax	$ —0—	$ —0—

The tax of $325,000 has been completely eliminated by using H's unified credit rather than the full marital deduction to shelter his estate from tax. By limiting the qualifying marital bequest, W's estate is reduced by $600,000; however, she has beneficial enjoyment of the full $1,200,000 during her lifetime.

The above example calls for an easy decision. However, if the size of H's estate is doubled, the decision would be more subjective and would force the estate planner to speculate on future events. If the marital deduction availed of does not reduce the taxable estate to $600,000 or less, the effect will be to voluntarily pay a tax before it need be paid. In the following example, the facts are the same except that the estate of H is $2,400,000. The illustration shows the use of all but $600,000 of marital deduction as compared to balancing the estates with a 50% marital deduction. In each case, the non-marital trust technique would be used to eliminate the non-marital amount from W's estate.

Example 2: Plan A — Use of all but $600,000 of permitted marital deduction.

	H Estate	**W Estate**
Total estate	$2,400,000	$1,800,000
Marital deduction	1,800,000	— 0 —
Taxable estate	$ 600,000	$1,800,000
Tentative tax	$ 192,800	$ 690,800
Unified credit	192,800	192,800
Estate tax	$ — 0 —	$ 498,000

Plan B — Use of 50% marital deduction.

	H Estate	**W Estate**
Total estate	$2,400,000	$1,200,000
Marital deduction	1,200,000	— 0 —
Taxable estate	$1,200,000	$1,200,000
Tentative tax	$ 427,800	$ 427,800
Unified credit	192,800	192,800
Estate tax	$ 235,000	$ 235,000

The combined tax for both estates is as follows:

Plan A	$498,000
Plan B	470,000
Difference	$ 28,000

It can be seen that Plan B has reduced the combined tax by $23,000. However, upon the death of H a tax of $235,000 has been paid which need not have been paid. The extent of this detriment will depend upon how long W survives. In this situation, failure of H to take advantage of the higher marital deduction is clearly unwise. If the $235,000 tax were deferred as under Plan A and invested at a compound 6% after-tax yield, it would take less than two years to recoup the estate tax saved by Plan B. Of course, if W does not consume this income, it would be included in her estate and reduced by estate tax.

GIFT TAX

Marital Deduction

Consistent with the estate tax marital deduction, an unlimited gift tax marital deduction will now be allowed. Thus the system of totally tax-free interspousal transfers is complete. This replaces the old rule whereby the first $100,000 of gifts received a 100% marital deduction, and the remainder 50%. The unlimited gift tax marital deduction will be effective for gifts after December 31, 1981.

The unlimited gift tax marital deduction will play an important role in the rearrangement of estates for optimum estate tax advantage. For instance, in larger estates it may be desirable to make substantial transfers to a spouse to assure that enough property is in his or her hands to take advantage of the unified credit.

Example: H has an estate of $1,600,000 while W has no property. If W predeceases H, the estate tax picture in both estates would look like this:

	W Estate	H Estate
Taxable estate	$ — 0 —	$1,600,000
Tentative tax	$ — 0 —	$ 600,800
Unified credit	192,800	192,800
Estate tax	$ — 0 —	$ 408,000

Although W could have passed $600,000 of property tax-free, this opportunity was wasted because of the absence of property. The estates of H and W may have been well-planned, assuming the prior death of H. The unanticipated prior death of W upset the plan. H's estate was forced into high estate taxes because of absence of the marital deduction.

Consistent with the economic well-being of H and other family circumstances, substantial tax can be saved by the following technique. H makes a lifetime transfer of $600,000 to W. The transfer is tax-free because of the 100% marital deduction. W's will directs that her property go directly to their children. If W predeceases, the estate taxes will then look like this:

	W Estate	H Estate
Taxable estate	$ 600,000	$1,000,000
Tentative tax	$ 192,800	$ 345,800
Unified credit	192,800	192,800
Estate tax	$ —0—	$ 153,000

It can be seen that estate tax of $255,000 has been saved. In effect, the unified credit of W has sheltered $600,000 of H's property from tax and made an additional $255,000 available to their children.

Tax-free interspousal transfers can also solve joint tenancy problems. Joint ownership can seriously restrict the options available in planning estates. This is because the property, by nature of its ownership, must pass to the surviving spouse. Often, by the time the estate planning professional arrives at the scene, large amounts of property have already been accumulated in joint tenancy. The separation of these interests may be vital to the estate plan. In the past, however, division of joint ownership could result in gift tax. The new unlimited marital deduction will eliminate the risk of this occurring.

Annual Exclusion

The gift tax rules have long provided an amount which could be transferred annually free of gift tax. Since 1942, this amount has been the familiar $3,000. Recognizing the ravages of inflation since that time, the Act increases this amount to $10,000. The procedure whereby spouses can consent to have gifts made by one treated as made one half by each still exists. Therefore, $20,000 can now be given to each of any number of donees. For example, a husband and wife with four children can give way $80,000 per year. Over a ten-year period, this would effect a substantial estate reduction of $800,000. Thus the annual exclusion has been restored as an effective estate planning tool.

A gift tax return is not required for gifts not exceeding the annual exclusion. Therefore, a return will not be required where gifts to any individual do not exceed $10,000. Note, however, that a gift in excess of $10,000 does require a return even though gift-splitting may eliminate any taxable gifts.

Gift Tax Rates

Continuing the system of unification of estate and gift taxes, the gift tax rates are adjusted to conform to the new estate tax rates. Accordingly, the maximum gift tax rate will be 50% after phase-in.

Gifts to Decedent Within One Year of Death

If a decedent receives property by gift within one year of death and it passes to the donor or donor's spouse, the basis of this property will not be stepped up to fair market value at date of death.

This provision is effective with respect to property acquired after date of enactment by decedents dying after December 31, 1981.

ACKNOWLEDGEMENTS

This book really could not have been completed without the expertise and assistance from our colleagues listed below. To them, we are grateful for their time and enthusiasm in assisting us to collect the most important information to date on all the different areas of tax shelters.

Leasing

Larry Lucas
Leastec
Walnut Creek, California

Equipment Leasing

Paul Ronan
Phoenix Leasing, Inc.
Mill Valley, California

Cattle

George Morrow
G. S. Morrow & Company
San Francisco, California

HUD

Bob Christensen
Sierra Pacific
Seattle, Washington

HUD

Jeff Zoldoss
American Development
Corporation
DenvLos Angeles, California

Stamps

Bruce Stone
Stamp Portfolios, Inc.
Stamford, Connecticut

Coins

Don Kagin
Kagins Numismatics
San Francisco, California

Research & Development

Jim Steffey
Energy Sciences Corporation
Seattle, Washington

Agriculture

Dan Stephenson
Rancho Consultants
Rancho, California

Residential Real Estate

Hal Morris
Hal Morris Seminars
Los Angeles, California

Cable TV

Thomas A. Marinkovich
Daniels & Associates